CHARLES THE KING

By the same author

IMPERIAL HIGHNESS
CURSE NOT THE KING
FAR FLY THE EAGLES
VALENTINA
ANNE BOLEYN
ELIZABETH
ANNE OF AUSTRIA
VICTORIA
CLANDARA
THE HEIRESS

Thrillers

THE ASSASSIN
THE LEGEND
THE MALASPIGA EXIT
THE OCCUPYING POWER
THE PERSIAN RANSOM
THE POLLENBERG INHERITANCE
THE RETURN
THE SILVER FALCON
THE TAMARIND SEED
VOICES ON THE WIND
THE GRAVE OF TRUTH
THE DEFECTOR
THE RENDEZVOUS
THE AVENUE OF THE DEAD
ALBATROSS
THE COMPANY OF SAINTS

CHARLES
THE KING

EVELYN ANTHONY

REISSUED 1987

CENTURY
LONDON MELBOURNE AUCKLAND JOHANNESBURG

First published in Great Britain in 1961 by
Museum Press
This edition published in 1987 by
Century Hutchinson Ltd
Brookmount House, 62–65 Chandos Place
London WC2N 4NW

Century Hutchinson South Africa (Pty) Ltd
PO Box 337, Bergvlei, 2012 South Africa

Century Hutchinson Australia Pty Ltd
PO Box 496, 16–22 Church Street, Hawthorn
Victoria 3122, Australia

Century Hutchinson New Zealand Ltd
PO Box 40–086, Glenfield, Auckland 10
New Zealand

ISBN 0 7126 1556 3

Printed in Great Britain by
WBC Print Ltd, Bristol

Author's Foreword

THIS is the story of a glorious failure. Charles 1 was the last absolute monarch to reign over England and one of the most ill-fated Kings of the tragic, splendid dynasty of the Royal Stuarts. It is the story of the public and personal life of a strange man, who came to an ingnominious end and turned it into a triumph of courage and faith which still has the power to touch and exalt the human heart after the passage of three centuries.

I have tried hard to give the reader a true picture of the King and the woman he married and lived with in shining fidelity for over twenty years, and of the circumstances which ended his reign after a savage and bloody Civil War. It is a love story because the passionate, abiding love Charles and Henrietta Maria bore each other influenced so much of his life and the history of his country. I have used documents and letters wherever these were available, and I have based the King's letter to the Queen at Berwick on his known opinions and words used in a different context at the time. I have shortened the account of war with Scotland and the tortuous negotiations with Parliament during his captivity at Carisbrooke, and given an account of his meeting with Cromwell which is not substantiated. But Cromwell was the principal negotiator of the Army treaty, and he was present when the King saw his children at Caversham, not Hampton Court as stated.

The Countess of Carlisle was the reputed mistress of Strafford and Pym, and she was and still is accused of betraying the King and Queen as I have described, though no definite proof has been found.

All other events, personalities, times and incidents in this book are true.

London, 1961   EVELYN ANTHONY

Chapter 1

THE King of England was waiting for his bride; he was twenty-five and also the sovereign of Ireland, Scotland and Wales, and she was fifteen, the daughter of a King of France who had been assassinated a few weeks after she was born. They had been married a month, but they had never met.

He had seen her once when he was still Charles, Prince of Wales, but he had been on his way to Spain to arrange a match with someone else and the little French Princess dancing in a court Masque in Paris had made no impression on him —he could not remember anything about her. Like his father's favourite, the Duke of Buckingham, who was travelling with him, Charles had spent his evening watching the stately red-headed Queen of France whose beauty and dignity eclipsed all the other ladies and Princesses of the Blood. They had then left Paris and gone to Spain, where the Spanish Infanta delighted the young prince, who was inexperienced enough and lonely enough to fall in love with anyone, but quite unprepared for the Spanish custom of courtship in the presence of the lady's household. He was also unprepared to reverse the Anti-Catholic laws of England on which his dynasty depended and to forswear his own Protestant religion; these were the conditions Spain asked in return for the hand of her Princess.

Charles and the Duke of Buckingham had abandoned the negotiations in an atmosphere of hostility which owed a good deal to Buckingham's efforts to seduce some of the impeccable Spanish ladies. They returned to England without a treaty or a bride, and Charles's father, King James, threw his arms round his son and hugged him in his undignified way and promised to find him someone else.

Charles accordingly retired to his apartments at St. James's Palace, and resumed his self-effacing life of study, without friends or intimates of either sex except the boisterous, bumptious, splendid man whom he had come to like against his will, Buckingham, the son of a poor country squire, who was a millionaire and a Privy Councillor and a Duke because he had taken the old King's fancy.

Charles and his father had nothing in common and there was no tinge of the unnatural in the Prince's response to Buckingham's friendship. Charles was lonely and shy and in his soul the Court and the King disgusted him and increased his isolation. He stammered when he was excited or nervous; he was small and slightly built and too modest to appreciate his own refined and sensitive good looks. He had the features and the bearing of a King and the mentality of a knight of the Middle Ages. It amused the cynical, amoral Steenie Buckingham to force himself upon the younger man and to make him the unwilling victim of his charm. For Buckingham possessed charm in an extraordinary degree. He was witty, he was generous, he was an acknowledged bravo who could suddenly laugh at himself; he radiated confidence, and in spite of everything Charles was flattered that such a man should seek him out. Though he was lonely and disappointed after his return, he now loved Buckingham more blindly and trusted him further than the crafty old King had ever done. And the King had kept his promise. He had found another bride for his son, the Princess Henrietta Maria of France, and then, two months before the proxy wedding, James sickened and died and Charles was king of all three kingdoms.

Charles turned away from the window and began to walk up and down the room. He wished there had been a mirror, or time to change from his riding clothes which were covered in dust. He wondered whether his wife had been impressed by the massive walls and fortress guns of Dover Castle, and then thought anxiously that perhaps the Castle was a depressing place in which to meet for the first time. Buckingham had gone to France to bring the new Queen back, and he had written to Charles telling him that she was gay and pleasing and pretty and well enough developed for her age. And though she was a Papist, the terms of the marriage treaty had been reasonable. She must have freedom for herself and her retinue to practise their faith, and also her husband must promise to alleviate the hardships suffered by her co-religionists in England. They

8

had been married by proxy, and then she had gone on a long, stately progress through France accompanied by the King and Queen of France, the Queen Mother, Marie de Medici, and all their attendants.

The delay had irritated Charles; in spite of his quiet manner he had inherited the volcanic temper of his Stuart ancestors with the dark red hair of his grandmother, the unhappy, controversial Mary, Queen of Scots. He had been hurt by the reports that Henrietta was in no hurry to leave France and join him. He had been extremely angry when he received a message from her when she arrived at Dover, begging him to wait before presenting himself as she had been sea-sick and needed time to prepare. He had ridden back to Canterbury, very pale and silent and obviously furious, and left her until ten o'clock the next morning before he presented himself.

Now he was not angry any more, only nervous and excited, and glad that he had sent everyone away, even Buckingham, because he must not let anyone see how much this meeting and this marriage meant to him, even before it had begun. Princes were not expected to be in love with their wives; they were not supposed to need support or companionship, and if they did they sought it outside marriage. But Charles had never had a mistress. He had seen the women at his father's Court, painted, immoral and loose in conversation. Some of the highest born could only be described as drunken whores. He had seen mothers leading their handsome sons up to King James, hoping to advance them by way of the King's bedchamber, and he had known that for himself there could be no happiness or self-respect in such a mode of life. He had been laughed at as a prude, and a ribald verse was circulating, offering condolences to the new Queen for a marriage bed as clumsy as the tossing ship which carried her across the Channel. He knew and he pretended ignorance. The Court would change; already conversation was more guarded and two gentlemen had been dismissed from their posts for coming into the King's presence tipsy, forgetting that their master was no longer the bibulous King James. The new King had a very cold eye when he looked at something or someone he disliked, if he stammered at some moments, he could express himself only too clearly when he was annoyed.

He had been King for three months, and already it was

understood that he would not tolerate an open scandal. At the same time the Duke of Buckingham, freed of the vigilance of the dead King, seduced and philandered to his heart's content, while his censorious young master behaved as if he were blind to the conduct of the most infamous relic of the disreputable past. Within three months Charles had established his authority over his Court; it was taken for granted that the fifteen-year-old French Princess would do exactly as her husband wished.

He was standing in front of the fireplace, kicking nervously at the smoking coals with his boot, when the door suddenly opened. Charles' first sight of his wife was somehow confused because of the crowd of women who were pushing behind her through the open door. When they separated, a small, very slight figure advanced towards him. He had a fleeting impression of a pointed face and enormous brown eyes, and then the new Queen of England sank down in a curtsy in front of him. She was much smaller and much more childish than he had imagined. He ignored the curtsying group of women round them and lifted the little Queen to her feet and kissed her before he had even really seen her face. She did not return the kiss. She stared at him with her extraordinary eyes, fringed with long black lashes and looked over her shoulder with an expression of panic. A tall, angular lady, her cheeks bright red with rouge, moved a step nearer and said encouragingly, "Sire, I am come. . ."

Henrietta Maria turned back to the King and began to make her formal speech. She had been rehearsed very carefully for her entry into England; she had been strictly brought up in a Court where etiquette bound every word and action of the Blood Royal, and she was accustomed to protocol. She had expected a formal reception which would take place before their attendants, when her husband the King would meet her suitably dressed and accompanied and she would come forward with dignity, wearing one of her magnificent trousseau dresses and her jewels. She stared at the handsome young man in his dusty clothes and muddy riding boots, waiting in the ante room like a common courier without even a gentleman in attendance, and she forgot every word of her speech. It was not what she expected. She was married and she was a Queen and she had landed after a wretched journey and found only a representative to meet her and been lodged in an appalling Castle which was only fit for prisoners, without proper apartments, heating or light, and with a disgusting antiquated bed left over from the reign of Elizabeth Tudor. Her suite had been grumbling. Madame de St. George, who had tried to prompt her a moment ago, had been outraged by the inadequacy, the shabbiness of the reception of a Princess of France, and with the words fleeing her memory and the young man who was her husband standing there looking at her in surprise, the Queen of England covered her face with her hands and burst into tears. They were not tears of fright as Charles supposed; he put his arms round his wife and this time he kissed her ceremoniously on both her wet cheeks, and taking his handkerchief, wiped her tears away.

"If your Majesty will permit me. . ." He looked up and the same Frenchwoman, obviously the principal lady-in-waiting, was standing with her hand on the Queen's shoulder.

"I will attend to Madam," she said firmly. "You must forgive her, Sire. She has had a long journey and her reception here was not one which made her feel at ease."

For a moment Charles looked into the woman's eyes; they were brown and they were bright with hostility. He was outraging every custom known to Madame de St. George and every self-respecting member of the French nobility. He was embracing his wife in public and fumbling with his handkerchief instead of retiring tactfully and leaving her to recover her composure with her women. She did not like the King of England. She did not like men with red hair and she detested the contemptuous expression in his eyes. When Charles answered his voice was very curt.

"Thank you, but the Queen will recover her spirits sooner with me than with you; it would be a poor omen for our marriage if her husband failed to comfort her."

He looked down at Henrietta and his rather stern face softened in a very warm smile. It was the first time she had seen on his face a look of anything but surprise or anxiety and then the unpleasant glare which had sent Madame de St. George to the other side of the room. Henrietta gave him her hand and he kissed it. He was really very handsome, as handsome as the portrait sent to her before their marriage. He had very fine eyes of a deep blue which at first appeared as if they were hazel, and she liked the little pointed beard he wore. She was proud and spoilt and she had cried with pure rage because she felt she had been slighted from the moment she landed at Dover Harbour, but she was also entirely feminine and innocently vain.

"Welcome to England, Madam. And forgive me for coming to meet you dressed like this. I was too anxious to see you to wait for ceremony."

Henrietta smiled at him, and the eyes which had been swimming in petulant tears, sparkled and a dimple appeared in one cheek.

"I am not as I would have wished myself," she said. "I had a special gown for you, Sire, and that speech which I fear I shall never make properly now. And I am not wearing stilt heels!'

To the horror of her ladies and the amusement of Charles, she lifted her skirts and showed her small feet in low silk shoes. He had been anxious that she should reach his shoulder; like most men of small or middle height, the King was sensitive; he wanted neither a giantess nor a dwarf, and someone must have repeated the remark to his bride. He blushed, and Henrietta decided that she liked him better every minute. For a moment neither of them spoke; they appraised each other with something close to the candour of children, the inexperienced bridegroom of twenty-five whose whole life had been a struggle against his own shyness and the physical delicacy which had robbed him of his childhood—and the proud, warm-natured, high-spirited girl who had been bartered in a marriage with a man she had never seen for the benefit of England and of France. She had expected a handsome Prince and in that at least she had not been disappointed. No one had bothered to inform her of his character or his tastes; he was a King and she was his wife, and would share his bed and his throne and bear his children. She would count herself supremely fortunate if she even liked him; love was a word used in letters and speeches, and it meant nothing. Nobody took such sentiments seriously. She would be faithful and obedient, provided that he asked nothing beyond the terms in her marriage treaty, and she would enjoy the full sum of the happiness allotted to Princesses on this earth. It had never occurred to her, or been suggested even as a joke, that Charles

Stuart might fall in love with her or she might find herself in love with him.

After a moment Henrietta remembered her obligations, and, with an apology, she presented her ladies to the King in strict order of rank. Madame de St. George came first.

"My Principal Lady of the Bedchamber," Henrietta announced, "and my very dear friend and mentor," she added as a hint to Charles to be especially gracious. He ignored it; he gave the Frenchwoman his hand which she kissed and then turned away without speaking a word to her. He disliked her, and he never changed his first impressions.

"La Duchesse de Chevreuse, La Comtesse de Touillère, Madame de Lanton, Mademoiselle de Berrand."

He received them one by one and did not find a single face he admired or a suggestion of a personality he could like. He addressed them in general; he was not going to be overawed by them, or allow them to take his wife away until he had finished speaking to her.

"Welcome to my Kingdom, ladies. I trust that you will be happy here and give your mistress all comfort and devotion, as I shall," he said, turning to Henrietta. "Come and sit down with me for a few moments, Madam. I was sorry to hear you had such a vile journey."

"It was a nightmare, Sire. The ship rolled and tossed until I felt sure we should all be drowned—indeed there were times on that crossing when I wished we might be, I was so sick!"

"It soon passes," Charles said kindly. "The moment you disembark the sickness disappears; I'm not a good sailor either, Madam, so we will do our travelling on land in the future. Are you comfortably lodged?"

Henrietta hesitated; this was not the moment to complain. In spite of her youth she was sophisticated enough to know that her husband was favourably impressed by her, but she felt the disapproval of her ladies, all of whom had grumbled and protested at the conditions at the Castle and knew that she would be accused of cowardice and lack of pride if she evaded the question. Having made up her mind, she was inclined to speak it without any saving tact.

"My lodgings are terrible, Sire," she said. "They are dark and cold, and I have a most terrible bed with a mattress like a board, and filthy hangings which squeaked in the night; I am sure there are bats in them. We were all too terrified to shake them out and look."

Charles felt himself reddening. She had a bold and haughty little face, far too set and determined for a comparative child and his discomfort was increased by the satisfied expressions on the faces of her women.

"I am sorry," he said stiffly. "I thought you occupied the State apartments; there must be a mistake."

"So I thought," Henrietta answered. "But it seems that is the name for them. I hope that my rooms in London will not be of the same kind."

"You will find Whitehall Palace compares with any of your homes in France."

He stood up and she curtsied; they kissed each other's cheeks with a coolness that delighted the jealous heart of Madame de St. George, and the Queen left the room with her attendants.

Charles followed after a few moments, going to his own apartments, where his valet, Parry, helped him change into a suit of red velvet with a wide collar of fine Belgian lace. Parry had been his servant since he was a boy; he was a gentle, understanding man who was devoted to the Prince. In all the years of his service, Charles had never once rebuked or punished him. Parry would have given his life for the King.

"The Duke of Buckingham is waiting, Sire."

"Send him in," Charles said. He felt weary and depressed; he had somehow mismanaged that important meeting with his wife. He had allowed himself to be annoyed by a childish lack of tact and good manners, instead of treating the complaint with indulgence. The Castle was gloomy, and she had probably been uncomfortable and homesick. Steenie would know how to put it right; he understood women.

A few moments later Buckingham stood in the doorway, dressed in green satin with an enormous plume in his hat; he looked like a splendid pagan god.

"Your Majesty! Behold your humble servant returned from France! Must I kneel or may I claim a friend's privilege and embrace you?"

Charles came to him and put his arm round his shoulder. In spite of his depression, he laughed. "You may be many things, Steenie, but you have never been anyone's humble servant! How are you, my dear friend. . . I'm so glad to see you, I've been as lonely as the devil while you were away."

"And now I'm back," Buckingham laughed. "With my mission accomplished and the bride delivered to her husband. How do you like her?"

Charles sat down and pointed to another chair for Buckingham. No other man was allowed to sit in his presence, irrespective of age or rank.

"She is much younger than you said," he confessed. "When she saw me she mumbled a speech and then burst into a torrent of tears."

"Nerves," the Duke suggested. "All women are subject to them. And with respect, most husbands are treated to that on their wedding night. Does she not please you at all? She has beautiful eyes—didn't you notice them?"

"They're magnificent," Charles said slowly. "She is far prettier than I expected. There's no fault to find with her looks at all. But she has a pert tongue which surprised me; you didn't mention that."

"Another feminine failing," the Duke grinned at him. "Alas, Sire, all women have tongues; it's the least useful part of their anatomy. She's spirited and she's apt to think the French created the earth, but she will learn, if you're firm with her."

"Are you firm with your wife, Steenie?"

King James paid that much respect to the conventions; his favourites had all been allowed to marry if the bride had a good dowry and kept in the background.

"I don't think so," Buckingham answered. "How could I be when she had so much to forgive—and still has, poor woman! No, Sire, I was never firm with women; I am not interested in moulding their characters. But you must shape Madam a little; believe me, she will love you all the better for it."

He smiled at the King; he was amused and cynical but not unkind. Personally he thought the bride he had recommended was a spoilt little minx, too thin and unformed to be bedworthy, with an insufferable sense of her own importance. He hoped that when Charles had recovered from his initial nervousness and inexperience he would have the sense to break her spirit. He would never have advised the marriage except that the Exchequer was dangerously low and she brought a dowry of 800,000 francs, and an alliance with France which would be useful in the war they were about to declare upon Spain.

Buckingham did not like Henrietta, and he knew that the feeling was mutual. He had chaffed her as if they were equals and then ignored her once the treaty was signed and abandoned himself to a violent pursuit of the Queen of France, the same red-haired beauty he and Charles had admired so much two years ago.

He was sitting at his ease now with his own sovereign, but in fact he had left France in the most unfriendly and inauspicious atmosphere, having almost involved the helpless Queen Anne in a scandal which brought her close to divorce and imprisonment at the command of her husband. Buckingham had scandalized everyone by making the proxy marriage and the negotiations leading to it the background for his own well-publicized love-affair with the French Queen, and the young girl who had become Queen of England had conceived a mortal hatred for him before she even sailed for her new home. Her enmity and the censure of her compatriots did not disturb the Duke. She had been bought, part of a settlement of money and a treaty; her purpose was to breed the King's children, and a few minutes of concentration at regular intervals could achieve this. He saw no reason to fear her and therefore he tried to revive Charles' enthusiasm.

"Don't worry about her, Sire," he insisted. "Everything will turn out well between you; I have a feeling, here, in my heart, that you will be perfectly happy with her!"

"I must be," Charles answered him. "And I feel that since I'm so much older than she, it will be my fault if we fail to love each other and be happy. I need happiness, Steenie; I'm not like you. I shall never go from bed to bed in search of it."

Buckingham leant forward and shook his head.

"You say so now, Sire; but you may change your mind. The taste grows on most men."

"Promiscuity will never grow on me," the King said.

"Please God you will never feel the need of it," the Duke answered. "When do you meet the Queen again?"

"We will dine together this evening. Then we go to Canterbury tomorrow, and I have arranged that the second marriage ceremony shall take place there at St. Augustine's. The following day we will proceed to London. I have decided to go by barge; the Plague has broken out in the City and it's unsafe to travel through the open streets. However disappointed she is with Dover, she cannot help being impressed by London."

"She cannot help being impressed by *England*," Buckingham said. He was becoming irritated by the King's anxiety over the opinions and feelings of a fifteen-year-old foreigner. The chill in which he had left France had wounded his vanity more than he would admit even to himself. His handsome face grew sullen at the memory. The man who had administered the bitterest snubs at the French Court was a priest who was also a Minister and the dour King Louis' only confidant. Armand du Plessis, Cardinal Richelieu, was a cold, polite diplomat with a head of iron and a heart of vinegar. Reputed to have been perversely touched by the voluptuous beauty of the Queen who had inspired Buckingham to so much vulgarity and indiscretion, he had been rebuffed, and he had changed from the admirer into a mortal enemy, pledged to the maintenance of the virtue which had withstood him and to the utter ruin of the Queen's relations with her husband. He was dangerous and clever and Buckingham spoke of him bitterly to the King.

"Like all these Papist priests, Richelieu's a schemer," he said. "And no friend to this country. He drove the devil's own bargain over the Queen's freedom of religion, and not, I assure you Sire, because he is religious!"

"The terms are not unreasonable," Charles remarked. "You know very well that I am not a persecutor."

"No, Sire, but the people and the Parliament are too suspicious of all Papists to allow them any tolerance. If the clauses in that marriage contract are made public, there'll be a most damnable outcry."

Charles listened to him without answering. He had summoned his first Parliament within a few months of his accession and found them as intransigent as his father had often described. They had been gracious, the elected body of gentlemen, lawyers and nobles and squires, and had made speeches expressing their loyalty and devotion to their new King and the approval of the war he was about to declare against Spain. It was not a war which roused much enthusiasm in the King.

His temperament inclined to peace; bloodshed and destruction did not excite Charles.

Parliament's idea was to wage the kind of war which the great Elizabeth Tudor had conducted so successfully against their old enemy. They wanted ships and troops to attack the Spanish ports and capture the treasure ships returning from the Indies. In this way the Catholic oppressors of Protestant Germany would be weakened, and the pockets of the godly in England enriched at their expense. The enthusiasts for war had a sentimental as well as a practical reason for demanding an end to neutrality. The King's sister, Princess Elizabeth, had married the Prince of the Palatinate and was in the centre of the religious conflict. Thanks to the imprudent ambitions of her husband, she had now neither throne nor resting place, and lived in exile in Holland with her three sons, urging her brother Charles to be true to his Protestant faith, and regain what the Prince Palatine's incompetence had lost. But the representative bodies at Westminster, who had been so clamorous in their demand for action, showed a sudden reticence when they were asked to vote the King enough money to equip the ships and the men who were to venture out so gloriously. He had never valued money in his life; he had a natural appreciation for everything that was artistic and rare and beautiful, but he felt nothing of the reverence for actual currency which was shown by many of his Puritan subjects. Charles had been born and educated as befitted a Prince; he was ignorant of other values and inclined to despise men who showed an ungentlemanly interest in trade. Without knowing that he did so, Charles had approached his Parliament with a total lack of sympathy and understanding of their motives or their scale of values. They had screamed for war and action against the Catholic Powers, and he was shocked and disgusted when they avoided their financial obligations. The sum voted was ridiculously small; he knew that Buckingham had fitted out ships and men with money borrowed from place-seekers and from his own income, and that he was sending out a badly-equipped, poorly-trained expedition against the Spaniards at Cadiz. If the Duke failed, the King had no doubt that some of those Members of the House of Commons who had cut him down to the last halfpenny, would be the first to blame the favourite rather than their own meanness. There were times when the new King longed for a full Treasury and a system of revenue which gave the Crown independence of that unnecessary and officious body. He had deliberately made concessions in his marriage treaty with the French which promised toleration to the English Catholics without informing Parliament or any of the Crown Ministers except Buckingham. War between one nation and another was not confused in his mind with the disembowelling of priests and laymen for the crime of practising their religion. Unlike his father, whose beliefs were dictated by policy, unlike most men of enlightened views at his own Court, Charles held his Protestant faith with passionate sincerity. He was unique in his ability to respect the opinions of others without sacrificing any tenet of his own.

He thought of his Catholic bride and felt sure that under the benign influence of the clergymen at his Court and his own example she would see the error of her beliefs and embrace the Church of her adopted country. If she did not, then it was not in his nature to make her; nor was he capable of allowing her views to corrupt him or the children he hoped she would bear him. That had been clearly understood. The heir to the throne of England and his brothers and sisters would be strictly brought up in their father's religion. He had assured a sceptical House of Commons on that point and he intended to keep his word.

Steenie had said he must be firm with his wife. He sat on, thinking of that advice after the Duke had excused himself and gone away to change his clothes and prepare for dinner at the Royal table.

The more Charles thought of the girl he had seen for such a short time, the less he felt inclined to take a stern attitude with her. Her lapse of good manners seemed less significant as the time passed; his irritation and misgivings faded until he remembered nothing but the sweet, piquant little face and the lovely dark eyes full of tears.

He had never been in love, and he was not in love then, but he felt a curious disposition towards it, almost a longing for the emotion which was so lightly roused and as lightly blighted by immorality and cruelty and betrayal between men and women. He was not like Buckingham, as he had pointed out. He had never felt the least inclination to sample women indiscriminently, but that did not mean that his blood ran colder than in the veins of other men. He was not libidinous; he was incapable of the mental leer and the unclean experiment, but the passions of his Stuart ancestors slept lightly in his nature. They were as inflammatory as his temper. If those passions woke with the new Queen of England, if his hopes were fulfilled in her, then his love would follow. And love with Charles knew no limit of prudence or generosity.

In her own apartments, Henrietta Maria was being dressed for dinner with her husband. She had spent a long time choosing what she would wear, over-ruling the advice of Madame de St. George, to the surprise of that lady, who thought she saw signs of needless enthusiasm for the stiff young English King.

"I think you should have worn white, Madam," she said. Henrietta sat down to look at herself in the dressing mirror on the oak chest by the wall. To her annoyance there wasn't a full-length glass in the room.

"Pink suits me better," she answered. "You yourself always told me not to wear white when I am pale. And I am pale. More rouge, please, de Berrand."

The dress was made of the finest Lyons silk, dyed a soft, coral pink and cut low over her tiny bosom and thin shoulders, with a wide collar of silver lace. There were pearl buttons on the bodice, and two rows of very fine pearls of a delicate rosy colour arranged in the curls of her black hair. She had very pretty hair and Mademoiselle de Berrand had dressed it in the style made fashionable by the beautiful Queen of France. It was drawn back from her face in soft waves and fell in curls and little wisps round her shoulders. She looked like an exquisite doll.

"It is not wise to make too much fuss of these people," Madame de St. George said angrily. "After all the King himself appeared in front of you without even changing his dusty coat!"

"You said that before," Henrietta answered. From the moment they left Charles, her lady of the bedchamber and the other ladies had been complaining about her husband on her behalf until she burst into tears and told them to stop or she wouldn't go down again that evening. They had fussed round her with wine and rose-water and some of the less vindictive had said half-heartedly that he was rather a handsome man and seemed quite kind. . . Praise was what Henrietta wanted to hear. She thought him handsome; she had thought it odd but pleasant when he kissed her and wiped her tears with his handkerchief, and she was desperately anxious for some word of approval or encouragement from her few friends in the strange country where everything, even the manners of Kings to their wives, was so different from France. She had an indomitable will when she felt it opposed; it was strong enough on that occasion to withstand Madame de St. George and she silenced her by saying that she had made her complaint over her apartments, and she did not intend to spoil her dinner by sulking.

"I wonder what the King will wear," the Comtesse de Touillère remarked.

"God knows," de St. George said acidly. "Let us just hope that it is the custom in this dreadful country to change one's clothes at all!"

"You look very beautiful, Madame," the Duchesse de Chevreuse whispered, bending close to Henrietta. She was a kind woman, and she thought it a pity to upset the Princess when she was committed to life in England. She thought the English uncouth and unlikeable, but there was nothing to be gained by prejudicing the child and urging her to take a hostile attitude.

"The King your husband will be enchanted by you," she added.

"I hope so," Henrietta frowned. "Thank God he speaks French so well; it would be so difficult otherwise, because I shall never learn this awful English language. It's nothing but grunts and coughs, like a lot of pigs at feedingtime!'

"All educated people speak French," Madame de St. George said. "No one expects you to learn their ridiculous language, Madam. As for the King being enchanted by you—how could he help it? It is much more important to me that he should please *you*."

"I shall know better after this evening," Henrietta stood up. "After all, one can't judge anyone by a few minutes' conversation when we were all upset."

"Reserve your judgement, Madam, until after the final marriage service the day after tomorrow," the senior lady-inwaiting said significantly. There was silence then until the

King's personal equerry, Sir James Paget, came to escort the Queen and her women to the dining-hall.

They left the next morning for Canterbury. The dinner had been a success; even the most hostile of the French entourage admitted that the King of England treated their Princess with courtesy and charm; carving the meats and waiting on her himself. They had sat together talking and laughing; Henrietta very animated like an excited child, with her cheeks flushed till she looked positively radiant, and the grave young King watching her with an expression of increasing tenderness and delight. They had looked so well matched in their youth and their preoccupation with each other, the handsome young man, very regal and splendid in crimson velvet and lace, with a huge jewelled order blazing on his breast, and the exquisitely pretty French Princess in her shining rose-coloured dress. He asked her many questions, and listened with amusement to her graphic descriptions of the stormy journey and the sea-sickness which had reduced her and her ladies to a state in which they looked like half-drowned cats. The remark was Henrietta's, but the Duke of Buckingham looked pointedly at all her ladies and burst into a roar of laughter. She had managed to ignore the Duke, but she did it cleverly, giving all her attention to the strange, intense, yet charming man who was her husband. He thought she was amusing, and he told her, somewhat shyly, that he thought her very beautiful; she had made a conquest of him in one evening, and her vanity and her optimism soared. The threat of Madame de St. George lost all its potency during that delightful dinner and the hours that followed. The day after tomorrow she would truly be his wife, and there was nothing in the prospect to frighten or repel her. Charles came up the stairs to the door of her suite, accompanied by Buckingham and all his gentlemen and the English ladies, some of whom were quite handsome and painted as much as anyone she had seen in France. He bowed low over her hand and kissed it, and to her surprise, he kissed her gently on the lips. It was a pleasant kiss, the first she had received in her life from any man, and she went straight to her detestable, dingy little mirror and looked at her mouth as if she expected to find it altered by the experience.

It had been perfect, and she slept happily and long through

the night, while her husband lay awake until the dawn, thinking about Henrietta, and thinking very impatiently about the night after the next when he would be able to go through the door with her.

But it was all spoilt on the journey to Canterbury. It was a small thing, relatively unimportant in the lives of both of them, but it disrupted the harmony between them as if someone had thrown a charge of explosive into the carriage.

In the State procession to the Cathedral City of Canterbury, in the presence of the English Court who had assembled there and the ambassador of France, Madame de St. George demanded to sit with the King and Queen, and the Queen supported her. Faced by two furious, insistent women, joined by the French ambassador anxious to preserve the honour of his country, Charles refused to allow his wife's attendant to take precedence over a high-ranking English lady. He was white and tight-lipped with anger; it was inconceivable to him that his wife should so far forget her dignity and the obedience she owed him as to argue with him in public and question English custom. He glanced away from Henrietta's flushed, furious little face; she was holding on to her attendant's arm and urging her to step into the carriage, and he saw the annoyance and astonishment of his courtiers and the disgusted look of the Duchess of Newcastle who was being deprived of her rightful place by a foreigner. Buckingham came towards him at once.

"What is the matter, Sire?" He turned and glared at the Queen of England, who had the grace to stop arguing, and Charles, stammering with anger and embarrassment, explained the situation.

"The Duchess should ride with us. The Queen insists upon this woman de St. George. I cannot allow it, Steenie. I will not have her in the coach with me."

Buckingham addressed Henrietta's lady-in-waiting.

"Get back to the second carriage, Madam. Go of your own free will or I will remove you by force."

Then Henrietta stepped in front of him. She was so angry that she could have struck him. Madame de St. George was the first of her ladies, the highest ranking, her inseparable companion; she had been warned to give no concessions in precedence to any of the English nobility or their wives.

23

"You overreach yourself, sir," she snapped. "Madame de St. George rides with me."

Out of the corner of her eye she saw the English Duchess shrug and move away. She turned towards the carriage door and climbed in. The first battle had been won. Then she heard Charles speak in a voice which was as cold as ice.

"Lady Newcastle, follow the Queen. And you, Madam, go to the other carriage where you belong."

They had made the journey to Canterbury in silence. The King stared out of the window after trying to speak to her and receiving no answer; protocol forbade the English Duchess to speak at all unless she was first spoken to, and after a few words which Henrietta suspected were an apology but could not understand because Charles was rude enough to say them in English, the King said nothing to anyone for the rest of the journey.

The route was lined with crowds who cheered and waved, and the King acknowledged them, and his new bride stared out of the window through tears of rage and waved her hand, but nothing would induce her to smile. She glared at the Duchess of Newcastle, who was sitting beside her looking fixedly at the scarlet cushioning above the King's head, and bit her lips until they stung to stop herself from digging the hated interloper in the ribs. How dare they; how could Charles, the attentive, doting husband, humiliate and hurt her by sending poor de St. George away and forcing her to sit with this odious stranger? Didn't he know how de St. George would cry and complain and play on her mistress's nerves until she felt ready to scream with tension . . . ?

And why did he summon that monster, that vulgar, bumptious Buckingham and allow him to threaten one of her ladies as if she were a common drab from the streets?

She was so painfully young and, in spite of her upbringing, sadly undisciplined; she had been taught so much of pride and protocol and ceremony without knowing how to control herself or bend with dignity in any kind of crisis. She reacted and she behaved like the child that she was, in spite of her fashionable dresses and her jewels and the fact that she would no longer be a virgin by the same time tomorrow.

They went through a ceremony of presentation at Canterbury, and she had recovered herself sufficiently to nod her head to the English officials who came up and kissed her hand. She could not reply to their speeches welcoming her and wishing her a happy life and reign with the King because she did not know or understand one word of English. Charles guided her through everything; his attitude was conciliatory because he had already begun to excuse his wife and blame the whole incident upon her lady-in-waiting. Be firm, Steenie had said, and he had been firm. He had made her give way but to his surprise he found that in the process he himself was downcast and disturbed and troubled by a most unreasonable feeling of guilt. And an hour before their marriage, which was to be a Civil ceremony in St. Augustine's Hall, neither Catholic and therefore offensive to the English, nor Protestant and so invalid to the French, Charles went to see her. An attempt was made to refuse him. However, her attendants, though furious at the treatment given to de St. George that morning and plainly disapproving, did not dare to disobey the King when he ordered them to leave him alone with Henrietta.

He saw at once that she had been crying; she had such luminous eyes and they betrayed her emotions. He had seen them flash with anger and sparkle with laughter, and now they were red and tragic with tears. Immediately he felt that odd sensation of pain and disquiet as if he were entirely responsible for her unhappiness. She was dressed in a long velvet wrapper; her white wedding-dress was laid out ready on the bed and the skirts swept down to the floor like a waterfall, blazing with diamond embroidery. He saw the little satin shoes on the floor beside it, and his own magnificent present, a diadem of pearls and diamonds and a rope of pearls which had belonged to his own grandmother, Mary Queen of Scots, and been sold to Elizabeth Tudor by the rebel Lords of Scotland. Henrietta curtsied, but her expression was stubborn.

"You must forgive me," Charles said gently, trying hard not to stammer, "for intruding upon you like this, but after—after what happened this morning, I felt I must see you and explain."

"I apologize for making you angry, Sire, but I understood that my ladies would receive the due of their rank in this country. As my principal lady, Madame de St. George felt that her place was with me and I agreed with her. If I was mistaken, I am sorry."

25

It was a very stiff, haughty little speech, but she spoiled it by blushing and covering her face with her hands to hide the tears which overflowed again. She had been determined not to argue, to be dignified and distant and aggrieved, and certainly not cry in front of him when he was so deeply in the wrong. But after only two days, Charles could not bear to see her weeping. He came and took her in his arms, one hand stroking her hair, while she sobbed against his shoulder like an overwrought child.

"It was my fault," he insisted. "It was all my fault. I should have explained English protocol to you but I thought it had been done. . . Please, dearest heart, don't cry and distress yourself."

He sat down on a chair and lifted Henrietta on to his knee.

"I couldn't leave things unmended between us," he said. "I have been so unhappy today when I hoped to be full of joy and pride, showing you to my people for the first time. And I could not go to our marriage service without telling you how tenderly I feel for you and begging you to forgive me for upsetting you this morning."

Henrietta sat up and borrowed his handkerchief for the second time since they met.

"Madame de St. George is the person who is injured," she said. Madame had indulged in a fit of minor hysterics as soon as she rejoined the Queen; her tears and reproaches and threats to return to France had overwhelmed Henrietta who was tense and tired out and quivering with humiliation.

"I am not marrying Madame de St. George and her injury does not concern me in the least," he said firmly. "She should have been sensible enough to efface herself at once rather than cause such a scene. But we are not going to talk about her; she and her rights of precedence can wait, but misunderstandings between us must not last a moment longer."

"She was terribly angry," Henrietta continued, trying to make him understand the ordeal to which she had been subjected. "And she ended by telling me a most dreadful story about what will happen after the banquet tonight."

Charles looked at her in horror.

"What dreadful story? What has that woman been saying to you?"

"She told me," Henrietta said, "that it is the custom here

for the King and Queen to go to bed in front of the whole Court! If all those strangers are going to come into my bedroom and watch me undressing, I shall die of shame! "

After a moment Charles smiled.

"It is the custom," he admitted, "but not as terrifying as you think. The ladies prepare you and the gentlemen help me and then we are escorted to our bedroom, wished many blessings, and after we are in bed, everyone leaves. There is no harm in it, my poor little Henrietta, but if it distresses you, I shall forbid it."

"Oh, do you promise me?" She put one thin arm round his neck and leant her head against his shoulder. There was something very comforting about him, something very tender and protective and not at all forbidding. She could not understand why all her French attendants thought him so reserved. She felt at that moment as if she had found an affectionate elder brother.

"I promise," he said. "You have nothing to fear."

She was so slight and so defenceless that he restrained his desire to anticipate the marriage service even by kissing her, and was surprised at the strength of the temptation. It was so strong that he set her down and got up quickly.

"I must leave you," he said. "It is time to dress now, and we have the rest of our lives to be alone. Until one hour, my dearest Madam."

He went back to his rooms where his valet and his gentlemen helped him into a suit of white satin, cuffed and collared in priceless lace, and fastened the bright blue sash of the Garter across his chest. Buckingham, dazzling in scarlet and gold came to escort the King to St. Augustine's Hall, and he left leaning on the Duke's arm.

He looked rather solemn and nervous, and Buckingham watched him shrewdly. Everything he had depended upon this inexperienced upright young man who was taking his marriage and his wife so seriously, and he had heard of Charles's visit to the Queen that afternoon. That was a bad sign, a sign of weakness in the King. A sign that the stupid little spitfire had established an influence over him which had already countered Buckingham's advice. He had been firm in the coach with the Duke as a witness, but weak and conciliatory when he was alone. Buckingham watched them take their marriage vows in the old Cathedral Hall and there was a coldly unpleasant expression in his eyes. There was no room for a wife who was anything but a cypher; there was no room for any influence with the King but his own. If Charles fell in love with his wife he would no longer need Buckingham.

The Duke joined the stately procession from the Hall to the waiting carriages, and smiled his congratulations to the King whose face was suffused with happiness. He had arranged this marriage. He knew then that in his own interests he must make sure that it was a permanent failure.

Chapter 2

THE banquet following their marriage lasted for nearly five
hours and dragged through twenty courses. The King and
Queen sat at a table on a raised dais, under a crimson and gold
canopy embroidered with the Arms of England, and they were
served by the Marquis of Winchester who carved the meats,
and the Earls of Pembroke and Essex as Stewards. Three
Countesses waited on Henrietta, and she was surprised to see
that these exalted nobles and their wives served Charles and
herself on their bended knee. The tables were set down the
length of the enormous dining hall which was very tall and
draughty, and a company of three hundred members of the
Court and her own attendants dined with them. The plates
and cups were solid gold, and after each course she and the
King washed their fingers in little golden basins and wiped
them on the finest linen napkins. It was her first experience of
English ceremony, and Charles watched her anxiously to see
whether she approved. She did not like the food, which was
coarse and heavily spiced in her opinion, and her appetite
was naturally small. She picked at the dishes and sent them
away uneaten. Charles ate heartily; he was very happy and
attentive to her, and he assured her in a whisper that he had
not forgotten his promise: she had nothing to fear. He could
not help looking at her and touching her arm and leaning
close to her. His feeling of love and tenderness and expectation
overcame his shyness and his dislike of public display. He had
the prettiest wife in the world and he was overwhelmed with
pride. She was so delicate, like some fragile creature in a fable,
her luxuriant hair blazed with his diamonds, and the famous
Stuart pearls roped round her slender neck. He told her again
and again how beautiful she was and how she had won the
hearts of his Court and his people, and she smiled up into his
face and asked him questions about London and the Palace
of Whitehall which he had assured her was the most splendid
building in the world. He had seen Versailles and stayed at

the Escorial, but he made the claim in all sincerity. To him, his kingdom, his Palaces, his religion and his traditions were superior to anything inherited by other Princes. He was passionately proud of England, as proud and as insular in his own way as the great Elizabeth whose claim to be mere English was a national boast. He loved it all and he was painfully anxious that the girl he already cared for so deeply, should share his love and join in his pride. He told her that she must learn English when they were in London, and Henrietta made a naughty grimace and said that she would try but made no promises. Privately she thought it a silly suggestion since everyone of consequence spoke French.

Charles glanced down at Buckingham, his only friend and confidant, who was not quite so superior to him now that he was married and about to round out his experience of life. He was deeply grateful to Steenie for choosing such an admirable wife, and he sent for him in the middle of the meal to tell him in English how happy he was and how appreciative of his service.

"I am the happiest of men," Charles whispered to him, one hand laid affectionately on his shoulder. "I defy you to point out one woman in this room more beautiful than the Queen!"

Buckingham laughed easily. His heart was bursting with jealousy and fear and he could have named at least fifty English women in the Hall who obliterated that sallow brat for beauty and for charm. For a moment their eyes met, and Henrietta stared at him and looked away. Buckingham's eyes did not change, nor did his smile. He turned smoothly to the King again.

"All men are envious of you tonight, Sire. All except me, for I love you so well I feel as if your happiness was my own." He bowed very low and went back to his place. The Duchess of Buckingham looked at him. In spite of everything she loved him deeply.

"His Majesty seems very happy," she said.

"Too happy," Buckingham snapped under his breath. "Did you see her glare at me and turn away? I've got an enemy there, by God, and she'll do her damndest to turn the King against me."

"No one could do that," Kate Buckingham said. "He's besotted with you, like his father."

"Not quite like him," he sneered. "There's a mighty difference, and you should be glad of it, though I begin to wonder if I am. The old King wouldn't have sat ogling a woman like a sick pupppy. . . She's not even worthy of him!'

"She's very young," the Duchess said. She knew all the details of her husband's conduct with the Queen of France, and she tried to be fair.

She was a wife herself.

"Leave them alone, for the love of God," she said. "She cannot hurt you, and he deserves to be happy with her if he can. You should be thankful to have a Queen as a rival instead of watching every page and groom of the bedchamber! "

He touched her cheek suddenly with one finger and for a moment the mocking, lazy look she knew presaged desire flashed at her like a bribe.

"You were very patient then," he whispered, "And you must be patient now. And good. Good wives get loving husbands. Leave the King and Queen to my discretion and think only of yourself and me."

At the end of the Banquet, Charles rose and gave his hand to Henrietta. Then they left the table together, stepping down from the dais and walking slowly to the end of the long room, followed by the peers and gentlemen in attendance in order of rank, headed by the King's favourite, the Duke of Buckingham and his Duchess, with the French ambassador and the members of the Queen's household. They mounted the stairs and at the head of them they separated, each going to their own apartments to be undressed by their attendants. They would meet again at the door of the State bedroom, for the ceremony of bedding down which had horrified Henrietta.

In her own rooms Madame de St. George and the Comtesse de Touillère helped her out of the heavy gold embroidered dress worn for the Banquet and locked away her jewels. They bathed her face with scented water and combed out her long black hair, and all the time the Principal Lady of the Bedchamber wrung her hands and wiped her eyes and muttered under her breath as if the tired, nervous bride were going to her execution instead of her husband.

In a corner the Duchesse de Chevreuse held up the fabulous pearls and exclaimed over their beauty.

"Pearls are tears," Madame de St. George declared. "Especially *those* pearls! Oh, my God, Madame, how could the King have given you such an unlucky gift? They have no imagination these people, no sensibilities!"

"Unlucky?" Henrietta's tired eyes opened in alarm. "But how could they be—he told me they were part of the Crown jewels of England."

Madame de St. George shrugged.

"They are the pearls which Mary Stuart brought with her from France—the pearls belonging to the Queen of Tears who lost her life in this barbaric country."

She went on her knees in front of her startled mistress whose cheeks were as white as her nightdress.

"I beg of you, do not wear them!"

"That would be a pity," the Duchesse came forward. The whole scene appeared quite ridiculous. Madame de St. George ought to be ashamed of herself for playing on the feelings of the Princess they were supposed to guide and succour in a foreign country.

"You must always wear the King's present, Madam." She said briskly. "Forget Mary Stuart wore them and remember that they hung round the neck of Queen Elizabeth and she never came to any harm! You will be late, I hear the King's Groom of the Chamber coming."

In his own rooms, Charles submitted to some good-natured but ribald mockery from his gentlemen while he changed into his nightrobe and bedgown. Normally only Steenie made jokes or used coarse language, but tonight was hallowed by custom; for once the King was the prey of his courtiers. He had taken a wife and proved himself a mere man like other mortals. There was laughter in his rooms, unlike the malice and conflict surrounding Henrietta, and he came out to meet her with both his hands outstretched. Noticing her pale and anxious face, he squeezed her fingers reassuringly and they walked together down the long corridor, lit by torches in the walls which flickered and flared in a cross current of draughts, until they reached the doors of the State bedroom. The King's two personal pages opened them wide and he stood back to let Henrietta enter first. Then he followed her and turning, faced the crowd of grinning and expectant Courtiers.

"We bid you good night, ladies and gentlemen," he said

and before anyone could move, he shut the doors himself and locked them.

When he turned round, she had moved away from him into the centre of the room. Her long blue velvet night robe was tightly fastened from the neck to the waist, and Charles wondered suddenly whether he was supposed to undo the complicated bows of gold thread or if Henrietta could manage them herself. He had never buttoned his own coat or tied his own shoes in his life. He came towards her uncertainly.

"Can I assist you. . ."

Henrietta stepped back quickly. "No!" she said. "No; I want my ladies."

"But I have locked them out," Charles said; he was so nervous that he sounded very irritable. "You said you didn't wish to be undressed in public and you can't have your ladies unless I have my gentlemen!"

"Then I will manage by myself," she said. She began pulling the gold strings and as she saw his eyes upon her, she blushed and turned her back on him. Charles also turned away and took off his own dressing robe, not without some difficulty and let it fall on the floor. When he looked up Henrietta was already sitting in the middle of the bed, the covers modestly held up to her chin, looking at him with such an expression of timorous curiosity that he forgot his own nervousness and came towards her with his arms outstretched. In his eagerness he forgot to snuff the candles; when he touched her she stiffened, but the feel of her small shoulders, covered in the heavy silk gown suddenly aroused him, and in the intensity of his excitement, he pushed her back upon the pillows and pressed his mouth over her closed lips. They did not open to him until he began caressing her, and then it was to cry out in protest. It was a frightened, querulous cry, smothered by clumsy, eager kisses, and as he exposed her body, she began to tremble and tears ran down her cheeks. In trying to rouse her, he outraged her modesty, and for a few moments she fought him as if he were committing rape. He had no knowledge of women and he made love to her by instinct, blindly and hurriedly, and horrified her by consummating the marriage in the lighted room. When he kissed her again it was a gentle kiss, full of gratitude and tenderness and raising himself upon his arm he looked down at her with wonder. Her eyes were closed, and her beautiful hair fell in disorder over the pillows; she had the body of a child, with little breasts and narrow thighs, and suddenly Charles covered her, and gathering her into his arms, with his head upon her shoulder, whispered his passionate love and thanks for the joy she had given him. He fell asleep without realizing that it was a joy she had not shared or understood. In his own inexperience, he had neglected to awake her passions, reaching a furious finale which left her cold and shaken and feeling as if she had been outraged. When she could move without waking him, Henrietta inched away to the far side of the bed and wept bitterly into her pillows. The candles burnt themselves out and she lay for a long time, crying with disappointment and disgust. Madame de St. George was right; she would never love or trust a man who could have subjected her to such indignities. She fell asleep determined to avoid a repetition of them for as long as possible.

" The French Ambassador is here to see you, Sire." Charles turned to Lord Holland with a frown. He was always frowning in the last few weeks; he was silent and distracted and the high spirits he displayed after his wedding night had never reappeared. His gloom matched the obstinate depression of his Queen, who wandered forlornly through the rooms at Whitehall Palace, surrounded by her French ladies and gentlemen who behaved more and more like bodyguards determined to shield her from the attentions of the King.

The marriage was not a success. Everyone knew that Charles was unhappy with his wife and that his wife avoided him. When they were together they quarrelled or sat in awkward silence, and it was rumoured that at night Henrietta refused him conjugal rights. She was thin and pale and openly hostile to anything or any person belonging to her husband's country and religion. Religion had become the means whereby they expressed their disappointment and antagonism towards each other. The Queen caused as much scandal as she could by attending Mass openly in the private Chapel provided for her at St. James's House and encouraging Charles's Catholic subjects to do the same. She had been allowed to practise her faith on condition that she did so unobtrusively and without subverting English Protestants, but encouraged by her priests

34

and her women, she staged a public display of Catholicism whenever an opportunity arose. The faith and its adherents had been proscribed in England under pain of death since the reign of Elizabeth Tudor. English public opinion in all classes was united in horror and suspicion of Rome and its practices. Her position had been delicate from the first and her own attitude was making it impossible. Charles told Lord Holland to admit the French Ambassador and resigned himself angrily to yet another discourse on the rights and privileges of his wife and the honouring of the marriage Treaty. He was beginning to hate France because French political interests were yet another factor in the unhappy circumstances of his personal life. The Duc de Thouairs cared nothing for the feelings of the Queen he was supposed to champion; Charles argued bitterly that if the Ambassador were genuine he would have tried to reconcile his mistress with her husband instead of constituting himself her advocate in all her grievances.

"Sire," the ambassador came forward and bowed low. He was a dark distinguished-looking man with a very courteous manner which remained unruffled and enabled him to come again and again before the King and deliver his monotonous complaints. Charles stared at him, his blue eyes cold with dislike.

"If you have requested this audience to discuss my wife's imaginary grievances, then I must tell you, Monsieur de Thouairs, that you are wasting your time. And what is more important, wasting mine!"

"God forbid," the Duc said, "that I should inconvenience your Majesty. Your Majesty knows that you have no greater friend than my humble self and my only wish is to see the differences dividing you and the Queen settled peaceably and with honour. This could so easily be done if you would only permit her to visit her Chapel in the proper manner instead of insisting that she goes there in secret like a criminal."

"In my country, sir, the Queen's co-religionists *are* criminals!" Charles snapped at him. "Her religion is treason against the law and I need hardly remind you that every time the Queen encourages my subjects to join her at Mass and makes a public procession out of a private devotion, she is placing these same subjects under the penalty of the law! I cannot help feeling," he continued icily, "that if she were better advised by

35

you, sir, and by those surrounding her, she would remember that wifely obedience is a Christian virtue common to Catholics as well as Protestants."

"The Queen owes allegiance to her Church as well as to you, Sire," the Duc pointed out. "And she feels that you are not fulfilling the promises made in the marriage treaty. That treaty is also the concern of His Majesty the King of France. In it you undertook to ease the lot of your Catholic subjects, and I have had to inform His Majesty that the Penal Laws are still being enforced. He is disturbed, Sire, and disappointed."

"Repeal of these laws is impossible," Charles said stiffly. "If I wished to do away with them, and I assure you I have no desire to persecute any man for his belief, I could not do so. My Parliament would not accept the proposal and the only result would be a stricter enforcement which might seriously endanger the safety of the Queen if she persisted in her present attitude. It is impossible, you understand."

The Duc shrugged slightly.

"It is difficult for His Majesty of France to appreciate that a subsidiary legislative body has the power to deflect a sovereign from his will; we have no such problems in France."

"You are fortunate," Charles said shortly. "In that case may I enquire why my brother of France has failed to carry out his part of the agreement and show some toleration to the Huguenots?"

"He sees no reason to do so, while Catholics in England are still persecuted," de Thouairs answered. He judged by the furious expression on the face of the King of England that he had better revert to the original subject. Where the honour and laws of his own country were concerned, Charles was implacable; obstinate, imperious, sometimes threatening, but he had a fatal weakness where his relations with his wife were in question. He had blazed with anger on that subject before now, but it was more malleable than his hostility as a sovereign; it could be deflected and turned against himself until another concession had been wrung from him for the Queen. Privately de Thouairs thought him a perfect fool where Henrietta was concerned, and he thought that her conduct was inexcusably irritating and unreasonable. But his duty was to use the situation for his country's advantage, and he encouraged her and reproached Charles without a qualm of conscience.

36

"The Queen tells me," he said quietly, "that she is in great disfavour with you because of a walk she took in Hyde Park two days ago. She tells me you received a report of that walk which was quite untrue and that you reprimanded her in a most violent manner. She is quite overcome with grief."

"I doubt that," Charles retorted bitterly. "The Queen may sulk but she is never overcome. As for the walk, as you describe it, it was a procession, headed by her and her attendants and priests to the gallows at Tyburn where some Catholic malefactors were hanging, and it was reported to me, by persons I believe implicitly, that my wife went down on her knees and prayed for them publicly. I did indeed reprimand her; I also told her that she might well be torn to pieces by the London crowds if she ever makes such a demonstration again. If that happens, sir, I hope you and her priests will be truly satisfied."

"The Queen assured me that she did not approach the gallows."

"She assured me also, and I do not believe her. I do not believe," Charles' voice rose suddenly, his temper rising after months of humiliation, nightly rebuffs and unremitting strain, "I do not believe that she cares a tinker's damn for her religion or for anything but causing me pain and embarrassment. If that is her intention, you can tell her from me that she has succeeded past success!"

"I would rather tell her that she is forgiven," the ambassador countered. "Please, Sire, have pity. Go to her this evening and be reconciled. She is so young," he added, "and so eager to learn."

"Oh, my God! Eager to learn? Learn what, may I ask? Certainly not the English language for one thing—she refuses to speak a word—certainly not my wishes, everything I say is disregarded."

"If I may interrupt this conversation," the voice of Buckingham broke in upon them and the Ambassador swung round. The Duke had come into the room from a small antechamber. He had been standing in the shadows listening for some moments. He bowed towards Charles who looked relieved, even pleased to see him, and continued; "If I may interrupt on behalf of His Majesty, who clearly needs a champion since the Queen is so ably and, er—constantly represented by you,

Monsieur, might I suggest that since the Queen is at fault, she should come to the King and ask his pardon? I have no doubt she'd be given it?"

He turned towards Charles, and Charles nodded. He was not in the least angry with Buckingham for interfering or for standing unannounced in his presence. Steenie was his friend, as he had been his father's; Steenie could sit in his presence and wear his hat and interrupt a private conversation and he felt nothing but gratitude and admiration for the way he had put his point of view. Buckingham always brought his quarrels with Henrietta into proportion. Buckingham had pointed out to him the enormity of what she had done by her pilgrimage to Tyburn and inflamed his anger against her until he was ready to give her a suitable rebuke. And Buckingham agreed with him that when she denied it she was lying.

"If the Queen comes to me, I shall receive her," he said. "You may tell her so. Now be good enough to take leave of us, sir."

When they were alone he turned to the Duke. His handsome face was weary and drawn and Buckingham put his arm round his shoulders.

"Don't go to her," he advised. "Let her come to you, Sire. And when she does, insist that she stays for the night this time."

He knew that Charles's pride had been flayed raw by the aversion she had shown for him; he guessed that most of his antagonism and even his hatred of her attendants was due to the conflict of suppressed desire and injured feelings.

"You know I can't insist on that," Charles said wretchedly. "I cannot force myself upon a woman."

"Better to use force than be made a laughing-stock and have those sniggering Frenchwomen writing back to Paris and saying that you are not man enough to make your wife submit to you. I tell you, Sire," he said quickly, "you are too gentle with her. Take the advice of one who knows more women than is good for his soul, and do two things. Get rid of these women of hers, and tell her that if she deserts your bed and refuses you an heir, you will divorce her."

"She knows I cannot divorce her," Charles said. "It would mean a war with France as things are at the moment. And we have troubles enough if we're going to fight Spain."

"If not divorce," Buckingham answered slowly, "then prison. Queens have been disciplined before without making a public show of it and sending them home. Try it, Sire."

Charles shook his head. His anger had gone; he felt oppressed with a sense of agonizing personal failure and despair. There were times when he closed his ears to Buckingham and admitted that the fault must also be on his side, the failure his responsibility. He had known nothing of women; he had spent his life in retirement avoiding his father's worldly, dissolute Court in the hope that he could escape the mistakes without learning by experience. He had not learned and he had ruined his marriage after only a few months and half a dozen nights, each one more fruitless and unhappy than the last until his wife held the sheets to her chin and burst into tears if he came into her room. He came no more, but his longing gnawed at him like a worm of wounded pride and suffocated passion. He sometimes sat with her and looked at her slight, pretty face and body and felt afraid that the day would come when he would throw himself upon his knees and beg. And if he ever did and she refused him, he would probably kill her. . .

He stood up suddenly.

"Something must be done. I can't hurt her, Steenie, I can't bring myself to do the things you talk about—I can't take by force what I only want from love and I can't threaten her with punishments I'll never carry out. So what am I to do? Tell me, in God's name?"

Buckingham smiled. Charles was still sick with love, so soft at the core with his emotion for her that he couldn't come to his senses and pummel the little brat until she shrieked for mercy. And this was just as well because the ways of women were inscrutable, and tougher shrews than this petulant minx had fawned on the men who tamed them. He did not want Henrietta to fawn. He wanted her to spit defiance and weep tears of homesickness and woe until she had killed her husband's love completely and driven him to cool his physical thirst at a less dangerous well.

"You could always take a mistress, Sire. That is one alternative to suing at Her Majesty's door. But before you do anything, dismiss her suite. There are over four hundred of these damned French parasites living at Whitehall alone. Without

39

their support she might listen to reason, and I'll be your spokesman if you like."

If Charles followed his advice, she would never forgive him. And he, Buckingham, would be safe; he would remain the favourite, privileged and inviolate in the King's confidence. And with such a domestic life and such an experience behind him, Charles would be unlikely to remove that trust in favour of another woman. And if an embassy went to France to explain the King's action, then he would be the leader. Having made his plans to blight Charles's chance of happiness, he allowed his mind to stray to his unfinished courtship of the Queen of France, whom he had sworn to see again even at the cost of war. He actually laughed, he was in such a good humour at the neatness of the plot. From the humiliation and ruin of Henrietta Maria whom he hated and the destruction of her life with her husband, the fulfilment of his own desires must surely follow. It never occurred to him that if he saw the Queen of France again, her virtue would hold out against him.

"I will wait until my Coronation. One more month, and then I will do whatever must be done. I cannot go on in this way much longer."

It was the twelfth of January, the old feast of Candlemas, and on this the morning of the Coronation, Charles knelt alone in the Chapel at Whitehall Palace. There were two tall wax candles burning on the altar before a golden crucifix, and the sun shone outside, streaming through the mellow stained glass high above his head, patterning the floor with the gorgeous reds and blues of the windows. The chapel was very quiet; the noise of the crowds did not reach him; he might have been many miles away from the life and activity of his sprawling Palace, filled with courtiers and officials, and he had gone to the Chapel alone early that morning to spend some time in prayer, like a knight keeping vigil before he received his accolade. He had been King for almost a year, but in his heart Charles felt that the sanctity of Kingship had yet to be bestowed upon him. That moment was to come in the Abbey this morning, when he would be anointed with the holy oil and the Crown of the Confessor placed on his head. He had worn it already in a strange defiance of all precedent when he opened his first Parliament. He was the King and the Crown was only a symbol of the inherent sanctity of his position; the sacramental anointing, the taking of his kingly vows, these were the confirmation of his birthright, the seal put upon sovereigns by God who had appointed them His deputies to rule over men. He believed this. He believed that his degenerate father, slobbering and drunken and perverted, was yet touched with the finger of Almighty power by this mysterious selection. Nothing a King did or was could wash away that solemn oil, or reduce him to the level of other men, however worthy and even superior they might be to the living embodiment of sovereign power. He knelt with his head bowed, his heart and mind concentrated in pure prayer, prayer untrammelled by thoughts of outside things, by worry over the arrangements or the expense which he could ill-afford or even by the anguish of going to his Coronation without his wife beside him. Henrietta would not attend a Protestant service. Obstinate, hostile and irresponsible to the last, she had inflicted this deep wound upon his feelings, but at that moment as he knelt before the altar of his Church there was no thought of her in his mind. He was alone with his God and his responsibilities, alone in the solitude of his extraordinary destiny, a man on his knees to the Supreme Authority, as men would kneel to him all through his life. He prayed for wisdom and for a sense of mercy; in his natural humility he also prayed for strength to govern worthily and to protect the interests of the nation which God had placed under his care. He had put aside his own unhappiness, his own doubts, even his own desires, and he made an almost Christlike surrender of himself to the demands of his destiny as King.

He had been born for this day, chosen to survive his ailing childhood, to outlive the splendid elder brother who had seemed born to be King, because God had intended him to reign. God, not the Archbishop of Canterbury or the bloodline of the Stuarts or the wishes of the people, God alone had given him the Crown of England and he was responsible to Him for the power and the use he made of it. It was a terrible accounting, a thing unknown to ordinary men, even to those ordained in Holy Orders, for there was no power as close to the Almighty as the power of Kingship.

He had refused the royal purple customary at a Coronation; he wore white, the colour of purity and sacrifice, the symbol

41

of his humility before his only Judge. He was the King, protector of his people, interpreter of their rights and laws, father and guide to all his subjects, champion of the Church established by his predecessors. And to that Church he came for comfort and for refuge, to pray and recollect himself in peace.

At last he rose from his knees and walked slowly back into the main Palace buildings. He went to his own rooms where his gentlemen and nobles were waiting, and one hour later, riding through streets lined with a cheering crowd of people, Charles passed under the windows of his wife's apartments on his way to the Abbey. He did not look up, and though she watched behind the curtains, Henrietta did not show herself or wave. For a moment her heart softened as she saw the lonely, upright figure in the coach. He looked so withdrawn, almost sad, a single man whose weaknesses she had already come to know so well, a shy, uncertain man in many things, travelling to his solemn Coronation, and her eyes filled with tears when she remembered how he had described its meaning for him and begged her to come with him. Spite and the advice of the people she loved and who hated him, had made her refuse, taking refuge in a bigotry which had little to do with real religious feeling. He had not insisted; he had looked at her with an expression of such pain and disillusion that for a .moment she was frightened, then he turned away and left her. Everyone else discussed it, and she felt the hostility of the English nobles who considered her attitude a deadly insult to the King and to the whole country, but after that evening Charles had never mentioned it again. She glanced at the skies which had been bright and sunny and were now clouding over with banks of rain. The superstition in her Italian blood stirred at the ill-omen. He should have worn the Royal purple; white was unlucky. White was the colour of mourning.

"I should come away from the window, Madam."

She turned to the Duchesse de Chevreuse and saw the disapproval on her face. She alone had advised the Queen to go to the Abbey with her husband and at least sit in the enclosure prepared for her, where she could have seen the service without taking part in it.

"Do not let the people see you, it will only aggrevate their feelings."

"I care nothing for their feelings," Henrietta retorted. "I care nothing for anyone or anything in this horrible country—I only wish there was some way I could go home!"

"As things are with you and the King, Madam, that wish may soon be granted."

The Duchesse curtsied and stood back to let the Queen pass. She pulled the window curtains and joined the other ladies who were sewing by the fireplace. She had a devoted husband who had been driven to distraction by her love affairs and her political meddling, but she understood men and the extent to which their patience and their pride could be attacked with safety. The Queen had overreached herself this time. She had quarrelled with Charles, flouted his orders, rebuffed his advances and presumed upon his love and his desire for reconciliation to behave like a spoilt, unfeeling child. But now she had affronted his kingdom and his people, and the Duchesse felt that this was an insult he would not forgive. She felt no longer interested in Henrietta and she would not try and give her good advice when it was always disregarded. She took up her embroidery and wondered how soon she could return to France.

Two months earlier an English expedition under the command of Sir Edward Cecil, seconded by the Earl of Essex, sailed for a rendezvous with a Dutch fleet and set out to attack Cadiz and capture the Spanish treasure-ship which was on its way back from the Indies. Crippled by lack of funds, forced into a hasty embarkation before the levies had been given more than rudimentary training in drill and the use of their arms, the attempt failed miserably. The fleet abandoned Cadiz, losing the treasure ship which sailed round them to safety.

In London, Charles heard the news of the failure of his first venture in war, and the sorry tale of disobedience, indifference and lack of fighting spirit among the troops was soon spreading over London. He sat with Buckingham in his privy Chamber at Whitehall. It was a spacious room with a lovely view over the river Thames; the King sometimes sat for an hour or more watching the traffic of boats passing up and down the great commercial waterway into the City. He loved the river and he particularly loved Whitehall, set in acres of parklands which were stocked with birds and every kind of flowering shrub. The walls of the room were hung with magnificent Flemish tapestries, and he had banished the heavy Elizabethan furniture and replaced it with graceful walnut cabinets, designed by the new Court craftsmen, and tall-backed, slender chairs, cushioned in velvet and brocade. It was a sumptuous room, typical of the fine artistic taste of the man who spent so much of his time in it and had chosen every item himself. He had so often regretted that Henrietta never shared it with him, never sat by the window and watched the busy river boats and the teeming life of his capital passing below them on the tide.

One of his agents in Holland, introduced by his sister the Queen of the Palatinate, had sent him a painting by one of the Italian masters. The Virgin and St. John was one of the loveliest of all Veronese's religious studies and it hung like a jewel upon the wall. The dark, sweet face of the Madonna gazed at him, and he turned away abruptly. The beautiful eyes, full of light and expression, reminded him of Henrietta.

He looked at Buckingham.

"We are disgraced," he said. "We send a fleet to join the Dutch and the Dutch do what fighting there is while our soldiers run away and their commanders bicker like dogs and come home empty-handed!"

"Sire, you know the cause of it, as well as I do," Buckingham answered. The disgrace of the expedition was already reflecting upon him, and for once in his life he did not deserve the blame.

"Thanks to Parliament's meanness, the fleet was badly provisioned, the ships were not fitted out as they should have been, and the men were the rag tags of the docks and gutters, ready to sign on for anything that promised money. The first sight of bloodshed and the smell of powder and they ran like the scum they were! That is the truth Sire, if any man can be found brave enough to tell it."

Charles looked at him. "I can," he said. "I can tell my Commons and your critics that the fault is not yours, not even the commanders. The fault is the parsimony of men whose hearts are in their pockets! With money we could have sent a proper fleet, properly manned! I shall tell them so!"

"Wait, Sire," Buckingham interposed. "There's no sense

44

in making enemies in Parliament; I remember that your father used to say they were a cursed nuisance but it was as well to be on good terms with them in case they had to be summoned in a hurry."

Charles turned away impatiently.

"It is their duty to be on good terms with *me*, Steenie, and I have no intention of pandering to them as my father did."

"King James was wise," the Duke began.

"The Wisest Fool in Christendom," the King said bitterly. "I know; I heard what people called him when his back was turned. What is Parliament? A gathering of members elected for the purpose of assisting the King to govern. Their assistance to me so far has been a refusal to grant enough money to prosecute a war which they demanded and the passing of a Bill which limits my right to the Customs revenue for *one year* instead of for life. That was a precedent which should have warned me of their real attitude towards the Sovereignty of the Crown."

The total collected from the Customs had always been voted to the King as a matter of course. Tonnage and poundage was the chief means of Royal income, the only independent source of revenue open to the Crown, and without it the sovereign must suffer constant financial embarrassment. The King's personal wealth had steadily diminished since the Reformation, and Charles was in debt as a consequence of the extravagance of Buckingham and his predecessors, and even the money allotted to him by Parliament was whittled away in the process of collection which permitted every intermediary to take a percentage for himself. The whole system was antiquated and corrupt; the City Guilds and the families who had become millionaires through the Reformation controlled the economic wealth of the country, and their representatives were sitting in the House of Commons, doling out a beggarly allowance to the King for the maintenance of every department of his Government. Money is power, and the Commons were no longer a submissive assembly, easily overawed by a peremptory command from their Prince.

Parliament wanted war with Catholic Spain and assistance for the Protestants in Germany and Bohemia, but they had unconsciously adopted the moneylenders' attitude and refused to make a sufficient loan without an increasing rate of interest, and the rate, as Charles saw clearly in his anger and disappointment, was growing interference in the government of the country. But Buckingham was not concerned with the larger issue; he had friends and protégés in the Commons who would speak for him, and he was ready to go down to the House and speak for himself.

"The Commons can be won over," he said. "All they need at the moment is evidence of your good faith, Sire. They are clutching the money-bags so tightly because they're not sure what you will do if they open them."

"My good faith?" Charles stared at him in surprise. "What the devil do you mean by that?"

"I mean that much of this atmosphere is caused by the conduct of the Queen," Buckingham said bluntly. "It is all very well to embark on a war with Spain and talk about aiding the Protestant struggle against the Hapsburgs, when the whole of Whitehall is crawling with French priests and English converts, and the Queen sets a public example of Popery. I've seen many of the news-sheets which are circulating and they all say the same thing. The Queen is suborning you and her influence is spreading to the Council. She did not attend the Coronation, and she has never been crowned Queen according to the rites of the Established Church. She and everyone connected with her has broken the Penal Laws from the moment she arrived here and you have done nothing to stop her. The whole country is afraid of Popery and they see a positive movement towards it taking place under the protection of their King. That is the trouble Sire. They will keep you short of money because that is their only means of defence. If you stop the Queen parading her religion and deliver the English Catholics to the penalty of the law, Parliament will grant you whatever you ask. I swear it!"

For a moment Charles did not answer. He knew how much his wife had injured him in relation to his people, but he was unable to accept that she must be persecuted and with her many men and women whom he knew and whose integrity and courage he respected, in order to placate the groundless suspicions of an assembly who had done nothing to prove their own loyalty. They had no right to question him in anything relating to his Kingly function.

"The Queen is not answerable to anyone except me," he said

at last. "Come, Steenie, I've had enough of Parliament for this evening. I am going to visit my wife. I told her to expect us after dinner."

He sometimes rebelled against Buckingham; he even pretended that his relations with Henrietta were improving, but Buckingham was not deceived. The visit would not do Charles any good; he would not find a sympathetic wife to comfort him and take his mind away from his anxieties, though he came again and again in a humiliating quest.

They heard music outside Henrietta's rooms, and when they entered Charles saw her sitting on a low chair, surrounded by three French ladies, the detested Madame de St. George at her elbow, watching a group of her women dancing to the lute. It was a warm, charming scene, filled with the colour and scent of pretty women and the sound of the gay little tune. Henrietta was smiling when he saw her, but the smile faded and the music stopped as he walked into the room towards her. She stood up, followed by her ladies, and the dancers moved away from the centre of the floor. She was not pleased to see him. There was no welcome, no warmth and relaxation for him. He stood for a moment, an intruder amongst all these foreigners, facing his wife who looked cool and irritated and never said a word.

"I have come to keep you company this evening, Madam," he said, and he stammered helplessly in the middle of the sentence. To his embarrassment Henrietta waited, leaving him stranded and stuttering at the mercy of his impediment, and when he had finished she looked coldly towards Buckingham.

"I see that as usual the Duke comes with you. Truly, Sire, if all men have a shadow, he must be yours."

"I may have one shadow," Charles said suddenly and he said it very clearly this time, "but you have at least two dozen in this room. Buckingham will leave us if you send your ladies to another room. I came to see you and I would like to see only you, if you do not mind."

"But I do mind," Henrietta looked up at him boldly. "I like my ladies' company; I am even prepared to endure the Duke of Buckingham rather than dispense with them this evening." They had been married for nearly two years and she had defied him and snubbed him more times than he could possibly remember. She had often refused to see him alone and

47

wherever she went, her attendants followed her. Nothing had changed, nothing had been said or done that evening which was a greater hurt or humiliation to him than he had suffered on dozens of occasions. He suddenly saw the angular figure of Madame de St. George moving closer to her mistress and the women still crowding the room in defiance of his request. Henrietta noticed that he had become very pale. He turned his back on her and she looked at her principal lady-in-waiting and nodded in triumph. But he did not leave as she had hoped; he went to the Duke of Buckingham and she could not hear what he said.

"The time has come," Charles spoke very quietly. "I have decided to take the first part of the advice you gave me last December. Go out and order the guard. Have every member of the Queen's household gathered together and moved out of Whitehall. If they resist, have them arrested." He turned round and raised his voice.

"Ladies, you will obey my command and leave the room. Stay where you are, Madam."

Henrietta had stepped forward but he moved in front of her and suddenly she stood still. He was livid with anger, his bright blue eyes were blazing as he looked first at Madame de St. George and then deliberately at all the others. One by one they went to the door, curtsied and left. When they were alone Charles walked over and turned the key in the lock.

"What are you doing? Why are you locking my door? St. George, St. George, come back!" She lost her head and began to scream.

He put the key in his pocket and said loudly, "Stop making that disgraceful noise. She is not coming back. She is leaving Whitehall and all the rest are going with her. I have given orders to take them away by force if necessary. This is the end, Madam. There will be no more insults and defiance from you. I have suffered enough because of these people you brought with you. You will never see any one of them again!"

Henrietta stood in front of him, her eyes widening in horror. She had never seen him look at her with such an expression of anger and disgust. She gave vent to a flood of tears, letting them pour down her face, and she sobbed and choked with her hands pressed against her mouth, but there was no alteration, no softening in her husband's eyes, only a cold and furious glare and a frightening gleam of triumph. Fear overcame her, fear that in spite of everything he had said and done to show that however she behaved to him he loved her still, he meant to carry out his unthinkable threat and separate her from all her friends, leaving her isolated, at his mercy and the mercy of all the enemies she had made at his Court in the past eighteen months. She forgot her wilfulness, her overblown pride, everything in fact except the need to avert the dreadful punishment he had pronounced. She threw herself on the floor and clasped her hands in abject supplication.

"I beg of you, I beseech you, Charles, don't do this to me! Don't be so cruel. . . You can't send my people away—they are my friends, I cannot live without them! I have no one else in the whole world!" She was weeping hysterically, and she sank down in a pathetic heap on the floor. "Don't, don't, I implore you . . . I will do anything, I promise, anything if you'll only let them stay."

"If you cannot live without them that is a pity," Charles said bitterly. "Because you will have to learn to live with me instead. Get up Madam, and compose yourself. My mind is made up and nothing will change it. You will have English-women to wait on you, chosen by me and loyal to my interests. You will do as you are told from now on, please understand that. And you will begin by remembering that the Queen of England does not fall on the floor and scream like a kitchenmaid. Get up."

She raised herself and glared at him, her face contorted with tears and a violent resurgence of temper. She spat at him like a cornered cat.

"You monster! You unspeakable beast—how dare you treat me like this! How dare you threaten a Princess of France! I hate you, I hate you . . . I will do nothing you tell me, now or ever!" The sound of voices, male and female came through from the courtyard below her room. There were shouts in French and English and the note of rising protest from the crowd of French attendants who were being driven out of the Palace before a guard of soldiers. The noise became a tumult of screams and yells and before he could stop her, Henrietta scrambled to her feet and flew to the window, shrieking for help. He reached her before she could open it, and caught her by the shoulders, trying to force her back. She wrenched away from him and tore at the catch to open it.

"Let me go! St. George, St. George! For God's sake don't leave me, come to me, he's locked me in!"

Charles seized her arm and pulled her and she caught the attention of the crowd under the window by driving her fist through the glass to the accompaniment of piercing screams. The gathering below became a riot of struggling, shouting men and women, shaking their fists at the Palace, pushing against the armed men surrounding them in an attempt to reach the door and re-enter the Palace, while their mistress fought with the King of England in full view. She kicked and struck out at him, and the indignity of the situation made him completely lose his temper. He had never touched a woman in anger in his life and he was unaware of his own strength. He swore at her fiercely, and wrenched her hands away from the window frame and dragged her back into the room. For a moment he held her in a grip that made her scream with pain and suddenly he shook her like a tattered doll.

"Now stop," Charles shouted. "Stop shrieking, you little virago. Stop it, or I'll have you taken where no one can hear you . . ." Her hair was down over her shoulders, her face was streaked with tears and the hands tearing at his coat were bleeding from cuts caused by the broken window glass. Her dress was torn, exposing the thin, heaving bosom, and suddenly she sagged, cowering and trying to cover herself. He released her and she fell, sobbing and breathless, her strength exhausted. For a moment Charles stood looking down at her, the long months of humiliation and neglect hardening his heart. He had broken her spirit; there was no fight or defiance left in the weeping, bedraggled figure, and he knew that he would never again hesitate to assert his rights or his wishes with someone who had shown herself so irresponsible and lacking in self-control. He had not wanted to hurt her; he would never have used force of any kind against her if she had not made it impossible to deal with her by any other means. Now it was done. The façade created by ceremony and custom had been destroyed between them in a scene of degrading violence and abuse. They might hold Court, obeying the rules of etiquette which governed the public life of a King and his Queen, but they had resolved their personal struggle in a physical fight between an incensed man and an infuriated woman, and the man had established his mastery on the most basic terms of all. Whatever happened between them in the future, nothing could protect her from the consequences of her defeat.

"I shall leave you," he said at last. "I will send someone to look after you. If you go back to the window or show yourself or make any more disturbance, I will have you removed to a suite of rooms in the inner courtyard of the Palace. If I have hurt you," he added stiffly, "then I ask you pardon. But you have only yourself to blame."

He unlocked the door and went out, turning the key after him. He was met by Buckingham in the corridor. The Duke was grinning and jaunty, but when he saw the marks on Charles' satin coat, he actually whistled in surprise.

"Good God, Sire—you've cut yourself."

Charles shook his head. He felt suddenly assured and triumphant. "The Queen cut her hands on some broken glass, that's all. She needs attention. Where are Lady Essex and Lady Scrope?"

"In the green ante-room. I told them and several other ladies to wait there in case you needed them. I had begun to think you'd need help to get her away from that window before she threw herself out."

"I managed it alone, thank you Steenie. Be a good fellow and tell the women to go and take care of the Queen. And pack her clothes and necessities; she will be sent down to Oatlands tomorrow and kept there until these people of hers have been returned to France."

Oatlands was an old Tudor Palace some miles outside London; the red brick buildings were sprawling and mellow, surrounded by a large park which was stocked with game for hunting. It was wild and beautiful and Charles chose it as Henrietta's prison and accompanied her there himself.

He took a small suite of gentlemen and a retinue of English ladies and servants for his wife; his musicians joined them and played in the evenings and during dinner, when Charles and Henrietta dined on a raised table under a canopy and there was nothing in the atmosphere to suggest that when the King was out hunting, the Queen was locked in her room under the guardianship of the Countess of Essex whom she detested, and that she was not allowed to walk or ride out in the grounds alone. She was surrounded by every comfort and treated with such studied courtesy that it made her want to scream with tension. Nobody quarrelled with her. Once when she began to abuse Charles to Lady Scrope, the Englishwoman rose, curtsied to the ground and left the room, bolting the door behind her. That was the rule of her confinement. She must not be upset or hurt or restricted in anything except her liberty to escape or receive visitors from the outside world, and if she attacked her attendants, they were forbidden to reply. They merely walked out and left her locked up until she had recovered her temper. In this atmosphere, devoid of comfort or support, surrounded by people who actively disliked her and would have treated her outrageously if they dared, Henrietta was thrown on the mercy of the man responsible for her plight. Charles was as kind and as polite and considerate as he had been when they first married. He spent many hours of every day with her, impervious to snubs and sulks and tears and quivering silences. He could afford to ignore her when she defied him because he was able to make her position intolerable with a word to her attendants; he was even capable, as she believed, of committing her to the discretion of that hard-faced, beady-eyed Lady Sussex, and going back to London. She hated Charles, she told herself; most of all she hated his new confidence which nothing could shake. She would have to give in; when one of those horrible Englishwomen came and told her to expect the King's Majesty one evening, she would have no one to tell him she was ill, or too tired or did not want to see him. No one would carry that message; no one would even listen if she gave it. They would just stare at her with their stony eyes, and curtsy and stand aside to let him in. And he knew it; he knew that from sheer desperation and anxiety she was speaking to him and making herself agreeable, and there were moments when she felt horrified at her own weakness, particularly in respect of the rights she had refused him and for which he was quietly and fiendishly suing. She wept into her pillow at night so that her attendants would not hear, and without knowing it, she clung to him a little more every day. She capitulated after only two months, when her impassioned plea to her mother to be allowed to return to France was unsympathetically refused. She must do her duty, the answer said. Divorce was an unthinkable disgrace for a Princess of her birth. She must accept her husband and submit to his wishes. There would be no welcome for her in France if she were repudiated and sent home.

Her French household had been embarked for France after remaining in Somerset House and in a state of siege, demanding arrears of salary and refusing to leave without payment. Buckingham obliged the King by moving them forcibly out of London and packing them aboard ship. In revenge they took most of Henrietta's elegant trousseau and a great part of her jewels. Their defection and the dishonesty of their claims robbed the unhappy Queen of her last defence against her husband. She was now in the wrong and the people she had defended so vigorously had helped to put her there. On the evening when Lady Scrope announced the King's visit, she accepted the inevitable and submitted to the experience which was quite the most disagreeable part of her disastrous married life.

He was still in love with her. He knew that as soon as he took her in his arms, and his triumph melted immediately into remorse for the way he had treated her. She lay beside him with tears running down her thin cheeks, so much thinner and paler in the last few weeks, and he felt suddenly sickened and ashamed as if he had committed an outrage. She was his wife and so much weaker, so much younger than he was and he had taken a cruel advantage.

"Forgive me," he begged her. "Forgive me for everything I've done to hurt you and make you unhappy. I did it because I believed it was the only way we could find happiness." He bent and kissed her, his heart aching with tenderness, and as she did not turn away, he gathered her into his arms and began to stroke her hair.

"I love you, Henrietta. I have always loved you from the moment I first saw you at Dover. I beg of you to believe that."

"You have separated me from all my friends," she answered, her voice trembling. "I must accept that because you are the

King and I have no redress. But if you really cared for me at all, you would never deny me a priest and force me to live like a heathen. I have not heard Mass or received the Sacraments for all these weeks. You go to your Church here at Oatlands, but there is no place where I can worship or ask God for comfort in my wretchedness."

"Why didn't you come and ask me before now?" he whispered. "I'd no idea it really meant so much to you—I thought much of your religion was just another means of defying me, another barrier between us. I would never deprive you of your faith, you know that."

"You promised," Henrietta wept, annoyed with herself because she was allowing him to hold and comfort her when she had made up her mind to remain like ice. But she felt warm and safe, and in spite of everything she cuddled into him a little like a lost and frightened kitten. His response was generous out of all proportion.

"I will send for Father Philip tomorrow," he promised. Father Philip was a gentle, studious Scot, with whom Charles had a great deal in common by temperament and nationality. He had liked the kindly old priest and never once suspected him of encouraging the excesses of zeal which had caused so much comment and resentment in a society which would have hanged, drawn and quartered him but for the Queen's protection.

"I want you to be happy," he said desperately. "If you will only trust me, only try to love me a little, I promise you I will never fail you. . ." She put her arms round his neck.

"I will try," she whispered.

At the end of the week Charles took her back to London, and everyone remarked on the change in their relationship. He was tender and protective, and his attitude forbade any reference to the circumstances in which he had left for Oatlands to subdue his wife. It was obvious that he had succeeded; it was also obvious that unless they were deceiving their household, there might soon be an heir to the throne. Charles unburdened himself to Buckingham, thanking him profusely for the excellent advice which had resolved all his difficulties, and admitted contentedly that though his wife remained unresponsive, she was angelic in temperament and acquiescent

54

to his wishes. The Duke listened and congratulated and took the credit with every appearance of satisfaction and told everyone he could trust to repeat it to the Queen that he was responsible for the dismissal of her servants and her subjection to her husband. She might have given way to Charles, but she would never accept him. He did not want acceptance, and above all he did not want the reconciliation to continue. He pressed invitations upon Charles and Henrietta which the former insisted were a proof of his affection, and before a month had passed, the Duke was able to complain to him that the Queen was hostile and insulting and trying to separate the master from his servant. He offered to go to her and placate her, and wearied with dissention and an atmosphere of discord, Charles agreed. It was unreasonable to bear the Duke such an unremitting grudge. He ordered his horses and went out to hunt at Hampton Court.

Henrietta was sewing in her Privy Chamber overlooking the herb gardens and the river when the Duke of Buckingham was announced. She liked the old Tudor Palace better than Whitehall; the air was cleaner and the life was more leisured. There was time to walk and go for trips up the Thames which she and the King enjoyed, and she had found a friend among the English ladies, the beautiful, vivacious Lucy Carlisle. She was happier than at any time since she left France and the last person in the world she wanted to disturb her was the insolent author of her humiliation in the past.

"Tell the Duke I am unable to receive him," she said angrily.

"Madam, do you think that is wise?" The Countess of Newport was an amiable, pretty woman who had made herself agreeable to the Queen and was advancing in her affections as quickly as Lady Carlisle. "He will only complain to His Majesty and try to cause trouble. Why don't you see him for a few moments, Madam? No harm can come of that."

"And no good either," Henrietta retorted. "I detest the creature; he has no right to thrust himself upon me when the King is absent."

"Newport is right, Madam," Lady Carlisle advised. She had once been Buckingham's mistress though the Queen did not know that. Unlike most of her lovers, the Duke had tired first and she nursed a malevolent hatred for him. This hatred, and a passion for fomenting trouble and participating in intrigue were the motives behind her friendship for Henrietta with whom she had little in common. "Don't give him the chance to accuse you of anything. See him and make an excuse after a few minutes and send him away."

"Very well." Henrietta stood up. "Admit him, but stay close to me."

Buckingham came towards her and bowed. She did not offer him her hand, and instead of waiting to be spoken to, he said shortly, "I come on the King's business, Madam, and at his command I desire to see you without witnesses." He glanced at Lucy Carlisle and gave her an impudent grin. "Your servant, my Lady, and yours," he added, turning to Lady Newport. "I shall not detain the Queen for long."

To Henrietta's surprise, they curtsied.

"If the King has commanded it, we must go, Madam," Lady Carlisle explained. "Ring if you need us; we will be in the ante-room."

When the door closed, Buckingham turned to her. There was a sneering, unpleasant expression in his eyes as he looked at her, giving her slight upright figure an expert and insulting scrutiny. There was no child as yet. She was as skinny and small-breasted and sallow as ever.

"I trust you are well, Madam?"

"I am no better for seeing you, sir. State your business, and be good enough to do it briefly."

"It is not my business," the Duke said coolly. "It is the King's. But perhaps you are right; the King's business is mine too. Most people recognize that and behave accordingly. You would be wise to do the same."

"How dare you speak to me like that! Leave the room at once."

"Don't pick up that bell, Madam. I haven't even started yet. And I shall say what I have to before witnesses if necessary. That is, if you want them to hear the King's complaint against you."

Henrietta glared at him. He pulled a chair forward and sat down in it with his legs sprawling and his hat on his head. She turned so pale that he laughed.

"I sit in the King's presence, so why not in yours? Contain

56

your ill-temper, my dear Madam, or you will choke on it before you have heard me out."

Henrietta's hands clenched; her impulse was to step over to the chair and strike the hat off his head. But she did not move. She looked into the cruel, aggressive face and knew that if she touched him or retaliated, he would find a way to ruin her completely with her husband. He was confident because he knew the extent of his power over Charles, a power which she had not diminished in the slightest. She made a visible effort and controlled herself.

"Bravo," the Duke said softly. "You have learnt some wisdom after all. Now, Madam—point one. You do not like me."

"I detest you above every living creature!"

"Quite so. But you show it, and the King is displeased. Crossing swords with me can be a dangerous business; there are many people, some still living, but in uncomfortable, not to say restricted, circumstances who could tell you that. You may detest me, but you will have to hide your feelings. You will have to treat me with friendship and politeness because that is what the King requires. You must not try and exclude me from your little gatherings. They are full of amusement and delight, and I insist on participating. Now, point two is the matter of your coldness to the King. He has often told me how unsatisfactory he finds you in this respect."

Henrietta bit her lips, blushing from her forehead to her neck, and her eyes filled with tears of pain and disappointment.

"I do not believe," she said, "that the King would ever discuss me with you or anyone in such a manner."

"I assure you," he mocked, "the King tells me everything. We have no secrets, he and I. Now, Madam, try to take my advice in a spirit of friendship, the spirit indeed in which it is offered. Relent towards me—take me into your favour and your confidence and we will all be happy. And show some human warmth to His Majesty; he deserves it for all his forbearance to you." He stood up.

Henrietta said slowly, "No man has ever spoken to me as you have done, my Lord. Your intention was to insult me beyond endurance, and in that you have succeeded. I will never forgive you or cease to undermine your influence over my husband as long as I live."

"That is not a prospect which alarms me. You have a pretty

57

head, Madam, but remember when you threaten me, that you wouldn't be the first Queen of England to lose it. You may pick up your bell and ring it now. And give my congratulations to Lady Carlisle. She has improved since I left her."

He turned his back on her and walked out of the room. She heard him begin to whistle and the little sound became a sudden roar and a rushing and the floor heaved under her. When her women came back, they found that the Queen had fainted.

Buckingham had failed to make friends with Henrietta. The King stood in his private apartments with his favourite and listened to the Duke's account of how the Queen had snubbed him and refused his overtures of friendship.

"I tried everything," he said. "I begged her to believe me her friend, I told her emphatically how much this meant to you and how happy you would be if she was reconciled with me. You know me, Sire—I'm not in the habit of begging from anyone, but I positively crawled to Her Majesty, and she ended by telling me that I was the creature she hated most on earth and that she'd never stop until she had destroyed my influence with you!" He paused and looked at Charles. "I'm sorry, Sire, but I'm afraid I lost my temper. I said things to the Queen which I bitterly regret."

"What you said was probably deserved," Charles said. "I shan't blame you, Steenie, I know you did your best. I also know my wife, and dearly as I love her, I know how far she can drive the most patient man when she wants to be insulting."

He was so disappointed and so rent by the conflict of loyalties and affections, that he did not wish to discuss it. She had remained implacable; she had rejected Buckingham's overture and placed him, Charles, in an impossible position; a position where he was bound to inflict pain on her or on the friend he loved. He felt sickened and angry and disinclined to go near her that evening and doubtless hear a recital of Buckingham's faults. Behind his back, the Duke grinned. He felt a twinge of contempt for the unhappy, confused younger man, torn between love for his wife and devotion to his friend, and too blind to see the selfishness of one and the duplicity of the other.

He stepped close to the King.

"If it will give you lasting happiness with her," he said, "I will retire from the Court. I don't want to come between you."

"Don't be a fool, Steenie! What would I do without you? You've never come between the Queen and me—it's thanks to your advice we've had any happiness at all. God bless you for offering, my dear friend, but don't even think of such a thing again. The Queen will relent, I promise you, and I promise you something else. I will never abandon you for her or for anyone living. Now be a good fellow and leave me alone."

Buckingham paid him the unusual courtesy of kneeling and silently kissing his hand. When he was alone, Charles turned and sat down wearily by the window. It was a mild evening and the scent of the gardens drifted up to him full of sweetness, and down by the river a boatman called out as his barge came into its mooring.

He loved Henrietta; he loved her slight, graceful beauty and her infuriating courage and her sad, childish dependence which could change to intractable wilfulness and pride. He loved her and he yearned with a physical ache for agreement and union between them. There had been times since they returned from Oatlands when they had sat together, holding hands and talking or listening to one of his musicians playing the virginals, and his sense of peace and contentment had shown him the final joy of a marriage where mutual love was rooted and strong. At such moments he could forget Buckingham, he could forget his debts and the troubles in his kingdom which were a constant source of worry and frustration. But such moments were too few and too transient to protect him from the intrusion of the man he genuinely loved. He could not desert Steenie to please his wife, because he owed him everything. When he stammered, Steenie spoke for him and disguised his embarrassment; when his confidence wavered or his temper got out of control, Steenie sobered him and advised him and did it without impairing his self-respect. Charles knew very well that he was a ruthless, extravagant, immoral adventurer, but he loved him and he had never presumed to be his judge.

One of his hunting dogs came over from the fireplace and settled by his chair, its muzzle resting on his knee. Charles stroked it, and then rang the silver handbell which summoned his page of the bedchamber from the ante-room outside.

"I will be served privately here this evening," he said. "Send word to the Queen that I shall not be joining her this evening and she may retire when she wishes."

Chapter 3

A T the end of September the King of France sent Marshal Bassompierre as his ambassador to England to enquire why Charles had dismissed the Queen's retinue and was permitting the Penal Laws to function in England in defiance of the terms of his marriage treaty. The atmosphere between the two countries was as hostile as the situation between Charles and Henrietta, but it was unrelieved by any saving moments of reconciliation. They quarrelled, but less violently than before, and as Charles's experience increased and his tenderness guided him, Henrietta began to respond to the physical aspect of marriage, and to find in it a release from the tension and jealousy caused by her husband's defence of the Duke of Buckingham. But they needed the mediation of someone outside their own circle, and the worldly Frenchman arranged a compromise within two months of his arrival, the terms of which permitted the Queen a limited number of French attendants and a complete Catholic Chapel at St. James's, and released Charles from the impossible obligations of allowing freedom of worship to his Catholic subjects.

Bassompierre went back to France imagining his mission to be a success, and found that the French King considered it a failure and the mitigations of the agreement a victory for the bad faith and bigotry of the English who had promised everything to gain his sister and consistently broken their word. There was no toleration for the English Catholics and he considered himself free to turn his attentions to the strong and militant Protestant community in his own country. He was advised on this course by Buckingham's old enemy, Cardinal Richelieu. The bastion City of La Rochelle on the west coast of France was a Protestant stronghold. The forces of the French king, led by the Cardinal, invested it for a siege and cut it off from the outside world by a fleet of twenty-six ships. The treaty with England was broken, the mass of English public opinion saw the siege of La Rochelle as part of the anti-

Protestant campaign which was raging through Germany and Bohemia, and there was no alternative open to Charles but to declare war on Henrietta's country and go to the assistance of his co-religionists in France. The King summoned the second Parliament of his reign to vote the money for a fleet and an army to succur La Rochelle with Buckingham in command. Parliament, strongly Puritan and wholly Protestant, was in agreement with the war; it was in agreement with any measure aimed at the iniquitous followers of Rome, from a full-scale war, to the death of an ageing Jesuit whom the King had tried to pardon. But it was not in favour of the Duke of Buckingham as the expedition's leader. No favourite is popular, and his extravagance and immorality made him particularly hated by that section of the Commons who regarded a visit to the theatre as an unpardonable sin. If the Commons was asked to vote the money for the war, then the Commons felt they had a right to interfere in the choice of a commander, and to enquire into the failure of the last venture at Cadiz for which he was responsible.

Charles was holding a Council meeting at Whitehall. His second Parliament had been summoned the day before and he had opened it and made a speech, haltingly delivered because he was nervous in front of the assembly, explaining the financial needs of the Crown and the necessity of a generous grant to prepare for the war against France. The need of their fellow Protestants in Europe was being pressed upon him daily, and it was his Divine duty to come to the assistance of the Huguenots at La Rochelle. If he had not misjudged the temper of his people, they were in sympathy with that duty and anxious to see it carried out. He asked his Commons to vote the money for war with France.

Buckingham had sat in the Gallery, and he nodded approval at the King. It was a good speech, and the Duke decided that the King had made a good impression, very young and earnest and dignified. The Commons thanked him, flattered him, and promised to debate his requests. Charles went back to Whitehall, and he was discussing the needs of the navy, Buckingham proposed to take to La Rochelle when Lord George Goring was announced.

Charles looked up in surprise. He disliked being disturbed

at Council meetings; Lord Holland, the Duke of Newcastle and the Lord Treasurer, Lord Weston, were seated down each side of the table, and Buckingham was at the end, facing the King.

"What is it, Goring?"

"Sire, forgive me for intruding but I dared not wait another moment! I was down at the Commons this morning—the Queen wanted to know how the debate was progressing when one of the members began attacking the Duke of Buckingham!"

"Which member?" Charles said sharply.

"I enquired, Sire. Sir John Eliot, the member for Fothering."

"Eliot?" Buckingham said slowly. His face was slowly reddening.

"Eliot is one of my creatures—he's been under my patronage for several years. . . Good God, I got him elected!"

Goring turned to him.

"Well, he denounced you this morning. And that is not all. The whole House joined him. And they have impeached you for High Treason."

"What!" Charles pushed his chair back and stood up. He saw the Duke's colour fading, and his temper blazed. Impeachment was the only means open to Parliament of attacking a Minister of the Crown. And impeachment for High Treason carried the penalty of death.

"That is impossible—they wouldn't dare!"

"They did, Sire. They said the Duke was responsible for the Cadiz disaster—they accused him of taking money from the Exchequer, of selling offices and bribing his enemies. And someone, Eliot I think, accused him of giving some potion to the late King which hastened his death!"

Everyone was standing, and slowly they turned to the Duke, the man hated by most of them and feared by all, who was suddenly attacked and called a traitor and a poisoner and called to stand a trial he would never survive. It was incredible that a secondary assembly composed of members of the middle classes and the younger sons of the nobility should have dared to do what was beyond the power of the greatest peers in England.

Buckingham was standing with them and suddenly he laughed. He came round the table and put his arm round

63

the King's shoulder and faced them all. He was betrayed by nothing but his ashen colour and even that was changing to his usual ruddy complexion. There was not a sign of fear or surprise or of anything but amusement when he spoke.

"If they've impeached me, Sire, then I'll stand trial and answer them. I should like to send such a pack of curs running with their tails between their legs." Even his enemies, and Goring was among them, had to admit that in that moment Buckingham was worthy of respect. Charles turned to him; he was white and strained with fury.

"You will do nothing of the kind. You are my Minister and answerable only to me. This impeachment will be stricken from the records. Goring, send someone back to the Commons and let me hear everything that is being said. Now, my Lords, we will interrupt our business to make our will known to our subjects at Westminster. Sit down, please. Lord Holland, kindly write the following.

"To the Commons at Westminster from Charles, King of England. I am willing to hear your grievances, as my predecessors have been, but I must let you know that I will not allow any of my servants to be questioned by you; much less one who is of eminent place and near to me. I see you specially aim at the Duke of Buckingham. Your business is to hasten and grant me the supplies I ask or else it will be the worse for yourselves."

"Sire," Lord Goring protested, "you cannot send such a message. . ."

"I am not aware," the King said, without looking at him, "that I asked for your advice. I thought you had gone to send an observer to Westminster as I ordered. When you have written that, Holland, I will sign it."

He wrote his signature at the bottom of the letter and a messenger took it to the House of Commons. Then he resumed his seat and continued with the Council meeting. No one spoke of the Parliament's action again; Charles behaved as if the incident were closed and re-opened the question of the Fleet bound for La Rochelle. All his life he had disliked friction; he was genuinely peaceful and inclined to avoid conflict if he could see an honourable way to compromise. But there was one principle which he could never yield without surrendering everything he believed in with absolute fanaticism. That principle was the authority of the anointed sovereign. He might regard himself with humility, even with dissatisfaction and doubt, but he would never admit to error as the King of England. He would never admit that any human agency had the right to question him or to impose a limit upon his Kingly power. If he had hated Buckingham, instead of loving him, his answer to the Commons would have been the same. The King's Ministers were an extension of the King's authority, and responsible to him alone for the way in which they discharged it. The attack upon Buckingham was a criticism of his master; the attempt to arraign him for treason was an infringement of the rights of the King to govern through his Ministers and thereby create a precedent which brought those Ministers within the jurisdiction of the House of Commons. And they had no such jurisdiction. Their function was to assent to the laws their Sovereign made and to provide the means of putting them into effect. If the price of their support for the war with France was an encroachment on the authority of the King, then he would fight that war without them.

Henrietta was waiting for him when he dismissed the Council. Goring had come to her with the news; he was a member of her household and one of her circle of intimates, of whom Lady Carlisle was the leader and her inseparable companion. Much of her antipathy to the English had vanished in the past few months; she found many of them amusing and agreeable and ready to respond to any sign of favour. And in spite of everything she was happy with Charles and was desperately hoping for a child.

Charles came to her and kissed her and, without being dismissed, Lady Carlisle and Lady Newport curtsied and left them alone together.

"Goring told me what had happened," Henrietta said. "I can hardly believe it!"

"Nor can I," Charles put his arm round her. She showed no visible sign of triumph at the attack launched on her enemy and he was deeply grateful to her.

"I sent them a message, and I don't think we will hear any more of it. Steenie has offered to stand trial, but of course I wouldn't think of it."

"How you must love him," she said slowly. "One is tempted

65

to suspect that in striking at him, they are really aiming at you."

He sat down and held on to her hands, looking up at her.

"That is exactly how I see it," he said. "They *are* striking at me. They are striking at my authority, and that, my love, is just as important to me as Steenie himself. On my way here I prayed to God that you would understand that. I know you dislike him," he went on, and turning her hands upwards he kissed them tenderly, "But I relied on you to see that much more is at stake than personal enmity."

Henrietta knelt beside him, and gently touched his face.

"Six months ago I would have rejoiced to hear anyone, even the common people, do what this Parliament has done. Don't look hurt, Charles, you know I'm not a hypocrite and nothing has changed in my feelings for that man. I can never forgive him for what he has said and done to injure me, but I too am royal, and I know that, whatever happens, he must be protected against this impeachment. The men in this Parliament are subjects; they have no right to attack him because he is your servant. That is what matters. So you needn't fear I shan't support you, even though it means supporting him."

He gathered her in his arms and held her closely. "God bless you, my love."

She knew that war was inevitable between her own country and his; she and her family would be enemies within a few weeks, but she had not protested or reproached him. He was so relieved to find that her miraculous tolerance and control extended to Buckingham that he could have wept. She had changed, slowly perhaps and with much pain and difficulty, but there was little left of the unruly, wayward child who had caused him such unhappiness when they first married. She no longer shrank from him as a husband, and the understanding they shared in the nights was influencing every aspect of their life together. There were times when he found the magnetism of Buckingham an oppression and secretly resented it. He knew now that his wife and his favourite were in mortal competition for him and he also knew instinctively, and with relief, that his wife was slowly winning.

He began to caress Henrietta, touching her soft shoulders and her hair, drawing strength and confidence from the physical contact. Whatever happened he would not falter.

Without money, without legal sanction, he would go to war and win it if he had to pawn the plate on his table and the jewels in his Treasury. And if his Parliament refused his demand and defied him, he would dissolve them and rely upon the loyalty and good sense of the English people. He pressed his wife against him and whispered, " Will your ladies come in . . ? "

"No one will disturb us," Henrietta murmured "until I ring."

Parliament defied him. The landowners and lawyers received his peremptory message with its ring of Elizabethan autocracy, and their resistance hardened. Most of them were honest men with a genuine sense of grievance and a conviction that the ineffective foreign policy which neither succoured the Protestant forces in Europe nor built advantageous alliances with anyone else was due to the influence of the King's favourite. Buckingham had always been unpopular; he was hated for his extravagance and his arrogance, and more simply because he owed his power to infinite charm. And the charm was not wasted on his inferiors. It was difficult for the members of the Commons to respect and trust the King when the King was tainted by his favourite's influence. The King had chosen the most hated man in England as his friend and an unpopular French Catholic as his wife. The tiny sect of Puritans that had been so cruelly persecuted in the preceding reigns had grown into a solid body of responsible men, many of whom belonged to the middle and professional classes and found sympathizers in the aristocracy. They believed passionately in the right of men to worship God according to their conscience, provided that it did not advise them to be Roman Catholics or even members of the Established English Church. They preached humility and virtue, but they burnt with the pride of the Israelites in believing themselves the chosen people and all others destined for hell-fire. To such people it was blasphemy to declare that a King, anointed by rites of which they deeply disapproved, was above criticism and that his immunity extended to his servants. Sir John Eliot, at one time Buckingham's protégé, was a typical example of a minor courtier drawn to the idea of a responsible legislative body where his oratory and knowledge of the law was not dependent upon the favours of a monarch or that monarch's friends.

He and others like him joined with members such as John Pym, a lawyer and a convinced Puritan, and John Hampden whose family had been Squires in Buckinghamshire since the Norman Conquest. Hampden was a rich man who had found an outlet for his energies and his opinions in election to the House of Commons; he was a Puritan whose religion was a consequence of centuries of independence and responsibility untouched by the atmosphere of Courts and the cult of the Sovereign. To him, and to all who made a study of the history of the Commons, it appeared that successive Kings had encroached upon its rights and powers, and that those rights and powers should be restored. The King's petition for money reminded them once again that he was unable to govern without them and inevitably posed a question of where his authority ended and their right to interfere began. There was nothing in the appearance or the mode of life of Charles which inspired love or loyalty in the Pyms and Hampdens of his Parliament. They suspected his youth, and they thought his lace and velvets and uncropped hair were the vanities of the Devil. The incarnation of the Devil was his Minister, Buckingham, who had once worn a suit embroidered with diamonds to the value of ten thousand pounds.

Pym rose in a packed House of Commons and once more demanded the impeachment of the Duke of Buckingham. Nothing would be granted to the King until the grievances set forth had been redressed. In the middle of a noisy and defiant debate, an escort arrived from Whitehall accompanying the Gentleman Usher of the Black Rod, the official empowered to dismiss Parliament in the King's name. His appearance in the Chamber brought the members to their feet and silenced the speakers. The Speaker himself was an officer of the Commons exercising the function of arbiter in debate, and it was hallowed custom that no motion could be carried without his presence in the Speaker's chair in the middle of the Chamber. Black Rod advanced into the centre of the floor and pronounced the King's sentence of dissolution to a silent and hostile House. It was an unfortunate part of the rights and usages of the Commons that the presence of Black Rod suspended their activities automatically and disbanded the members until the King chose to summon them again. They

68

had challenged Charles and Charles had answered them through the power of what was termed the Royal Prerogative, the right of the Monarch to dismiss his Parliament if they resisted his demands.

He had silenced them and deprived them of their only means of exerting public pressure on him. But if Black Rod was the King's weapon, money was the Parliament's, and the two hundred members returned to their homes all over England and waited to see how long he would be able to last without it.

"My Lords, you all know that what I intend asking of others, I have given myself. I have sent the gold plate to the Mint and sold some of the jewels belonging to the Queen and myself. Many of you who serve in my household have suffered a reduction in salary."

Charles addressed the members of the Privy Council who were meeting at Greenwich Palace. St. Stephen's Hall at Westminster was empty, the doors had been locked and the Commons were scattered. He was alone with his responsibility for the relief of La Rochelle, a half-empty Treasury, and a grumbling, discontented Court who found their amusements curtailed and their allowances suspended. He looked down the line of faces, at the men whom he had called to advise him and help him in his struggle to maintain the independence of his Crown. There was Holland he was able, but inclined to be lazy; there was the Duke of Newcastle, enormously wealthy, narrow in vision and inclined to act on impulse, but perhaps the loyalest of them all; the Lord Treasurer, Weston, who was already disliked for preaching strict economy in the Court itself; and the Lord Chief Justice, Nicholas Hyde, who was newly appointed because his predecessor had denounced Charles's proposals as illegal. Hyde and Newcastle had much in common. Both believed in the Divine Right of their King, and that its resistance or denial was a crime which deserved punishment by imprisonment or, in obstinate offenders, death. They would not hesitate to carry out the orders Charles was going to give.

"Our fleet will be ready in three months," the King continued. "But I need not tell you that it will never sail for France unless we get more money. I have considered many ways and means of raising what is needed. I tried in the first instance to appeal to the loyalty and generosity of my subjects by asking for free subscriptions from those who could well afford it. The response was shameful." His expression hardened. There was an enormous and unequal distribution of wealth among his people, and he had directed his plea to them in terms covering every contingency. He had called on the aristocracy and the immensely rich landowners to support him out of loyalty to the Crown, and made a less exalted appeal to the City of London, never notorious for generosity to the Sovereign, by explaining the danger to their trade if the wool markets of the Netherlands succumbed to Catholic arms. The response was shameful indeed. The money came in grudging dribbles, given in many cases by those who could ill afford it, and ignored by those whose homes and coffers were bursting with treasure. He was shocked and disgusted and then suddenly bitterly angry. If his people would not give to their country and their King and support them both in time of war, then he would take what he needed by force.

"The Lord Chief Justice has looked into the matter of a Forced Loan," he said, "and he finds that the Tudors had recourse to it more than once and thereby established a precedent. It is a precedent which has become part of my Prerogative, and I intend to make use of it now. Demands for sums of money will be sent to every person in the realm who has substance, under the authority of the Great Seal of England. If those demands are refused, the offenders will be committed to prison until they pay."

"I can think of some who will not," Lord Holland remarked. "If Your Majesty is including some of the wealthier members of the late Parliament in that list. . ."

"Then they will be punished," Newcastle snapped. "It may teach them to vote it without arguing next time."

"There will not be a next time until we've relieved La Rochelle," Charles said shortly. "That is the purpose of these measures. Now, my Lord Justice Hyde, the responsibility for enforcing the Loan will rest with you and your justices. In cases of contumacy, the Sheriff's Courts in each district will try the offender and extract the money without punishment if possible. I am not interested in being vindictive; I am only interested in collecting the money. We need at least a million pounds."

"We shall have it, Sire." Hyde rose from the table and bowed. "We will have it within three months, I give my word."

The Proclamation was drawn up and the Great Seal affixed to it in the presence of the King and the members of the Privy Council, and according to ancient and as yet unchallenged custom, the contents became law. Other proclamations followed; recruits for the Duke of Buckingham's army could be pressed into service against their will, and the townspeople and the villagers were bound to lodge them and provide for them out of their own resources until embarkation; soldiers and civilians came under the provisions of Martial Law until the King pleased to suspend it. Charles signed every document. He signed away the liberties and the rights of appeal which his people had begun to take for granted and which even his father, by no stretch of imagination a champion of justice for the common man, had never dared deny them. He did so because he had no choice. Their elected representatives had proved themselves disloyal and irresponsible, and the people themselves had not responded when the King appealed to their finer feelings. He had made up his mind and from that moment he never hesitated. And no one tried to reason with him. Buckingham, intent upon the expedition and triumphant over the failure of the attack upon him, praised every measure and encouraged more. And the Queen, violently partisan towards her husband and the rights of Royalty, curtailed her expenses, pawned her jewels and raised a little money for him among her English Catholic friends.

In the following months the Court lived quietly at Whitehall. Charles himself worked until he was exhausted, supervising the ordnance and supplies for the fleet gathered at Portsmouth and watching the money extorted from his subjects go out to the shipwrights and gunsmiths as fast as it came into the Treasury. The Lord Chief Justice had kept his word; those who refused to pay were imprisoned and kept there without trial and their numbers included John Hampden, Sir John Eliot, Denzil Holles, and other Members of Parliament. In the country itself, enthusiasm for the war was fading; it

71

was prosperous and lazy and primarily concerned with trade. If the King stinted himself in London, the Commander of his forces lived in sumptuous style at Portsmouth, where his excesses with women and his arrogance to the City officials mocked at what was supposed to be a religious crusade. When the fleet sailed at last for France, it did so at the cost of the King's popularity with his people and the liberty of hundreds of respectable citizens and gentry who had been thrown into prison without any prospect of release. Charles went to Portsmouth and said good-bye to Buckingham. The Duke knelt on the quarter-deck of his flagship and kissed the King's hand and promised to return victorious before the autumn.

But the spirit of the great Elizabethan captains Hawkins, Frobisher and Drake did not exist in the fleet Buckingham took to France; one man's courage was not enough; the Duke's worst enemies had never accused him of being a coward, but he could not hope to overcome the lack of enterprise and loyalty which poisoned his command from the officers to the lowest ranks of his troops. Nearly forty years of peace had softened English backbones; the defeat of the Armada was a tale told by old men over the fire, and the swords of Charles's people had long been beaten into ploughshares.

It was three months before the remains of the expedition returned to Portsmouth Harbour, leaving two thousand corpses in the salt marshes and the seas round La Rochelle. The blockade was unbroken, and Buckingham brought nothing back to England but disgrace and defeat.

Charles blamed himself. He received Buckingham at Hampton Court, holding Henrietta by the hand, and refused to listen to the Duke's apologies. Something had happened to Buckingham; some of his infuriating, fascinating buoyancy had gone, and his face was lined and tired. He had even gone down on his knee to the Queen, and when he tried to tell Charles how he had failed him, tears came into his eyes.

"It's not your fault," Charles said. "You did what you could with what I provided for you, but it was not enough! You begged me for reinforcements and supplies and I couldn't send them in time. . . I know it, Steenie, I know it all!"

"Ah, but you don't, Sire! It is useless to blame my defeat

on yourself. I led them there, and by God I had to take a cudgel and beat my own men round the head to make them disembark and face the fire of a miserable little force of Frenchmen. All the reinforcements in the world cannot make a fighting force out of a cowardly rabble—that is the Commander's responsibility and that is where I failed."

He looked at the serious face of the King, undarkened by reproach, and felt overcome with shame for the first time in his life. He had been so shamed by his men that his own initiative was broken; he knew nothing of the conduct of war except that courage and resource were essential, and the commanders who went with him, men like Sir Edward Cecil who had fought in the Dutch war, were too jealous of him and each other to supply the tactical experience he lacked.

The King had quarrelled with Parliament to protect him, staking everything upon the success of the venture, and even Henrietta whom he had hated and despised had proved that at last her loyalties lay with Charles and England.

"I beg of you both," the Duke said, "to forgive me. I also beg of you to give me one more chance."

"You are not suggesting you go back?" Henrietta asked.

"I must," Buckingham said. "I must go back and I must win, or I'll have done the King an injury which can never be healed. Believe me, Sire, I'll die at La Rochelle rather than have you stand before your people as a King who cannot win a war without the help of the Commons who defied you. You see that, Madam," he appealed to Henrietta, "you see that this is no scheme to glorify myself or excuse my own failure. I am a rich man, and every penny I possess will go into equipping another fleet—I will ask nothing of the King but his permission to go back to La Rochelle!"

"I am not thinking of myself," Charles told him gently. "I undertook this war on a point of honour; I gave my word as King and Head of the Protestant Church that I would help the Protestants at La Rochelle, and I cannot break that word. I do not know yet what must be done, but I do know this. I regret nothing except that I let you go too soon and without the money and men you needed to back you at the crisis of the battle. And I thank God you've come safely back to us." He squeezed Henrietta's hand. "I know the Queen joins me in that."

"I do," she said, and she said it for his sake alone, without looking directly at the Duke. They had been so happy in his absence that she wished Buckingham would sail to the end of the world.

"We will meet in Council tomorrow morning, and you can make a full report," Charles said. "And be sure that I shall support you in everything."

There was silence for a few moments after the Duke left them.

"He's right," Charles said suddenly. "He must go back. But God knows how we're going to do it without money. We've come to the end of the Loan and what we got from it was insufficient."

"Then levy more taxes," Henrietta suggested. She had little patience with people like Lord Holland and the dour Earl of Sussex quibbling over the need for Parliament's assent. If that was the law in England, it was a bad law and should be changed.

Charles sighed and put his arm round her. The simplicity of her approach was frightening; it offered the plain solution to all his problems, but at the same time it invested the Crown with powers which it had never had, even under the despotism of the Tudors.

"We'll have to wait," he said, and feeling her stiffen slightly with impatience, he pointed towards the window where the autumn sun was shining. "It's still early, my darling—I can't stay mewed up in here another moment. Let's order some horses and go out!"

Henrietta brightened. She was sick to death of worry and discussion and the blight of failure. Much as she loved Charles, there were times when his Stuart propensity for brooding on the unpleasant almost made her lose her temper with him.

"I'll ring for Lucy," she said quickly. "I can change my costume and bring some of my ladies with me and be ready in half-an-hour!" As she moved away, he caught her suddenly and surprised her by kissing her fondly on both cheeks.

"My sweetheart—what would I do without you? Thank you

for everything you give me so constantly that makes me happy. And thank you for being kind to Steenie when he was so low today."

A new fleet was assembling at Portsmouth. The press gangs were busy from one end of the country to the other, and the King's justices, ignoring his command that only the rich were liable, demanded money from the poor. The troops were unpaid, and they pillaged and stole, inflicting the crimes of an occupying army on their own people. Public protest became a roar in which the Puritan clergy joined, and the London mob attacked a pedlar in drugs and philtres, who claimed the Duke of Buckingham as a client, and tore him to pieces in the streets. The prisons were full of recalcitrants of all classes and the country was under the rule of martial law. But there was not enough money, and the fleet could not sail. Charles had gone too far to turn back and abandon the enterprise; as King of England he would not sue for peace with France and leave La Rochelle to its fate, and the only alternative was the one he had broken the laws of his kingdom to avoid. Even the extremists on the Council like Newcastle and Hyde saw no choice but to follow the advice of men like Essex and the Duke of Manchester and the Earl of Northampton, all of them courtiers and constantly near the King, but who believed it impossible to ignore the constitutional practices of England any longer.

At the beginning of 1628, Charles summoned Parliament to meet at Westminster.

The Chamber was crowded to the walls on that day in March when the King rode down from Whitehall to address them. Sir John Eliot had been released from prison; so had Hampden and Holles and an opinionated Yorkshireman called Sir Thomas Wentworth who was newly elected. There were several new faces in the crowd which watched the King read his speech from the Throne, and the member returned by the Borough of Huntingdon was the local squire, the middle-aged, thick-set Mr. Oliver Cromwell, whose great-great uncle had been a Minister under Henry VIII.

In the circumstances, the King's message to them was not conciliatory. If they expected a confession of failure or any

75

hint of humility, they knew very little about Charles Stuart. He spoke to them as their King, and as their King he made it plain that this time he expected obedience. In return he would consider their lawful grievances. They listened to his demand for money in silence; the Speaker made a formal reply and the House rose politely when the King and his attendants left the Chamber.

Sir John Eliot, the leader of the King's opponents, the spokesman of the Puritans, caught the Speaker's eye and was given leave to open the debate. He was a clever man and an experienced politician; he nullified any possible effect created by the King's speech by completely ignoring the war. For twenty minutes he attacked the rites and ceremonials used by the Anglican clergy and brought the Puritans to their feet with an accusing cry of Popery. Sir Thomas Wentworth had been watching Eliot intently and with increasing suspicion and dislike. The two men were old enemies united in an uneasy truce; he himself had gone to jail rather than pay money which he regarded as an illegal extortion but he had just listened to the King and been moved in spite of himself by his dignity.

Eliot had ignored the real issue for which they had been summoned; he was now pouring out a tirade of hate and bigotry and whipping up passions on the question of religion which did not interest Wentworth in the least. The country was at war, unable to secure a victory for lack of funds and suffering from the illegal and inefficient methods employed by the King; the whole system of constitutional government was threatened, and it was obvious to Wentworth that Eliot and his party had no desire to reach a settlement with the King.

At the end of Eliot's speech, while the Puritans cheered and the moderates and Royalists protested, Wentworth rose to speak.

"My Lords and Honourable members!"

He had a resonant voice and a lifetime of authority behind him as a large landowner, Sheriff and Justice of the Peace. The House quietened and prepared to listen.

"We are summoned here today to discuss matters touching the liberty and honour of the English people and to demand the redress of certain grievances and wrongs. Citizens are in prison without trial; many of us here, including myself, were among them not long ago. The country is under martial law and the war with France has brought us nothing but failure and disgrace. We are at odds with the King, but though he asks much of us, I believe we have a duty to consider it for England's sake."

"What of his duty to us?" Holles shouted.

"His duty is to govern his kingdom properly," Wentworth retorted, "and it is my belief, my conviction, that His Majesty knows now that he cannot hope to do it without the support of Parliament. The King has come to us, gentlemen, not we to the King. Let us remember that. Let us remember that we are here to save our country and our people from chaos and ruin and defeat at the hands of the French. The King wants supplies; well, I say to you that grievances and supplies go hand in hand."

"The King promised nothing," Eliot interrupted, jumping to his feet, but the Speaker rebuked him and he was forced to sit down until Wentworth had finished.

"We know what those grievances are," he continued. "I move that we draw up a petition naming them all and present it to the King for his assent. I also move that every effort should be made to mend this quarrel within our own kingdom and reach an understanding with His Majesty, without whom we cannot hope to achieve anything. Good will is essential! And if the honourable members expect their sovereign to come and beg upon his knees, then they are not merely fools but traitors! If the King restores our ancient freedoms, then we will vote him all he needs. If he refuses, the House will be right not to grant him one penny. But he will not refuse, unless the ill-will of some among us make it impossible for him to accept. I move that a Petition be drawn up and signed by every member present."

He sat down and the cheer that broke out announced that Eliot's leadership of the Commons was over. Wentworth had spoken for all but a small nucleus of fanatics when he emphasized that their primary task was to re-establish good relations with the King and restore sane government to the country. The motion was carried, and within a few days a list of reforms was tabulated and entitled the Petition of Right. No Englishman or woman was to be held in prison without a trial.

No taxes must be levied without the consent of Parliament. Troops must not be billeted on private citizens and martial law must end.

A week after Easter, when Charles had failed to placate them with verbal promises, the Petition was returned to the Commons with the Royal Assent.

And two days later, Sir Thomas Wentworth received a summons to Whitehall.

Chapter 4

CHARLES had made up his mind that he would not like Wentworth. Wentworth was determined not to be overawed by Charles; there was little in their tastes or their physical appearance to suggest that they would ever find anything in common. Wentworth was tall and raw-boned, with a strong-featured face and a choleric complexion. He was known to be rude and outspoken and opinionated, lacking in every quality that distinguished the polished courtiers like Goring and Holland. He came into the King's Presence Chamber at Whitehall and tramped up to him like a soldier, stiff and awkward and rather badly dressed, plainly dressed by comparison with the bright satins and delicate lace worn by the King and his attendants. He went down on his knee and kissed the King's hand. He saw Henrietta for the first time and thought what an insignificant little dark creature she was, to have caused so much trouble and made herself so disliked by the ordinary English people.

"Your Majesty sent for me," he said.

"Rise up, Sir Thomas."

Wentworth's expression was quite different from that of most people when looking at Charles. He looked the King in the face without fawning or trying to ingratiate himself. He was expecting an angry reprimand as the instigator of the Petition of Right.

"I sent for you, because I owe you thanks for the speech you made in Parliament," Charles said, and he was surprised to see the rugged face suffuse with pleasure.

"I only spoke the truth, Sire. If it accomplished anything, I'm humbly gratified."

"Your speech caused much comment," the King said. "My Lord Bishop of Wells was among many who recommended you to my notice." He turned to a stocky, grey-bearded little priest standing behind him and smiled.

Wentworth bowed to the Bishop. He was not aware that

Bishops troubled themselves with politics, but he liked the look of the homely old man, standing out among the elegant gentlemen and ladies like a sturdy weed in an exotic flower-bed.

"My thanks to His Lordship," he said.

"I understand that you have applied to the Court for some employment in the past," Charles said.

In the early days of the reign Wentworth had sought an outlet for his energies in the service of the new sovereign, but he had no influence at Court and his applications were refused without even reaching Charles. He had entered Parliament instead.

"I did, Sire, but without success."

Charles smiled at him suddenly; he could not help liking the man. It was all too rare to get such a short answer to a simple question.

"Then it pleases me to repair that omission and offer you a place with me now."

For a moment Wentworth was too surprised to answer. In his own eyes he was a Parliamentarian, the author of the Petition of Right which the King had signed against his will. He caught the eye of the Bishop of Wells and was further surprised to see him nodding vigorously.

"Come, Sir Thomas," Charles said gently, "are you willing to serve me as well as you've served the House of Commons?"

He had never been really at home at Westminster; he was essentially single-minded and honest, and the wranglings and intrigues got on his nerves. He had quarrelled with many of the members during that short session, particularly the Puritan element, which filled him with suspicion and contempt. He had an almost mystical belief in the virtue of authority, and he had failed to find it in its proper form among that crowd of ordinary men, few of them his equal in intelligence and energy.

He dropped on both knees before Charles. There was no-one at Westminster to whom a man could kneel, no-one to follow, and all his life he had been searching for something or some-one to serve to the full extent of his capacity.

"I am your servant, Sire, from this day and for all the days of my life."

"That makes me very happy," Charles said simply. It was

no effort to be gracious; he had a growing, intuitive feeling, all too rare in his choice of friends and councillors, that this blunt Yorkshireman might prove the most valuable servant he would ever have.

"Come into the Privy Chamber; we will talk alone." Charles went to the Queen and kissed her on the cheek; he kissed her every time he entered or left a room, and often for no reason at all except that he could not contain his affection for her. He was never embarrassed by witnesses; he was so much in love with his wife that his courtiers felt it was almost indecent. To Wentworth, a kindly husband and a devoted father, it made the King seem endearingly human. They left the room together, and the Queen and the rest of the Court dispersed.

They were alone for two hours, but though their voices could be heard the eavesdroppers could not distinguish what they said. At the end of the two hours, Thomas Wentworth backed through the double doors and found an excited and not altogether friendly little crowd of nobles and officers of the Court. He had come to Whitehall as a simple country baronet, and he had left the inner sanctum of the King as a peer and a member of the Privy Council. He could hardly believe it.

The Bishop of Wells came towards him and he stopped. "I am Dr. Laud," he said, "And if I'm not mistaken, you are now Lord Wentworth."

Wentworth nodded. "I am," he said. "By the King's favour and my own incredible good fortune."

"Congratulations;" the little bishop smiled. "I took careful note of you, and I told His Majesty very plainly that you were wasted in that rabble at Westminster, and he ought to attach you to himself. I am delighted that he has followed my advice. I hope, Sir, that we will be friends as well as Councillors."

He held out his hand. Wentworth did not kiss the Episcopal ring. It was typical of him and of Laud that when they parted they shook hands.

The Queen and Lucy Carlisle were playing cards, and as usual the Queen was losing. She had little value for money, and she was too impulsive to be a good card-player; her opponent had an excellent memory and a curiously systematic mind which was concealed by a vivacious, flippant manner.

Lucy Carlisle was one of the most beautiful women in England, and also one of the noblest born. She was the sister of the Earl of Northumberland, one of the proud, troublesome breed of Percys whose power had often rivalled that of their sovereigns in the past. She had thick dark brown hair which was profusely curled and ringletted and fell over her handsome shoulders, delicate features and large bright blue eyes. Only the small, sensual mouth betrayed her; it was mean and thin-lipped and startlingly red. She was full-breasted and tall, with lovely hands and feet, and the range and magnificence of her wardrobe was famous. She was amusing and charming, and men fell in love with her in such numbers that she told Henrietta once that it would have been impossible to accommodate them all. Henrietta was shocked and yet delighted by the gaiety and poise of her friend, her dearest friend, for she had fallen under the spell of a personality that attracted women as strongly as men. She scolded Lucy but she laughed as she did so, and she defended her obstinately to Charles when Charles showed his disapproval. He did not like the Countess. Behind the bright exterior he detected something heartless and cold which utterly repelled him, and he was not a man who hid his feelings. He thought her morals were scandalous and he noticed that she always chose her lovers from the first rank in position and importance. She took whatever was offered and gave nothing, just as she played cards with his sweet, but silly wife, and encouraged her to lose large sums of money to her. Lady Carlisle knew that the King disliked her. She was particularly charming to him, but she hated him because she knew she was not making an impression. She also despised him because he was so ridiculously infatuated with his own wife. She was questioning the Queen skilfully about the appointment of a leading Parliamentarian to the Privy Council.

"Two jacks, Madam," she announced, and picked up her winnings. "Whatever made the King choose this man Wentworth? Shall I deal again?"

"One hand more, Lucy," Henrietta said. "Bishop Laud advised it; he argued and argued with the King for days saying that Parliament wasn't to be trusted and that Wentworth would desert them if he was approached. You know what a dogged creature the Bishop is, and eventually he got his way.

The King thinks a great deal of him you know."

"I know," the Countess said, "they have a mutual interest in theology. I didn't know it was extending to politics."

"Everything is extending to politics," Henrietta retorted. "The word Parliament sounds in my ears like a curse—everything is politics and money and the war. Oh, I'm so utterly sick of it!"

"Of course you are," her friend leaned across and patted her hand sympathetically. "But I'm still curious about the new Lord Wentworth. What does the King think of him now that he's been at Whitehall for a month?"

Henrietta frowned. She had spent some time with Wentworth and she thought he was dictatorial and unattractive.

"The King has a wonderful opinion of him," she answered. "I haven't seen him so drawn to a man since the Duke of Buckingham. God knows what it is they have in common—he doesn't care for music or art or religion, in fact there's nothing one can discuss with the man except hunting and politics."

Lucy Carlisle trumped the Queen's hand and finished the game without mentioning the new Minister again. But she thought about him with great interest while she was talking to Henrietta about the new fashion for high collars on women's dresses. They covered the bosom, the Queen said, and the Countess said naughtily that the costume would not be popular with men. So Wentworth was not only the King's Minister but also his friend. He was a stern, outspoken boor, the last man in the world that she would have noticed or spoken to except for his extraordinary rise in power and importance. If the King liked him, he was worth cultivating. And there was only one way in which the Countess cultivated men. Later that evening, Wentworth was astonished to receive a note in the Countess's own handwriting, inviting him to dine at her house in the Strand. At the end of the evening he had impressed her with his energy, vision and abilities, and she had made him aware of his ambitions, warned him against those men near the King who were hostile to him and proved that she was not only beautiful, but alarmingly clever. He was not the man to be seduced at a first meeting and she did not make such an amateur's mistake. She offered her friendship, and in her position with the Queen it was of inestimable value to him.

She came to the door and gave him her hand to kiss as he left. She had a faultless instinct for those who were about to rise high in the world, and this strange man with his rugged face and domineering personality was going to be a great man and a very powerful force in the government of England. When she became his mistress, she would know his secrets and have a share in his power.

The King had signed the Petition of Right, and in return Parliament granted him an immediate subsidy of money as evidence of their good faith. But it was only a fraction of what was needed; now Eliot and the rest expressed their dissatisfaction with the way in which the King and his Bishops were governing the Church.

Exasperated, Charles ordered Parliament to adjourn, and went down to Portsmouth to see Buckingham.

It was August, 1628, and the expeditionary fleet was almost ready to sail. The streets were full of troops and sailors and the human rubbish which accumulates in ports. The town was packed with beggars and pedlars and prostitutes, and the King's arrival brought out the local gentry to present themselves and offer him hospitality. Among the crowd pushing and elbowing its way down the North end of Portsmouth High Street, was an unemployed ship's officer with a crippled left hand who had travelled from London the previous Tuesday. This was thirty-five year old John Felton, a poor Puritan who had twice made his way to Portsmouth when the first expedition to La Rochelle was gathering and besought the Duke of Buckingham to give him a command. He wanted to join what he believed to be a crusade against the anti-Christ and he had pestered the Duke's household and written letters to the Duke himself. He had been a persistent nuisance, and it was unfortunate that Buckingham received the last communication on a day when he was harrassed and short-tempered. Felton begged for the command without which, he explained, he could not live. Buckingham sent him the answer that in that case he would have to hang.

Felton borrowed tenpence and bought a knife from a cutler on Tower Hill and set out once more for Portsmouth, with the insulting dismissal of his faith and himself pounding in his head like an old Testament prophecy. At nine o'clock on that Saturday morning the Duke was breakfasting in public in the

Hall of his house when he saw John Felton for the first time, moving towards him in the crowd. He had an appointment to wait on the King, and as he left the table the pale and shabby young man who had been staring at him suddenly rushed forward, and before anyone could stop him he drove his knife into Buckingham's heart.

Henrietta had never seen a man prostrate with grief before. For a moment she stood looking at her husband; he was white and haggard and his eyes were red with weeping. When he embraced her he clung like a child, and now it was her turn to strengthen, her hand that wiped his tears and stroked his hair, and she held him against her and rocked him as if he were the child she had never born. Her greatest enemy was dead—her rival, her persecutor in the early days—and she sat for a long time without speaking, nursing her husband in his grief without anything but love and pity in her heart. She heard him mumble the Duke's name repeatedly, and she hushed him gently, and for the first time as she listened to his outpouring of sorrow and regret, she understood what that ill-matched friendship had meant to him.

His courage, his confidence, even his marriage, were in some part due to the influence of the man Henrietta had hated and despised. She could see the reason for Charles's love, and she was no longer jealous of it. She was his wife and at last she was in full and undisputed possession of his love. She could afford to be generous to the dead.

That autumn, the last expedition sailed to relieve La Rochelle under the command of Lord Lindsey. Its original commander had been given an almost Royal burial in Westminster Abbey, and his assassin had fulfilled his destiny and been duly hanged. His remains were rotting in chains at Portsmouth as the fleet sailed. Charles had kept his word, but the cost was crippling and the result was worse than failure. La Rochelle surrendered to the King of France before the English could engage in battle.

Charles had rifled his Treasury and shattered his people's confidence for nothing. And the Parliament that reassembled that winter was in a very different mood from the assembly which had been swayed by the moderate council of Wentworth. Charles had granted the Petition of Right in the hope that they would appreciate his good will and unite under his sovereignty. They repaid his concessions by refusing him the revenue from the Customs and launching a violent attack upon the government of the Church. Everything possible was said and done to convince Charles that he had gained nothing by signing the Petition and that the House of Commons was seeking to encroach still further on his power by interfering with ecclesiastical matters. Pym and Eliot denounced the King's Bishops, particularly Laud who was known to favour the Anglican ritual and the solemn Communion Service. They raised an issue which struck at the King's heart and his dearest belief, by pressing for the abolition of diocesan government, an extreme which had been regarded as High Treason even during the Reformation. Charles' father had quelled such an attempt with the remark that without Bishops there would soon be no King, and the Parliament of the day had agreed with him. James had been a politician first and a Protestant after, but his son was a man to whom religion and the purity of his English Church was not an expedient but an article of deep faith and sacred trust. He bore the titles, Supreme Head of the Church and Defender of the Faith, and there was no basis in any law or precedent in the whole history of England for what his Parliament was trying to do in nullifying his authority.

He found little help at the Council table; Newcastle suggested imprisoning the leaders and fining the rest; Holland and Goring disagreed without suggesting a sensible alternative; and the Earl of Essex made Charles his lifelong enemy by supporting the Parliament.

In the end he sent for Wentworth.

The King sat by a blazing log fire in Henrietta's Audience Chamber at Whitehall, and his Minister stood in front of him, his hands behind his back in the attitude Charles knew so well. He was frowning, and he had listened to the King for twenty minutes while Charles confessed his anger and disgust with the attitude of the Commons and increased Wentworth's anxiety by telling him simply that he would rather resign his Crown than perjure his Coronation oath and permit his Church to be defiled by heresy.

The two men understood each other well; they had come

from mutual respect to friendship, and finally to complete confidence and deep affection.

"As you know, Sire, I am not a particularly religious man," Wentworth said at last. "But that doesn't mean I cannot appreciate your point of view. However, if you'll forgive me, I know the Commons and you don't. For every one who talks sincerely when he attacks the Bishops and sees the Pope lurking behind every surplice, there are fifty who are only interested in attacking them because it is a means of attacking the authority of the King. Pym may be honest according to his lights—I know Eliot is a hypocrite and a liar. If any man were to accuse them of seeking to destroy you, they would rise and deny it with their hands upon their hearts. But I tell you this. I sat in that Commons and I know the machinery it uses. I used it myself to present the Petition of Right, that was the only concession any loyal subject could expect you to grant. You granted it. In the last few months I am beginning to think it was a mistake."

"I always thought so," Charles said bitterly. "I don't blame you, Thomas, but it was weakness, and weakness only breeds contempt. When a King submits to his subjects, he ceases to be a King. This is one lesson Parliament has taught me, and I promise you I shall never forget it as long as I live."

"You granted it, Sire, because you were in the one position which made you dependent upon them. You were at war. Now you have asked me for my advice and I am going to give it. Make peace with France. Make peace immediately. La Rochelle has surrendered and it is useless to continue. And dangerous, Sire. As long as that assembly sits at Westminster you are in danger. I know them, and I have been watching what they are trying to do. They are challenging more than the ritual of the Church. They are challenging the authority of the King to rule. So you will have to rule without them. Not for one year or two, but for the rest of your life."

Charles rose and walked a few paces across the room. It was dark and very quiet.

"No sovereign has done that for hundreds of years," he said at last. "Even the Tudors governed with Parliament."

"Not this Parliament," Wentworth said. "They ruled with the Council, and so must you. Parliament was never summoned except for money and then as seldom as possible. It was a good precedent and the Commons in those days were a flock of sheep compared to the wolves sitting at Westminster now." He came close to Charles, his tall heavy figure overshadowing the slender King. If he had dared he would have touched him, so strong was his emotion, his *conviction* that what he was advising was the only course.

"You are the King," he said. "You are God's Anointed. I may not have your faith, but I believe that above all things in the world. And you must *be* King, in the sense of that Divine vocation. Fulfil it, Sire. Rule England, and rule it alone. I swear to you it is the only way, and I swear that you can do it. You are the law; your word and your wisdom should be sufficient for your country. Dismiss this Parliament and let it be the last of your reign. So long as you keep England at peace, you need never summon them again."

"And that is your advice, Thomas?"

"It is, Sire."

Charles pushed a strand of red hair back from his forehead; he wore it down to his shoulders in the fashion described by the Puritans as lovelocks, a symbol of moral degradation and Satanic vanity.

"All my life I have known what I must *not* do," he said slowly. "It is easier than knowing what I *must* do. God knows, in the past year I have wished that the government of my kingdom depended upon me alone, and yet I never thought it possible to alter what has always been—from the days of Edward I who founded Parliament. I love my country and I love my people. I want to do what is right for both. Leave me, Thomas. I want to think on this."

He gave his hand to Wentworth who knelt and kissed it reverently. The door closed and Charles was alone. He went back to his chair by the fire and sat down, looking into the flames. He had been King of England for nearly four years, and his reign had brought nothing but discord and chaos at home and defeat in his enterprises abroad. Everything he did had been criticized and sabotaged by the representatives of his subjects; his wife was hated and vilified for her religion and her innocent love of dancing and play-acting; his wars had been fought against Parliament as much as the enemy, and he had been unable to win against either. A Puritan had murdered his best friend, and Puritans up and down the country were preaching sedition and heresy with the approval of the House of Commons.

He sat on, watching the logs blazing up the chimney, while the candles in the wall sconces flickered and died one by one, and his thoughts turned back to that day at Westminster Abbey when he drove out alone to his Coronation and made his solemn vows to defend his subjects and their liberty and protect the purity of his Church. He had walked down the long nave, following the path taken by his ancestors, by good men and tyrants alike, the younger son who had been chosen by God to be the King. He was the law, as Wentworth said. He was only a human being, with more than some men's burden of doubt and irresolution in his nature, innocent of personal ambition or love of power for its own sake. But he was the living embodiment of a Divine institution. Whoever attacked him attacked what he represented and if he capitulated anything to his enemies, his Coronation oaths were broken and his soul was stained with blasphemy. A King had founded Parliament. The time had come when a King must abolish it.

He rang his bell and his valet Parry came in from the antechamber. He lit fresh candles and poured Charles a cup of wine.

"Her Majesty sent a message asking if you would come and dine with her this evening, Sire," he said. Charles looked up at him and his face lightened. He had made his decision and already he felt relieved; nothing in the world would please him more than to leave the silent room and escape into the gaiety and cheerfulness of Henrietta's Privy Chamber, and eat and drink with her and lean across and take her hand. He loved her so intensely that his happiness was very close to pain; he could watch her for hours, admiring the vivacity and grace which seemed to increase with every day, his passions awaking at every touch and every glance they shared. The thought of her reinforced his courage and confirmed his decision. With the support of an idyllic marriage, he would govern his country as Kings were meant to govern—wisely and justly and devotedly, until the people who had lost their loyalty and their faith in Monarchy went on their knees and blessed his reign.

"Send word to the Queen that I shall join her as soon as I have changed my costume."

Half an hour later, attended by his Gentlemen-in-waiting, his page and his Groom of the Chamber, Charles went to his wife. They spent one of the gayest evenings they could remember and at the end of it he gave her a pendant of emeralds and pearls which had belonged to his mother and been specially brought up from the Treasury.

At noon the next morning he summoned Wentworth and the Council and announced the dissolution of Parliament. An hour later the Gentleman Usher of the Black Rod rode down to Westminster.

The Commons refused to be dismissed. The Speaker tried to obey the King's order and rise, thereby ending the debate which was in progress, but Ben Valentine, the member for St. Germans, and Holles, Lord Clare's son, held him in the Chair by force while the doors were locked and the House continued its business.

Outside, the soldiers accompanying Black Rod battered the doors open. On March 10th the third Parliament of Charles' reign was at an end. Eliot, Valentine and Holles were fined and sentenced to imprisonment, and the windows of St. Stephen's Hall were shuttered and the doors were barred. The House of Commons became a place of dust and silence for the next eleven years.

Chapter 5

WHITEHALL in the Spring was like a village, festive and noisy and full of activity. The Palace sprawled across the acres of parkland and gardens, its dome and turrets shining in the bright sun, while the river ran high past the western walls, carrying a constant traffic of boats and barges up and down from the City and out to the surrounding countryside. The shrubs and trees were in bud, sweetening the air and colouring the lovely gardens with the pastel pinks and yellows and the snowy May blossoms that the Queen especially loved. Henrietta had taken a great interest in the planning of the gardens at Whitehall; she spent hours walking through them, arm-in-arm with the King and followed by a crowd of ladies and gentlemen, all laughing and talking and flirting, and none of them more tender in their devotion to each other than their King and Queen.

Charles had changed very little; he was graver and at thirty-five he was handsomer in his prime than when she met him first. He walked and spoke with unhurried confidence as if time were of no consequence, and indeed the hours and days and weeks ran into one another in an endless succession of pleasure and amusement and tranquility, illuminated by the blaze of an unquenchable passion for the woman at his side. The thin, mercurial little Queen with her childish figure and dainty air had now become a warm and rounded woman, glowing with beauty and high spirits, and if her tiny waist had gained in inches, there was a sturdy Prince of Wales toddling in the Royal nursery and three more infants sleeping in cradles by the Palace windows. She was pregnant every year, and whenever he looked at her, Charles found her splendid fertility an added blessing to all the others she had brought him.

He loved his children because they resembled her; his eldest son was as dark as a gypsy, to his own amusement and Henrietta's distress. The second son was fair, with downy yellow hair

91

and hazel eyes, but his strong little nose and large mouth were Henrietta's, and the third boy had her colouring. Charles played with his sons and let them clamber on his knees, and hung over the cot where his little daughter slept, rejoicing because the tiny face and bright brown eyes mirrored the woman he adored. He lavished presents upon her, regardless of the fact that he was heavily in debt; he had been in debt for years and he had grown careless. It was impossible to refuse Henrietta new dresses or query the cost of one of her New Year Masques even if they were extravagant, when he spent so much money on his own art collection.

They had begun to indulge themselves after 1629, when the war with France was over, Parliament dismissed, and the country's economy returned to peace-time standards. He had redeemed the plate pawned to pay for Buckingham's fleet, and added to it, so that the royal tables at Whitehall and Hampton Court and Greenwich shone with the finest products of the goldsmith's art. He had given the Queen fabulous jewels in addition to the ones she had lent him when he needed money. Nothing delighted him more than to fasten a new trinket round her beautiful neck, and claim the reward of kissing her shoulder.

And while she amused herself with her ladies and her theatricals, he escaped from the trouble of governing his kingdom and spent long hours with his collection of pictures. He was passionately interested in art in all its forms, but the acquisition of the Italian and Flemish Masters occupied the major part of his energy and his time. The walls of Whitehall were hung with magnificent Correggios, and Rembrandts, and on that lovely day in spring the ceiling of the Banqueting Hall was being prepared for the superb paintings which Charles had commissioned from Rubens and which were waiting at Antwerp. Art dealers from all over Europe made their way to London and beguiled the King of England into purchasing more and more of the treasures scattered throughout the world, frequently stored away and unappreciated. His pictures cost a fortune but they gave him a joy and an absorption far more important than mere money, and he felt that they enhanced the prestige of the Crown. He had always appreciated beauty and tried to indulge his taste as far as his commitments would allow; in the last few years he had no commitments which could not be shelved or solved by some expedient thought up by his advisers, and his hobby became a passion which he pursued to the detriment of his pocket and the disapproval of his subjects.

The English people were not happy. They were prosperous, and they owed their prosperity to the good relations existing between England and her old enemies France and Spain. But they were not grateful; they regarded the two Catholic nations as instruments employed by the Pope, and their friendship with England as an earnest of a Catholic revival.

Public discontent was so inconceivable in the circumstances of peace and prosperity that Charles never considered it at all. He imagined that the things which were dear to him, things like light and cleanliness and space and beauty, were precious to the rough and insular citizens of London, and he was astonished when his plans for building a new church at St. Pauls and developing the fields of Long Acre into pleasure gardens were received with ingratitude and hostility. He was astonished and very angry; and he became very angry very quickly when his will was crossed by anyone except his wife. For years no one had said no to him or even expressed a contrary opinion. He was absolute master of his Court and his country, and, often without his knowledge, his Council and his judges quickly stifled a dissenting voice.

Charles loved his capital; he often stood by the windows at Whitehall and watched the fleets of ships and small craft sailing up the Thames.

London was rich and growing fast, and all he wanted was that it should mirror the beauty and grace established in his own home and his own life.

Charles saw no harm in the theatres which sprang up, or in the pleasure gardens at Hyde Park or Finsbury and the puppet shows and bear gardens along Bankside where the ordinary citizens amused themselves. Vice and robbery and prostitution were part of the life of a great city, and he could do no more against them than enforce the ferocious laws and maintain impeccable moral standards in his own Court. He could never share the Puritan's fanatical hatred of pleasure which was spreading like an insidious poison through the respectable members of the community. The fires of hell blinded them to the gleam of Heaven, and the trumpeting wrath and savage imagery of the Old Testament completely superseded the gentle teaching of the Christian doctrine. To thousands of his subjects Charles personified the levity and worldliness which the Puritan was dedicated to destroy. His love of beauty, his interest in the arts, even his devotion to his wife were only evidence of sin and idolatry and unseemly lust. His efforts to improve his people and induce them to share his tastes were resisted as an attempt to pervert the Godly. They hated and suspected him and everything for which he stood, and most of all they hated his Roman Catholic Queen. For this he could never forgive them. And on the occasions when they attacked her, and they did so in pamphlets and pulpits and street corners all over the country, Charles punished them with unremitting cruelty.

That afternoon Charles and Henrietta picnicked under some trees in the gardens at Whitehall. Henrietta had posed most of the morning for a portrait, one of the many her husband commissioned of her, and at last he had found an artist worthy of his subject. Anthony Van Dyck had come to London from his native Holland, and the King had been so pleased with his work that he induced him to remain, gave him the post of Court Painter, and knighted him. He had come to see the picture during the morning and expressed his delight. Henrietta was posed in profile, wearing a splendid dress of yellow silk collared in exquisite lace and with a single strand of enormous pearls at the base of her throat. The artist had captured the mobility of her features and the brilliance of her eyes; the mouth was slightly curved as if she were about to smile. Charles had turned from the portrait to the sitter and immediately decided that his wife still looked pale and needed a diversion. He sent word to Wentworth that he would not attend the Council meeting in the afternoon and ordered a picnic in the gardens instead.

Chairs and tables had been set up, covered with linen cloths and gold and silver dishes, and a canopy had been erected to protect them from a breeze. They sat together, their seats so close that Charles felt her elbow when he moved, and lunched on a dozen courses, all of which were served by stewards and cupbearers on bended knee. It was a lovely afternoon, made lovelier for him by Henrietta's gaiety; he could not forget that he had found her weeping bitterly only two nights before because someone had left an obscene pamphlet in her room. She had organized a Masque, very stately and beautiful, and performed it with her ladies in front of him and the whole Court, and within a week London was flooded with a scurrilous article condemning the performance and describing the principals as notorious whores. He had taken the filthy thing out of her hands and ripped it to pieces and caught her fiercely in his arms, wiping away the tears and promising a vengeance on the author that would be an example to every Puritan in England. He leant across and kissed her cheek, now pink with the fresh air, and begged her to tell him she was happy and enjoying his surprise.

"Of course I'm happy, my love," Henrietta gave him the warm and tender smile that always quickened his heart. "You take too much care of me—I tell you again and again that I'm the happiest woman in the world."

"You were tired this morning," he insisted. "I was so worried to have you upset like that so soon after the birth of the child."

He looked at her anxiously. His beloved, adorable, perfect wife whose life was so innocent, who did nothing but good and kindness to everyone who came in contact with her. He thought of that revolting pamphlet and his face grew hard and cold with anger.

"We will not mention it again, my darling, but I want you to know that the author of that paper has been caught."

One of Henrietta's closest friends was sitting on the other side of the table and he looked up as he heard the King's words. Wat Montagu was the son of the Duke of Manchester. It was odd to Charles and to Henrietta that the dismal and unbending man whom neither of them liked could have produced such an intelligent and charming son. He was especially dear to the Queen because she had converted him to Rome. He glanced at the King for permission to speak.

"Who is it, Sire?"

"A Puritan." The King's voice was like ice. "A barrister called William Prynne. He came up before the Court of the Star Chamber this morning."

Henrietta turned to him. "In France he would be broken on the wheel for what he wrote," she said.

Charles lifted his hand to have their cups refilled with wine.

"We don't use the wheel in England," he answered, "but you can rest content. I sent word to the judges what sentence I expected them to pass. Master Prynne will be fined to the last penny of his goods; he will have his ears cut off and stand in the pillory at Palace Yard for the amusement of the people. If he is alive when he is taken out, he will go to the Tower for life."

Henrietta raised her cup to him.

"Thank you, my love," she said.

"With your permission, Sire, some of us will go and watch," Wat Montagu remarked. "The last man I saw in the pillory was an old Papist, convicted for carrying a rosary. He was covered in filth and blood in a few minutes and the good ladies of London took turns to go up and spit in his face. I'll be interested to see what they do with this scum who has insulted the Queen!"

Lucy Carlisle, Henrietta's inseparable companion, leaned across Montagu and shrugged.

"Much as I should like to see you properly avenged, Madam, I hope you'll forgive me if I renounce the pleasure. I have a horribly squeamish stomach!"

There was a general laugh which died away when it was noticed that the King did not join in.

"I was not aware that you suffered many qualms, Countess. I am relieved to hear of one at least. Come, ladies and gentlemen. We will return to the Palace."

The Countess moved to the dressing table at the other end of her room and looked at herself in the glass hanging on the wall. She began to fasten a silk robe, and as she did so she was humming. Behind her, Thomas Wentworth, now a Viscount and first Minister in the Kingdom, was getting out of her bed and searching for his clothes. She heard him come behind her and for a moment they watched themselves in the glass, his face close to hers, his arms around her. It was gratifying to see such a man in love; she had never been in love with anyone herself and she was always interested to observe the weakness it revealed in others. He was the toughest, most ruthless and most hated man at Court, with dozens of enemies and very few friends except that plebian old Bishop Laud, who was now Archbishop of Canterbury, and, of course, the King. No one credited Wentworth with a spot of human feeling or a single human weakness. But then they only saw him in Council where he bullied his opponents and forced his ideas on men who found them too unconventional and far too taxing to put into effect. Wentworth was not lazy like Holland and Newport, that idiotic Mary's husband—how the Queen simpered over her and preached her wretched Popery in the hope of making yet another convert—Lady Carlisle had always hated Lady Newport because she was true to her mistress when her back was turned. Wentworth had more energy and courage than any of them; the trouble was he would not admit that the inertia and stupidity of His Majesty King Charles was the prime obstacle to all his plans for putting a foundation of rock under Whitehall instead of shifting sand.

She unlocked his hands and stood up.

"I hear that the little play at Palace Yard was not what their Majesties expected," she said.

"No," Wentworth frowned. He did not want to talk politics, and he was surprised that the woman he loved could rise from his embrace and spoil their hours of happiness by talking about the torturing of a criminal fanatic.

"It was a mistake," she said. The fire was alight and she stood in front of it, warming her hands. "If the King thought the people would sympathize with Henrietta, he knows better now."

"I did not see it," Wentworth said. "Where's the wine?"

"Over there, by the bedside. Pour some for me. Wat Montagu went there and he told me what happened. Two others were sentenced with Prynne for publishing an attack on the Bishops, and Montagu said the people strewed flowers in their path and gave them cups of wine on the way. They stood in the pillory for two hours and preached to the crowd at the top of their voices, and nobody threw a pebble at them. Montagu saw several women dipping handkerchiefs in their blood afterwards as if they were martyrs!"

"Why are you so pleased?" he asked her suddenly. "Why are you always criticizing the King to me when you know I love him? And how can you rejoice to see the Queen humiliated when you behave as if she were your dearest friend?"

"I criticize the King because *I* think he's human, even if you don't. All too human, alas, or he would never make enemies

97

of honest English Protestants for the sake of a Papist, whether she's his wife or not! As for the Queen—your opinion of her is much the same as mine!"

"I think she's a good woman and she loves the King," he said shortly.

Lucy Carlisle laughed contemptuously.

"You think nothing of the sort. You know perfectly well that she's an obstinate foreigner who won't curb her religion or her habits, and that all she tells the King is to do what he pleases and to the devil with his people!"

She got up and began to walk up and down. Wentworth's abandonment made her careless. He was in love with her and she could have made him beg if she chose; he had knelt and kissed her naked feet only an hour before. She felt suddenly reckless, with an unusual urge to speak her mind.

She came close to him and looked up into his face.

"Thomas, how can you have patience with fools? How can you be content to serve someone you know is so inferior to yourself!"

"The King is not inferior to anyone," he answered quickly. He wished she would stop and pursue something else. She was not a nice woman, she possessed none of the virtues he had expected of his two wives and she had no moral sense. But she was a source of wonder and fascination to him. He had never encountered a woman with brains before he came to Whitehall. He had associated her political judgment with men, and her amatory talents with whores. But she was a great lady, clever and important and unapproachable, and though he had been her lover for three years, he was still a little overawed by their relationship.

If she hated the King, he preferred not to know it.

"You speak as if you believed that nonsense about the Divine Right of Kings," Lucy Carlisle said scornfully. "The more I hear of it, the more ridiculous it seems. The king can do no wrong—one step further and we'll be told that the Pope is infallible!"

Wentworth began to redden. The persistent calumny that Charles was inclined to the Catholic Church always infuriated him; no one, except Laud, who suffered from the King's enthusiasm for theology, knew how staunchly Protestant he was better than Wentworth himself. Too staunch to please his critics and deform the liturgy and dogmas of the Established faith. He felt suddenly irritated to hear Lucy Carlisle repeat the accusation.

"You should be ashamed to say that," he said angrily. "And for your information, I do believe that the King can do no wrong, exactly that! I believe that the sovereign is above all ordinary men and that his subjects owe him absolute allegiance. And that should include you, my dear Lucy."

He turned away from her and went back to the table and poured himself another cup of wine; he did not ask her if she wanted any. He had come to her because he was in need of relaxation and affection, and, God damn it! because the woman had infected his blood. He loved her and he wanted her and he was prepared to overlook the defects in her nature which gave her a shrewish tongue and a tortuous mind. But there was a limit, and though she thought she knew him better than he knew himself, that limit was criticism of the King. He was not a man who gave his love or his loyalty lightly or transferred either without unhappy self-examination. And he loved Charles better than any other human being; better than his own family, better than the clever and beautiful woman who stood in front of him, her bright blue eyes narrowing with contempt. He did not like to feel a fool; he did not like being called one, or listening to lies and sneers directed against the King he believed to be noble and generous.

"I have a concept of how this kingdom should be governed," he said slowly. "An ideal, if the word does not offend you. I see that its salvation lies in a strong and absolute monarch and in a loyal Ministry. I have sat in the House of Commons and I know that real liberty and order will never come from them. I have taken my place with the King, and if you care anything for me at all, Lucy, you will not speak against him."

"Dear Thomas, what a simple soul you are! I thought you had ambition; now I see you are content to sit for the rest of your life at the feet of that arrogant egotist who thinks he is practically God made Man! You may see liberty and all the rest emanating from King Charles but I do not, not any longer. I see him growing more and more unpopular, idling his time away with his paintings and his hobbies and his nauseating

99

marriage. I think he will fall, and I think he deserves to." She came back and sat down by the fire.

For the last seven years she had been a jealous and irritated witness of a sublimely happy marriage, watching a man who loved his wife so much that he was blind to the charm or virtue of any other woman. And she could not understand it. She had never really cared for anyone; she had indulged in promiscuous affairs with many men, and though her body responded, it was a mechanical response, arid and untouched by emotion. She used her sexual power but in her heart she hated it because it had never brought her happiness or kept a lover at her side for long. And what she had just given Wentworth was not strong enough to wean him from his loyalty to the King.

"I see them together," she said. "Pawing and kissing and watching the clock. . ." She turned round quickly and pointed to the bed. "That's where the policy of the kingdom is decided! If she turned her back on him for a single night, he'd abandon every one of your splendid plans, to get her back. He's not a King, he's a besotted fool. By the living God, Thomas, sometimes I find it disgusting!"

Wentworth stared at her. She was not being malicious, she was telling the truth. And the truth showed him the value of the hours they had spent in each other's arms; they showed him the worth of her kisses and the horrible superficiality of her response. He came close and stood over her.

"So you are nauseated by a husband and wife . . . of all the women in the world, you sit there and turn down your mouth like some prim village virgin at the thought of the King and Queen doing in wedlock what you and I have just done outside it—less than half an hour ago! Good Christ, woman, your sheets are still warm!—— Or is it because you have been as false to me in them as you are to the King and Queen!"

She looked up at him and the colour rose in her pale face.

"Warm or otherwise, there's no place between them for a boor, my Lord. I thought you had learnt a few manners by now."

"I have learnt many things since I met you," he said roughly, "But, thank God, showing a double face is not among them. As a boor I thank you for the favours you've shown me

100

this evening. As a gentleman, I decline to enjoy them again."

She stood up and faced him, her pale eyes glittering.

"You may regret this," she said softly. "You are not so mighty that you cannot fall; and when you do I'll make you a prophecy. You'll find that Their Gracious Majesties are only human after all. Human enough to tire of a servant as I have tired of a lover. And I was tired of you a very long time ago!"

He fastened his sword and found his plumed hat and pulled it on his head. He looked older suddenly, and his eyes considered her with bitter disgust.

"Don't concern yourself with my future, Madam. I was going to tell you tonight; the King has appointed me Lord Deputy of Ireland. I shall be leaving before the month is out."

"Congratulations! You must have disturbed the King from his art collection and his dandling after his wife too often. So he sends you to Ireland where you won't be able to trouble him and make him take an interest in the dull grind of being King. Congratulations! Ireland has been the grave of better men than you. I hope it buries you alive!"

She went to the door and pulled it open. Her beautiful face was so contorted with rage and malice that he was shocked to see how pinched and ugly she had become.

"Get out," she said.

"My dear Wentworth. I was afraid you would never find time to come today."

Laud sat very straight in his chair at the head of the table and smiled at his guest. He had invited him to dine at Lambeth Palace before leaving for his post in Ireland; they often dined together when Wentworth was dismissed from duty by the King. They talked for hours and argued with vehemence about every aspect of the government which concerned them both so deeply. Laud was very proud of his establishment at Lambeth. He had redecorated the Archbishop's Palace and made many improvements to the Chapel which he found bare and ugly, unfit for the worship of God or the dignity of his office. He had replaced the Communion table against the East wall, removing it from the nave where the congregation sat with their feet and elbows propped upon it as if they were in an ale house.

He had ordered the lovely stained-glass windows to be repaired and sent the golden crucifix and altar candlesticks to the King's goldsmith to be mended and made fit for use. He had brought his love of beauty and ritual into the Archbishop's Palace, stripped and disfigured by his Low Church predecessors, and transformed it into a replica of the Lambeth which existed before the Reformation.

He intended to do the same with every Church in England, and the King agreed with him. He was rounder and greyer, and he wore a white linen surplice and long purple robes, with an Episcopal Cross of amethysts on his chest. He was a humorous, obstinate, affectionate old man, and he dearly loved Wentworth.

"Eat up, eat up," he said. "I've got a new cook from France and the food is like manna from Heaven. I have to tear myself from the table these days."

Wentworth laughed. "You're like some old Roman friar with a tun belly," he said.

"Nothing of the kind," Laud retorted. "I'm a devout and honest Anglican with a healthy appetite. God gave me a stomach and there's no sin in filling it. Friars fast, my friend, and I don't. Though that's not the only difference between us!"

"Some people say it is. You have candles and music in the Chapel and you make your congregation take Communion with their hats off. You're being called a Papist from one end of London to the other."

Laud's shrewd little eyes twinkled. "I'll make Puritans howl and Papists weep; I've no patience with either. Nor have you; boy, help my Lord Wentworth to some carp—they came from the river today and they're excellent."

Wentworth began to eat the fish; Laud had finished. He ate as quickly as he spoke; he was always hurrying, talking and gesticulating and bustling from place to place on his short legs, making uncouth little jokes and roaring with laughter at his own humour. He was as blunt and honest and uncompromising as the big Yorkshireman sitting opposite to him; he also had a brilliant theological brain and was a noted Oxford scholar in his youth. His father had been a draper. He washed his hands in a silver basin and dried them on a linen napkin.

"I saw the King today," he said. "I tried to persuade him to insist that the Queen is crowned at Westminster."

"And you did not succeed," Wentworth finished for him.

"No," Laud said seriously, "unfortunately I did not. The King listened and agreed with everything I said. The people would be pleased and it would raise the Queen in their estimation. It's unthinkable that the Queen should never be crowned, in whatever rite. I know the King sympathized, but he wouldn't commit himself without asking the Queen first. So he sent for her, and you can imagine the result. She refused, and the King would not press her."

"Has she no idea," Wentworth said angrily, "how dangerous her attitude is? Can no one explain to her that it might be worth imperilling her immortal soul for an hour or two just to still all these rumours about Popery and gain the King some popularity?"

"None at all," Laud answered. "She thinks the King is above trifles like the opinions of the mob. She also thinks that having her children reared as Protestants is sacrifice enough. She is a very stubborn woman and I sometimes wish she were less spiritual or the King less fond of her. Needless to say, she has never liked me."

"Nor me," Wentworth said. "She'll like me less after Lady Carlisle has finished poisoning her against me."

"I'm glad that that is over," Laud began peeling a ripe fig. "I never approved of it; that woman is a snake. She may shake the Queen but the King won't listen. The King loves you, and he never wavers from a friend or forgives an enemy. But I still think it's a pity to send you to Ireland. He needs you here in London."

"Ireland is vital to the King," his friend said. "It's in its usual disgraceful state, corruptly governed without justice for the Irish or discipline among the officials. A strong Ireland is essential to the strength and security of the King. And a prosperous Ireland would help the Treasury. I have unlimited powers, my dear Archbishop, and I intend to use them. I shall make Ireland the model of what England can be under a thorough system. It may even be loyal to an English King for the first time in history."

"You will become even more hated than you are now," Laud

prophesied. "Especially if you stop the nobility from filling their pockets and filching the land."

"I'm used to enemies," Wentworth shrugged. "The better I govern the more I shall make. But the King will be stronger and that's all that matters. My only anxiety is leaving him with fools like Holland and Newcastle beside him. Keep a close watch on him, Laud. He trusts you and he will need a man of sense."

They rose from the table and the little priest led him out of the dining hall into his private apartments.

"I shall watch over the King; we will watch together, Thomas, you in Ireland and myself in London. No harm will come to him. No harm has come in seven years since the day that accursed Parliament was closed."

Wentworth looked out of the window up the river; there was a mist rising and he could not see beyond Westminster Bridge.

"Whatever happens, he must never summon them again. Locking the doors was not enough. When I return from Ireland, I hope he'll be able to pull St. Stephen's Hall to the ground. Only then will he or anyone of us be really safe."

Chapter 6

THE new Banqueting Hall was finished, and the King and Queen were holding a reception and a Ball in honour of their nephews from Holland. Rubens's magnificent ceiling paintings were in place above their heads, filling the stately room with colour. The artist had painted an allegorical tribute to the late King James, depicting him dispensing justice and wisdom upon earth, attended by cherubs, and receiving his celestial crown in the presence of angels and the gods and goddesses of mythology. It was a splendid ceiling and Charles could not resist looking up at it and pointing out fresh details to Henrietta. They sat under a canopy on two thrones at the end of the room, their pages and gentlemen of the Bedchamber and the Queen's ladies grouped on either side. The dais was draped in scarlet and the canopy was heavily embroidered with gold; a superb Flemish tapestry covered the wall behind them. Henrietta was dressed in yellow satin and her bodice and skirt were worked with pearls and topaz, with a wide collar of exquisite Irish lace, the present of the new Lord Deputy Wentworth. Her black hair was curled and brushed back from her face, and a five-pointed star set with diamonds, its centre an enormous stone of canary yellow, flashed as she moved her head. Charles had paid her a compliment by wearing a velvet suit of deep green with a half cloak of gold satin. He took as much pleasure in her clothes as she did, and he was particularly careful to praise her appearance because she was pregnant for the fifth time and disappointed that she could not lead the dancing. The Royal musicians were playing in the gallery at the far end of the Hall, and in front of the dais a dozen ladies and gentlemen were performing the pavane. On the King's left, the younger of two brothers who had come over from Holland was watching the scene at the English Court and thinking how different it was from the shabby gatherings in his mother's home.

Prince Rupert was only eighteen, the second son of the unhappy Queen Elizabeth of Bohemia, and the nephew of King Charles. He had been a baby when his parents were driven from Germany and the fury of the Thirty Years' War broke out in Europe, but he had been brought up on stories of the grandeur and importance of his English mother's country, and he spoke English as well as French and German. He was half Stuart, and he had inherited the breeding and arrogance of the line, and much of their good looks. He was over six feet in height, with a powerful figure and the bearing of a soldier. He had fought in the German Wars when he was still a boy and shown such an aptitude for fighting and getting himself into danger that his mother had sent him to the English Court to see what his uncle and aunt could do to civilize him. He had come for a few months and stayed for almost two years. He towered over Charles like a young giant; the difference between them made Henrietta laugh and tease him until he blushed. He loved Charles because his uncle was so different from the men he had known, so much kinder than the rough, unscrupulous German Princes of his father's family, so much more dignified and gracious and genuine than anyone Rupert had ever met. And so generous that the penniless nephew was overwhelmed with money and presents as soon as he arrived. His elder brother Carl was with him, and as the heir to the vanished throne of Bohemia he had the place of honour at their table and on State occasions. But Carl was a calculating, rather envious young man with none of Rupert's fiery gratitude for all the kindness they received, and the young Prince knew he was his uncles favourite of the two.

He looked at the beautiful Englishwomen in their gorgeous dresses, dyed in every colour of the spectrum, blazing with jewels, as they moved through the graceful figures of the dance, partnered by men as colourful and lavish in appearance as themselves, and Rupert marvelled that his uncle and aunt were reputed to be heavily in debt. England was so rich; her palaces were so large and luxurious compared to the bleak Rhineland castles and the ugly buildings at the Hague. England was like paradise with its green countryside and its prosperous towns, untouched by the wars which had ravaged his own homeland and slaughtered his people in thousands. The English were rich and at peace and, in his opinion, they did not appreciate their good fortune or show enough gratitude to the King who ruled them so well.

He looked over his shoulder at Charles, and the King smiled at him affectionately. He was proud of his nephew. He was proud of his reputation as a soldier, and his fine horsemanship and he loved the boy because he was so touchingly grateful for being admitted into their lives. And in spite of his youth, and indeed sometimes Charles forgot what a boy he was in years, he admired him for his decisiveness and courage. He was not afraid of anything; he talked of the wars to his uncle with the joy and enthusiasm of a born fighter animating his handsome, haughty face. He was a German, and the Germans were the mercenaries of Europe, selling their swords to any cause for the highest pay they could command. Rupert was a Prince but he had the soul of a mercenary, but in the opinion of the King it was a better soul than that of his brother, the cautious Prince Carl, who seldom risked himself in battle and badgered his uncle to engage in the war on his behalf. Rupert asked him for nothing; Rupert gave instead, though he had nothing but his own energy and gratitude to offer. He amused Henrietta when Charles was forced to leave her for a few days and attend to his government; Charles gave her into Rupert's charge and knew that she would be watched over and cared for, and presented back to him as if she were a helpless girl and not the Queen of England and the mother of four children. It was foolish, but every time she was pregnant Charles imagined that some harm would come to her, remembering the first pregnancy after Buckingham's death, when a pack of dogs fought round her feet and she miscarried from fright and almost died.

Everyone told him she was exceptionally strong and healthy, but he loved her too much to take anything for granted. He turned to her and took her hand in his.

"You look melancholy, my love. What is it? Are you not feeling well?"

"Dear heart, I wish you wouldn't fuss over me so—I'm perfectly well, just a little piqued to see these creatures dancing and not being able to join them. You know it bores me to watch."

"I know," he soothed, "but it won't be long now. And then perhaps we'll have a rest from children."

Henrietta laughed and shrugged her shoulders. She looked into his face with her large black eyes, and they were full of mockery.

"You know perfectly well that will never be," she said softly.

"What would I have done if you'd never loved me," he asked her.

"You would have eventually come to hate me," Henrietta answered. "You almost did at one time."

"Never," Charles insisted. They often had heated arguments about who loved the other most; like most lovers their favourite topic of conversation was themselves. "I always adored you, even when you were your most impossible, my darling love."

"You were extremely unkind to me in spite of it." Henrietta could never resist bringing up their troubled past for the feminine joy of seeing him wince and beg her forgiveness. One day she meant to tell him that she had really begun to love him on the day he dragged her away from the window at Whitehall and threw her on the floor. But not until he was much older and had been apologizing for many years. . .

"Please," he said, and to her delight he looked as pained and guilty as ever. "Please, don't mention that. You know I would give anything in the world to make you forget it."

"Oh, I have forgiven you," she said gently. "You ought to know it by now. And do not look at me like that; half the room is watching us and trying to listen."

"I have just looked at the watch on your girdle," he said, "and within an hour we will be quite alone where no one can pry on us and I shall look at you exactly as I like."

"Lucy Carlisle is watching," Henrietta said. She had seen the Countess glance up at them quickly as she moved past the dais. She was one of the principal dancers.

"I detest that woman," Charles said. "I wish you would dismiss her."

"Oh, you expect too much," his wife answered. "Lucy is very fond of me, and she makes me die with laughter sometimes. I know you don't approve of her, but I never heard you blaming Wentworth."

"Wentworth was not to blame," he said stubbornly. "You are a sweet innocent, my dear, with no more experience of life than one devoted husband, and you know nothing at all about the Lucy Carlisles of this world. It was the only foolish thing that Wentworth ever did. I was talking to Laud about him yesterday and we both agreed on it."

"You agree on everything," Henrietta pointed out. "I don't know what you find to talk about—all Laud does is say ' Yes, Sire', and all you do is say ' Quite right, Laud.' Don't let's talk about him, sweetheart, you know he irritates me, and I'm not in a condition to be irritated."

"I wish you liked him," Charles said gently. "He's a very holy man in his way."

"His way is not mine," Henrietta said quickly. "Look at poor Rupert standing there; he's miserable tonight because he's going home so soon. I wish your sister had let him stay with us indefinitely. God knows why she wants the boy back in Holland, living that dismal life and going off to fight for that ridiculous Principality. It's not even as if he were the heir. You ask her, Charles, ask her if Rupert can stay with us for another year at least."

"She won't allow it. She's jealous, my love, and I know my sister well enough to tell you that she could never bear taking second place with anyone or anything. Even if she doesn't love Rupert, the best of her children, she will not allow him to love anyone else but her. He will have to go back. God knows, I shall really miss him."

"So shall I," she leant forward and smiled at her nephew. "I was hoping to find a rich heiress for him and have him settle down in England with us."

Charles shook his head. "He will never settle anywhere," he said. "It would be like caging a tiger. I will write to my sister and extract a promise that he can visit us again. I can do no more than that."

"He said he would come back," Henrietta said. "Poor Rupert! He's so splendid and so sweet. He makes me feel almost ridiculous helping me in and out of chairs as if he thought I was going to break!"

"He loves you," Charles said happily. "He told me once he thought you were the most perfect woman in the world."

"It's really you he loves," she said. "He looks at you with such an expression sometimes, almost like worship. It's very touching and rather beautiful to see it. I wish our eldest son would grow like him."

"He'll never have the chance, please God," he answered. "Our son will never be a disinherited wanderer, begging from relatives."

When the dancing was over, the King and Queen rose, and Charles beckoned his nephews to join them. They stayed on in the hall for a short time, moving among the crowd of courtiers. The brothers were not popular among the English. Carl was a nuisance and a self-seeker, and there were too many interested men surrounded Charles, bleeding him of favours and stealing his revenues, to welcome a foreign robber to the band. But they hated Rupert most of all. Nobody could accuse him of filling his pockets or trying to turn his kinship to the King to a profit. Nobody could bring out any fault against him except that he was bumptious to everyone, rough and aggressive with the men and indifferent to the women, and that he shadowed his uncle and aunt like a hired bodyguard, daring anything or any person to attack them. The Princes were leaving, and in that Court of winding passages and communicating rooms, the word was passed from mouth to mouth as soon as the Queen of Bohemia's letter was opened by the Queen. There were few secrets at Whitehall; everyone spied on their own behalf, and it was unfortunate for Charles that he had never encouraged spying or rewarded an informer, because the intriguers and gossips were working against him.

Henrietta and the King were too concerned with each other to develop genuine friendships among those who served them; their happiness had made them smug, and the perfection of their married life aroused envy instead of admiration. Everything had gone too well for them, and it was only human that so many of the men and women who were outside the tight little circle of dancing companions and dilettantes should begin to wish for adversity.

But there was no sign of it. England was at peace, and so was Ireland under the absolute dictatorship of Wentworth. The power of the Bishops was increasing under Laud, who used the Ecclesiastical Court of High Commission to discipline unruly parsons who deviated from the Book of Common Prayer and replace them with men of the Archbishop's views. It was no longer safe to denounce the King and Queen from the pulpit or to advise honest citizens they need not pay their taxes. The penalty was imprisonment, and if the King's Court of the Star Chamber did not punish a culprit sufficiently, the Court of High Commission intervened.

The King had instituted a new tax under the heading of Ship Money to maintain the fleet. He was determined that the rotten ships and untrained crews which had brought such shame on the Navy at Cadiz and La Rochelle should be replaced by an efficient force. The original tax had been imposed by Elizabeth Tudor on the coastal counties; Charles and his advisers saw no reason why the whole country should not contribute, and they made Ship Money obligatory to every county in England. Nobody wanted to pay. And a member of the last Parliament went to prison and offered to stand trial.

John Hampden was immensely rich; he had spent the last seven years travelling between his estates in Buckinghamshire and his house in London, where he had regular meetings with his friends and Parliamentary associates and which was the rendezvous of the leading Puritans in the city and surrounding counties. When Hampden was sent to prison, his house was still open, and there, one evening towards the end of January, three peers, the Earl of Warwick and the Lords Say and Brooke, were conferring with John Pym, and a distant cousin of Hampden's who had come up from Huntingdonshire.

Oliver Cromwell was not an important member of the group of men sitting in Hampden's room overlooking the Strand gardens. He was a gentleman by birth, but he had only sat in the last Parliament, and he was inclined to come to these meetings and say very little. He was a big man, ugly and blunt-featured, with an untidy appearance and very plain, old-fashioned clothes, a fond husband and a stern but just father to his five children. He had spent his life on his small country estate and served as a Justice of the Peace; it was a quiet, obscure existence, and he had been content with it until his late thirties, when he became afflicted with fits of depression and nightmares so terrible that he became afraid to go to sleep. Now he showed no sign of the mental crisis which had brought him close to insanity. He had lived as a sober, conscientious man, taking his guidance from the Bible, until the sense of guilt and oppression of the Puritan belief began to unhinge his mind. Evil had pressed in upon him, stifling every human joy, until the sunlight itself appeared as an affront to the terrible God of the Scriptures, and his own inactivity in the face of Evil became an abominable crime. He suffered and wrestled with mental demons, and emerged from it outwardly unchanged. But his mind was warped with zeal; he prayed and agonized like a mediæval saint and when the depression left him and he could rest through the night without fear he had made his dedication to reform his fellow men by any means that offered. The first means was a seat in the Commons of 1628 where the righteous were opposing the will of an idolatrous King. He had made little impression in that Parliament; only those who knew him well, like Hampden, appreciated his intelligence and fanaticism and introduced him to the highest levels of Puritan society. Now Hampden was in prison, the martyr of the King's injustice and disregard of the law.

If a judge could be found honest enough to acquit him, the King's demand for Ship Money could be defied by the rest of the country. Illegal taxation was bad enough in the eyes of the men sitting together on that wet January evening. They were all men of property some actively engaged in business partnership in the Caribbean, where their ships preyed on the Spaniards and traded in slaves, neither occupations offending the sensitive consciences which considered the masques and entertainments at Whitehall as abominations of the Devil. But the worst crime of all was the King's attempt to standardize the Church of England under one service and in obedience to the Bishops, and to permit his Archbishop of Canterbury to introduce Romish rituals and practices and force Puritan clergy to profane themselves or lose their livings.

And now he had directed the Church Assembly of Scotland to accept the English Book of Common Prayer and forbidden all other forms of worship.

John Pym was loudest and longest in his denunciation. He was thick set, rather a stout man, with grey hair cut short above his collar and shrewd brown eyes. He was astonishingly able, a born administrator, and a rousing speaker.

" We all know," he said, " what iniquities the King is committing in our own country. We also know of the orders sent to our brethren in Scotland. Well, my lord and gentlemen, I have had word that the King's Book has been rejected by the Scottish Kirk. The first reading at St. Giles caused a riot, and the people have signed petitions all over the country refusing to change their service to the idolatrous trumpery practised at Lambeth and Whitehall. My informant assures me," he added triumphantly, "that the nobility and the gentry are united with the rest of the Scottish people. The King's Scottish Council has fled from Edinburgh to Holyrood, and the Book has been suspended."

"Thank God," the Earl of Warwick exclaimed. "We must send messages of support. Who are the leaders of our brethren at Edinburgh?"

"The Duke of Montrose and the Earl of Rothes," Pym said. "They have sworn never to accept the Book and submit to the King's ordinance. At last, at last, my Lords, there is a gleam in the sky for the eyes of honest men to see. And it comes from Scotland, where there are no priests cavorting at liberty, free to poison men's soul and commit them to everlasting damnation!"

Cromwell raised his large head and made his first remark of the evening.

"We should take care in dealing with the Scots," he said. "I do not trust them."

"That is a rash judgment," Lord Say turned towards him. He thought Cromwell a boor and resented his intrusion. "Proceed, Pym."

The lawyer's bright little eyes rested upon his audience. "For nearly ten years we have been silenced by the King because we spoke out against his usurpation of our rights. We have been silent as a body but he cannot silence the discontent and apprehension of his entire people. And now part of that people, the people of Scotland, have found an opportunity of speaking out. They are in rebellion against the King's authority. It is our duty to see that they are encouraged to resist him to the limit."

Cromwell was listening, his head bent, his hands spread out awkwardly on his knees. He saw the direction of Pym's argument faster and further than anyone else in the room. He could have said in one short sentence what the professional rabble-rouser was saying with so many embellishments. If Scotland rebelled against the King, the King would probably make the fatal mistake of trying to subdue it by force. And with one half of the British Isles in arms against the other, he would have to call a Parliament to meet the cost.

"We can send assurances of our support," the Earl of Warwick said.

"We can do better; we can send money, if there is any question of resistance with troops." Cromwell made his second remark, and looked round at them obstinately. He felt their surprise at his temerity, and Lord Say was looking at his collar which he considered it a useless vanity to change when it was dirty. He had often felt shy and clumsy in their presence because they were courtiers and men of wealth and education, but the matter was too important to let his diffidence stand in the way of the cause. He had something of value to contribute and nobody was going to stop him.

"The King will never go to war," Warwick said shortly. "He will capitulate and withdraw the Book."

"You misunderstand the King, it seems to me." Cromwell's voice became strong, almost aggressive in the effort to assert his views. "The King believes himself inspired by God to rule this kingdom and dictate every detail of our lives. He will never withdraw the Book without admitting his own principle to be a false one. If Scotland resists, he will set out to subdue Scotland. He has had his way for ten years; he has forgotten how to withdraw anything. There will be a war. And then there will be a Parliament. That's all the care I have in the affairs of Scotland, now or at any future time. If this comes about, it will be the first real service they have ever done to England."

"As you say," Pym said quickly. He was annoyed at being interrupted and annoyed that Cromwell had distracted the attention from himself. "As you say, sir, and doubtless you are right. For the moment there is nothing we can do but send our message of support and wait to see what happens." He moved his chair a little closer to the Earl of Warwick and began speaking to him in a low voice. After a few minutes Cromwell got up and excused himself and walked out into the muddy streets back to his lodging in the City.

The Court was at Greenwich and Henrietta was sitting with her ladies in the Queen's apartments, trying to distract her mind from the anxiety of the political situation and the approach of yet another confinement. She felt extremely well during her pregnancies; her energy and her dislike of rest troubled the King who could not persuade her to care for herself properly and often brought an angry rebuke upon himself when he tried to restrain her. They were about to be separated for the first time in their married life, and this would be a matter of weeks or even months, depending upon the speed with which his army overcame the rebels in Scotland. Henrietta was not a wife who confined herself to pleasure and domesticity; she had always taken an active interest in the affairs of the Kingdom and never hesitated to advise the King. She was one of the few people close to him who had disapproved of the Prayer Book composed by Laud, and the only one who had dared to say so to his face. Charles had been pained and disappointed when she threw it down with an exclamation of contempt. To him it was beautiful in its uniformity and it embodied the best features of the Reformed religion with all the stately ritual of the Church of Rome. He had expected his wife to be sympathetic; he had hoped the similarities to her own faith would show her yet again that he was not a bigot and that his Church and not hers was the true means of offering perfect worship. Henrietta thought it was a muddled travesty, borrowing shamelessly from the ancient faith, and, with unusual foresight, she imagined how offensive it would be to the mass of his subjects across the Scottish border whose religion was as bleak and barbaric as the Puritan creed in England.

It would cause nothing but trouble, she said, and it lacked the virtue of being the truth. They had come very close to quarrelling about the Prayer Book; in the end he took it away from her and the subject was avoided for some weeks. Henrietta forgot about it; Laud was always shut up with the King and very few of his Council knew what they were discussing.

But the time had come when he could not conceal either his plan or the disastrous situation which had arisen from it. Scotland was in armed revolt, and at last the Council, for months bedevilled by rumours and officially in ignorance, had to be summoned and informed in full. And now, thanks to the meddling of that bumptious old churchman and the obstinacy of Charles, England and Scotland were at war. It was inconceivable to Henrietta that Charles should have allowed his zeal for his Church to have led him into such a danger; it was incredible that he should have forgotten the lesson learnt during the war with France, that his only hope of ruling without Parliament was to keep his country at peace. She blamed him, but it was human to blame Laud more. And now, while Charles prepared his army to march into Scotland, Henrietta had sent for the Archbishop.

She put down her sewing and stared round the room; immediately her ladies paused, waiting for some instruction, and Lucy Carlisle watched her cynically. The Countess hated her and the King more than ever. The Queen's dainty figure was swollen with her pregnancy; the royal nurseries were full of crying children and the lovers flirted and pretended to bicker and held hands in public as if they had not got a care or a responsibility in the world. They might cleave together, but the ground was cracking under their feet. She had made her prophecy to Wentworth and at last she could see it beginning to come true.

Troops were being levied up and down the country; the Court expenses had been drastically curtailed; there was talk of war and a great deal of boasting by the younger men who were joining the King and imagined themselves marching unhindered into Scotland to return with riches and glory in a short campaign.

"Where the devil is the Archbishop?" the Queen said at last.

"Shall I go and see, Madam?" Lady Newport rose and curtsied. She had rewarded the Queen by becoming a Catholic, arousing such a storm with her husband and family that the King had been forced to intervene and protect her. Henrietta had made a friend and a convert for life, and Charles had made a mortal enemy of the rich and powerful Earl.

"If you please, Newport."

"He has no right to keep you waiting, Madam." Lucy Carlisle picked up the Queen's needlework frame and put it away.

"I expect he's with the King again," Henrietta said.

"He's always with His Majesty," Lady Carlisle began winding the silks. "It's such a pity he has no other confidant in the Church."

"I have never understood the King's liking for him," Henrietta leant back in her chair; her back was aching and she felt vaguely restless and unwell. "He's such an ill-bred little creature—and that dreadful laugh—always guffawing, you can hear him two rooms distant! Ah, Newport, is he here?"

"Yes, Madam. I saw him coming down the corridor and I ran straight back to tell you."

"Good." Henrietta stood up, supporting herself on the arm of the chair. "When he comes, you will all retire. I have certain things in mind which must be said to his Grace alone."

The Archbishop came in, and kissed her hand. She did not return his smile or answer his enquiry about her health. She did not invite him to sit down and her dark eyes glared at him.

"It is not my habit to interfere," she said abruptly and she was too angry to notice the gleam in his little grey eyes. "Nothing would induce me to send for you and ask an explanation of your conduct, except the hope that you can somehow undo the harm you have done to the King before it is too late!"

Laud's ruddy face flushed a dark red.

"God forbid that I should do the King harm, Madam. I'm afraid I do not understand your accusation."

"You understand perfectly," she snapped. "I thought only Jesuits were guilty of casuistry, my Lord Bishop. I am asking you to withdraw this Prayer Book and persuade the King to treat with the Scots Covenanters. Do you realize that we are about to go to war on account of this piece of authorship you undertook?"

He folded his thick hands in front of him and faced her coolly.

They had fought many battles in the past, battles when he had tried to explain her championing the Catholics and displaying her religion in terms of the harm she was doing to the King, and he had never succeeded in moving her. Now she accused him on similar grounds and he was not prepared to lose his temper. He had his faith, and it was also the faith by which Charles lived and reigned. He did not expect her to understand why its enforcement was important.

"It is not a question of my authorship," he said quietly. "Believe me, Madam, I only put the Prayer Book into its form, and when I did so, I was following the King's instructions. The Church of Rome insists on uniformity among its people. Why should the Church of England be satisfied with less?"

"I am not interested in the Church of England," Henrietta retorted. "I am only interested in the welfare of the King. Your heresy and the Covenanters' heresy are one and the same to me; I do know that the King would never have proposed forcing this Prayer Book on Scotland if you had not suggested it."

"I did suggest it, Madam. And it was the duty of the King's subjects to accept it, whether they were Scots or English. I must point out to you that it is no longer a matter of my authorship or my opinions as Archbishop, whether they matter to you or not. It is now the King's authority which is in question. He cannot bow to the dictates of rebels; as a Princess of the Blood you see that as clearly as a poor commoner like myself."

"I see that there was never any need to put his authority to such a test," she said bitterly. "I see that you have encouraged him and brought him to the point where he must defend it with an army against some of his own people. I may be a Princess of the Blood, my Lord Bishop, but I am not a fool on that account! We cannot afford this war—we cannot afford any war! We haven't the money or the troops trained to bring it to victory. There is still a chance to stop it if you will go to the King and beg him to withdraw the Book. He will not listen to me; he may still listen to you!"

For a moment Laud did not answer. She lowered herself into the chair, feeling suddenly dizzy. Her time was very near.

"Madam," he said slowly. "I am an old man; old enough, saving your pardon, to be your father and near the father of the King himself. I claim the privilege of age by speaking freely to you. Many times I have wondered to what extent you love His Majesty. Many times I have tried to persuade you to make some compromise with your faith for his sake, and I have never once succeeded."

"Whatever my own beliefs," Henrietta answered, "I would not pursue them at the cost of Civil War. I have tried to protect my Catholic people from being butchered like animals on a public scaffold for going to Mass or taking the cloth of the priesthood. I have refused to attend services which I believe to be wrong as the King has always refused to attend my Mass. But if the time came when my practice of my faith put the King in the danger he is in at this moment, I would abandon anything and trust my soul's judgment to God! If you love His Majesty, go and beg him on your knees before it is too late!"

Laud looked up at her, and his round ugly face had softened. "Madam, no man except Lord Wentworth loves the King as much as I do. And if I ever doubted that you loved him, I beg your pardon for it now. I wish," he said simply, "that we had talked like this before. Much of our misunderstandings could have been avoided. The Prayer Book was my idea, Madam, and I made it in good faith, believe me. I wanted the King to rule as absolutely in his Church as he does in his State. I wanted the peace and benefit of that rule to shine through every aspect of his subject's life, beginning with the worship of God, where all men kneel as equals in His sight. But I had no idea that it could lead to this. And before I came to you this afternoon I went to see His Majesty. I went on my knees and begged, but he won't listen to me either."

There was no sound or movement in the room for some moments. He looked up at the Queen sitting awkwardly in her tall chair, her face sallow and lined with fatigue, and on a sudden impulse of remorse for his bias against her, the Archbishop knelt and lifted her hand to his lips. He did not understand women; he had never remotely understood her or appreciated the strength of her love for her husband when so many of her actions seemed to be obstinately selfish. He was not sure of anything about her even then, except she loved the King with all her heart, and for that he could forgive her everything.

"Trust in God, Madam, your God and mine, for He is the same in spite of all our efforts to divide Him up. And pray for the King and the success of his arms. I shall never cease to do so night and day until he returns. It may be that God will listen to us both."

Chapter 7

IT was late and Charles had sent his attendants away; it was the custom for one or more of his gentlemen to sleep in his room as a precaution against the Scots. He had crossed the border and was staying at Berwick Castle with what remained of his army, a defeated army composed of discontented, untrained men, grumbling against a war with which none of them was in religious sympathy, officered by nobles and gentry quarrelling amongst themselves and secretly in league with many of the Scottish rebels.

Lord Holland, Henrietta's friend and his favourite, had taken his cavalry and foot-soldiers into Scotland and run from the superior Scots forces without firing a shot. There was no battle, only a disgraceful rout, and what was left of the Royal army's tremulous morale collapsed.

They were surrounded by the Covenanters, and the discipline and fervour of the rebellious Scots were a merciless reminder to him of the disloyalty and cowardice of his own people. He had met the Scottish leaders to discuss a treaty—the rough, suspicious Earl of Rothes and the younger, more courteous Earl of Montrose, and Charles had received them graciously and disarmed them with promises he had no intention of keeping.

His power was threatened, and he was a man and a King in spite of his gentle upbringing and peaceful instincts. He had been betrayed and flouted and Laud was not with him to remind him of the sanctity of the Christian Princes word.

He did not want his attendants with him. He could hardly bear to speak to Holland and to Arundel, who had mismanaged his fleet; he was sick of their excuses and their attempts to lay the blame on each other. He felt that night that if one of his advisers counselled him to give the rebels what they wanted, he would strike the speaker in the face. The room was bare and draughty, and he walked up and down to keep warm, measuring the paces, his mind in a turmoil of intrigue and counter-intrigue. Rothes wanted to abolish the Bishops in Scotland and set up a separate Scottish Parliament, far more independant than the English Commons. He could do nothing but agree and return to England to reorganize his forces for a second war. That was his only hope and his only aim, and he did not trust any of his nobles not to warn the Covenanters or babble about it in their cups if he confided in them. The more he saw of the lay preachers and ministers moving among the Scottish armies singing psalms and quoting fiery passages of scripture, the more he hated and resented what he saw. To him it was religious anarchy, rebellion against God and defiance of the Lord's anointed. It was especially embittering to know that his only reliable officers were Catholics, who had joined him in gratitude for the lenience he had shown them during his reign.

He went to the fireplace, where a heap of logs were smoking and smouldering in the freezing draught of the old-fashioned chimney, and pulled on the bell rope. His valet Parry came into the room and bowed. He alone knew the King's mood, and he did not venture to speak.

"Bring me some pens and ink and paper," Charles said. "And tell Lord Hamilton I shall not need him in my room tonight; I don't think I shall go to bed at all."

"Yes, Your Majesty. Will you require him or any of your household? They are waiting in the ante-chamber."

"I want no one," the King said, "except only you, Parry. You can keep me company tonight when I have finished writing." The valet brought him paper and some freshly-cut quill pens and ink and did his best to coax the fire with a pair of ancient bellows which wheezed so loudly that Charles told him irritably to stop and leave the room.

He wrote first to his wife.

"My own Dear Heart, I think of you constantly in the midst of my troubles, and so my thoughts are the only consolation I find here. I am beset by vexations and quarrels and the demands of my enemies for all that is ungodly and rebellious, and I must perforce bear with them and even try to smile, for fear that they should see what is in my heart concerning them. God did not mean that His Princes should be tried as I am, nor that such a one should lie and forswear in order to preserve His peace, but so it is, and being so, mine own beloved, I do what must be done as fairly as I can, strengthened as always by my thoughts of you and the hope of being quickly in your arms once more. Do not distress yourself, or put the well-being which is dearer to me than life itself into peril by listening to rumours or losing trust in him who is your husband, and could not survive without support from you. I have left my kingdom in your hands; cherish it and guard it against my return for there is much to be done before this stain of shame is wiped away. I would to God that you were with me," he wrote, as he had written every day since leaving London, "I would that I might find the sweetness of my life in your arms and the strength of my soul in your wisdom. I beg of you with all the need of my love and the humility of my heart, that you will write to me as soon as you receive this . . ."

He ended as always in his letters to her, "Farewell, my dear Heart, from him who is your loving husband, Charles."

He sanded the letter and sealed it, and then wrote a short letter to the only man in whom he could put trust, the man who had accomplished in Ireland everything he had failed so wretchedly to do in England or across the border. He wrote to Wentworth in Dublin and ordered him to return to London immediately.

The summer passed and the King and his army made their way slowly back to London. It was a depleted force, thinned out by desertions, its loyalties shaken by contact with the Scottish rebels and their preachers, conscious of waste and failure and ready to blame the King for everything.

The nobles were no less affected. Those who had lost their reputations like Holland and Arundel, and those who had sided with the Covenanters like the Puritan Lords Brooke and Say and Essex, spread rumours of the King's perfidy in dealing with the Scots, for nobody believed in the validity of the promises made when he left Berwick. He was going back to build up his army and return to subdue them, and the rumours were confirmed by the news that Wentworth was returning. The iron disciple of absolute rule, fresh from his subjection of Ireland, was being brought back to perfect his system in England and prepare the King's army for war.

Wentworth had been the most bitterly hated man in England, when he was President of the Council of the North and the reputation he had earned in Ireland had preceded him before he landed again on the English coast. Here was the one man strong enough to put a sword into the King's hand; the one man rich enough and fanatical enough to override the corrupt officials and the lazy Courtiers who were weakening Charles and dividing his government. And the King was not chastened or hesitating, as so many of his people had hoped. He had not seen his reverse as a warning from the Lord to desert the unrighteous. He was committed to evil and beyond the reach of grace. His people hardened against him and huddled together in fear of his revenge upon them. Most of all they feared the ruthless actions of Lord Wentworth. The Court favourites trembled and busied themselves intriguing uselessly against the Lord Deputy and each other, and many of Charles' nobles began frequenting Lord Warwick's house and making contact with Pym and the Puritan leaders. They felt the approach of danger, each to their own interest, and all were united in a common resistance to absolutism. With the exception of the King himself, the only two people who were glad to see Wentworth were Archbishop Laud and Henrietta.

They had been separated for three years, and none of them were prepared for the change they saw in the Lord Deputy of Ireland. Charles and the Queen stood close together, her hand was resting on his arm, and the little figure of the Archbishop, rounder than ever, waiting a few paces behind them. It was no longer just the King and Laud; now Henrietta joined their conferences, and at last when the force of popular hatred against the Bishop and the Queen expressed itself in lampoons and pamphlets and ribald scribblings on the very walls of Whitehall and Lambeth, Laud and Henrietta had become close friends, bound by their common care for the King.

For a few seconds, Henrietta did not recognize the man who walked so slowly across the polished floor towards them. Her fingers gripped Charles and she felt him stiffen. Then he began to walk towards the Minister. Thomas Wentworth met them half-way down the room, and with some difficulty he fell upon both knees in front of Charles. His dark hair was thickly streaked with white. He was thinner than before, but the spare, athletic frame was gone; the body of a tired, enfeebled man replaced it, and his strong face was hollow-cheeked with an unhealthy jaundiced colour. He looked twenty years older than his forty-nine years; only his eyes, so full of light and intelligence, blazed out in defiance of his physical decay.

"Thomas . . ." Charles was the first to speak. He gave his hand to Wentworth and when he had kissed it, helped him rise to his feet. "Thomas, my dear friend, how truly glad I am to see you. . ."

"This is a happy day for me," Wentworth answered, and he smiled. Laud, who knew him so well, recognized the irony in the smile.

"You find me changed, Sire," he continued; the King was looking at him with such alarm that Wentworth felt tempted to laugh. "I neglected to mention to you that in the last few months I've been unwell. It's taken a greater toll of me than I imagined."

Henrietta came forward. She had never really liked Wentworth, and in all honesty she admitted that her only interest in him was his usefulness to Charles. But this sick, sallow wreck was hardly the mighty champion they had summoned home to put their troubles right. He looked as if he could hardly stand.

"Welcome home, my Lord. Sire, will you permit Lord Wentworth to sit down?"

Nobody would have dared suggest such licence except the Queen. Wentworth was given a chair.

"My humble thanks to your Majesties." For a moment his eyes met Henrietta's with a message of gratitude. His right foot was bandaged, and the swelling had crept up his calf.

"Gout," he explained. "An unfair affliction for an abstemious man. I crave your Majesties' pardon."

"I had no idea you were in such poor health," the King said gently. "You have lost much weight, Thomas. What have the Irish done to you. . ?"

"Given me new heart," he answered quickly. "Shown that with justice and authority they can be faithful subjects. What their water has done, besides give me the gout, is another matter, Sire. I have been suffering with a stone for some months."

"So you said in your letters," Laud came forward and the two men shook hands. The Archbishop beamed and his bright little eyes filled with tears of emotion. "Welcome, welcome, Thomas."

Wentworth released his hand and looked up at the King. Charles had changed very little; he was as slim and upright and handsome as the day Wentworth first came to see him at Whitehall. He would pass from youth to old age without the ugly transition of corpulence and greying hair which disfigured men in middle age.

"I should not sit in your presence, Sire. You did not send for me in your trouble to have an invalid lolling in a chair talking about his own ailments. Forgive me."

"Stay where you are," Charles commanded. "Come, I will sit with you."

"We are in straits," Henrietta said. "Our army ran away from the Scots, and the King was forced to concede everything. There is not one person who can turn that defeat into a victory except you."

"Their army numbers twenty-five thousand men," Charles said. "It is commanded by Rothes and Montrose and Argyle— Argyle is the most powerful of all, and he has taken the leadership from the rest. My Council in Scotland has no authority; my friends there have been forced to recant and sign this Covenant or else they are in prison. My Treasury is empty and my troops are scattered. My Crown is in contempt. That cannot be, Thomas, no matter what the cost. I must raise a new army and return to Scotland. I want you to command it."

Wentworth did not answer for a moment. He had been in communication with Laud throughout that disastrous campaign; he had written urgent letters to the King himself, begging him to wait until he was sure of success before invading Scotland, offering him troops from Ireland, money, ships, anything he needed if he would only show a little patience. Charles had not listened; the voice of sound sense was overcome by the clamour of hotheads, and the King's own irritable pride. Wentworth had watched disaster come upon his master, and at last he had dragged himself out of his sick-bed and made the long, exhausting journey back to England to save what he could before it was too late. He was so ill that there were times when he suspected he was dying. His body was wracked with urinal attacks; the poison from his infected kidneys ravaged his system, and gout robbed him of sleep and appetite and exercise. Only his will remained, forcing him to ignore pain and weakness and offer his services to the King he loved, who had sent him to Ireland and then forgotten his advice: never go to war on any pretext whatsoever.

He should have felt resentment for Charles but Wentworth did not blame him. He blamed his own absence, and the ascendancy of his good old friend William Laud, who had pointed his nose in the direction of a united Church and fired his King with his own mistaken zeal.

"We will raise another army, Sire. You can leave the organization of it to me. On my way here I studied the situation and I have a plan ready for your consideration."

Charles glanced triumphantly at his wife and she smiled at him.

Wentworth had not wasted time. The sound of his voice inspired confidence; sick or well, nothing changed the resolution or the ingenuity of his extraordinary character.

"What is your plan?" Charles asked him.

"We need a map, Sire."

The King's Secretary brought maps of England and Scotland and a third of Ireland, and stayed long enough to hear the Lord Deputy mention a sea blockade of Scottish ports and a landing of Irish troops. He was able to tell an interested audience of courtiers in the second anteroom that the King and Queen and the Archbishop were in high spirits and planning the annihilation of their enemies. Lord Wentworth might have the gout and a kidney ailment, but he had lost nothing of his fighting spirit.

That evening, when the King and Queen retired early, the Countess of Carlisle hid herself in a hooded cloak and slipped out of a side entrance to her carriage. She drove to a small house at the back of Westminster Palace Yard. It was the private lodging of John Pym, the Puritan leader. They had first met at a reception given by the Earl of Warwick some months before; the Countess had begun to cultivate Warwick and other peers she knew to be unfriendly to the King and Queen, and in their company she modified her dress and her conversation as a sign of her political leanings. She had been bored for a long time. There was no one at Court with whom she had wished to have an affair after her quarrel with Wentworth. There was no one among the Hollands and Gorings and Newcastles strong enough or intelligent enough to replace him as a lover of consequence or to do him the injury she would like to inflict upon him. She spent her time amusing the Queen, whom she disliked and despised more and more for not suspecting her, and began investigating the strata of Puritan society out of a sense of mischief.

Warwick was a boor; so were Say and Essex and the Earl of Manchester's heir, Lord Mandeville; they were all disappointed men who were out of sympathy with the Court and she knew them all too well to be interested in any of them. But at Warwick's house she met John Pym.

She had never forgotten that evening. She had dressed very cleverly in black velvet, covering her magnificent shoulders with a modest lace collar, and deliberately emphasized her classic beauty with a severe hair style and no rouge. Struck by the searching eyes and powerful chin of the stout, plain man in his sober Puritan cloth suit and short-cropped hair, she had asked to be introduced to him. She had a genius for appraising talent, and talent was what she found in the person of the famous Parliamentary leader. This was not a discontented theorist like Warwick, or a religious fanatic like Mandeville who should have been a parson. This was something different and exciting, a man who spoke with fire and enthusiasm and confidence; who was not overawed by men of nobler birth and not afraid to talk on equal terms with a beautiful woman from the circle of his enemies. Here was a Puritan with a thirst for power; she knew because she shared it like an addiction to vice. They met and they challenged each other without words, and that was the first of many meetings. It ended as all such meetings did with her. Pym surrendered his immortal soul, and she found in the guilty tempest of his passion a satisfaction which had eluded her through a lifetime of sexual experience. She seduced him and in return he converted her. She was his mistress, and no one in her circle or his suspected it. By this time she was not only his mistress but his spy.

There were other women at the house in Palace Yard. The Countess of Warwick was there with Lady Essex, whose husband was an open partisan of the Scots Covenanters and the

Puritans in England, and one or two other minor members of the Court. Pym came forward to greet the Countess of Carlisle and placed her in a chair with a glass of wine beside her. She spoke to Warwick's wife and to the Earl himself, and began to talk to John Hampden. They were all discussing Wentworth as if the devil himself had assumed human shape, and Hampden questioned her about his health.

He was a stern man, good-looking and extremely erudite, but unlike her lover, Pym, he lacked humour.

"He's certainly ill," she said. "I haven't spoken to him, and God forbid that I should if I can help it, but I see a tremendous change in him. He's not the man who left England three years ago, whatever the King tries to make out."

"But he's not sick to death," Hampden pointed out bitterly. "God may have stricken him but the devil sustains him yet."

"The devil always sustained him," she said. Ireland had not destroyed him; her curse had turned into a veritable blessing in terms of success and prestige for the man who had rejected her.

"It's common talk that he has come back with a large grant of money from the Irish Parliament, and with the offer of a trained army. That is, if it's possible to train those savages to anything."

"He is bent on war," Hampden said. "He and the King between them will never rest until they shed the blood of honest men in order to pervert their souls and steal their liberty. From what you have seen of him, my Lady, how long can he live under the strain the King will put upon him? Even a man in his full health must falter under the task of gathering that scattered force and training it to fight against its principles. To say nothing of conjuring the money out of the empty air!"

"It will be conjured out of our pockets," Pym interrupted. "By forced loans, by fines, by every illegal method he can devise."

"It won't be enough," Hampden said. "The whole country is against the King in this business. No one wants a second Scottish war; no one wants to fight it or pay for it. There is a war for Protestant freedom raging in Germany, and England has not contributed anything. If the King called for an army to fight for our brethren abroad, his coffers would be full and every man in England would enlist."

"The King is not interested in the Protestant cause," Lady Carlisle said. "The King is half a Papist already, thanks to his wife, and the Archbishop would rather persecute the members of our religion than stop the spread of Popery."

She had gained the full attention of everyone in the room. She glanced around her audience and met the intense, and critical scrutiny of an ugly middle-aged man sitting with his back to the wall, a little apart from the rest. She recognized Cromwell; he was often at Pym's house, always wearing the same crumpled clothes and looking as if he had not washed for weeks. He was not an important person, or a prepossessing one, and she had never troubled to speak to him. But his was the only face in which she sensed hostility. He was the only man in the room who was not impressed by her; she saw in his calculating eyes that he despised her, and for a moment she felt as if he knew the truth of her relationship with Pym. But she was not a coward, and she stared back without flinching, expecting him to turn away. To her surprise he looked over her head and addressed himself to Hampden.

"Cousin, why are the Covenanters keeping an army on the English border?"

"Because they do not trust the King's word," Hampden replied. "It is only a matter of months before he breaks the agreement reached at Berwick."

"In that case," Cromwell leaned forward, "why do they wait until Wentworth gathers his army and brings in his Irish mercenaries. You have friends among the Covenanters, Cousin. Put it to them that it is poor strategy to wait to be attacked, when at this moment they have all the strength."

Pym came behind Lucy Carlisle's chair; she felt him brush against her. Once or twice he had expressed his resentment of Cromwell. He disliked his habit of interrupting and he thought his opinions irresponsible. He was also a little jealous.

"You are not suggesting that the Scots should invade us?"

"I cannot see a better way of making the King call a Parliament. And after all, sir, that has been the object of treating with them behind the King's back. What is the good of a treason half committed? If Lord Wentworth takes an army over the border and wins a victory for the King, we will never see the light of freedom or reform in our lifetime or even in our children's. If we sit here idling and wasting our time with a lot of Court gossip, we deserve to have our religion and our liberties extinguished——"

"By God, he's right!" the Earl of Essex burst out. "The King must be stopped; Mr. Cromwell uses the word 'treason', and I beg leave to quarrel with it, however much I agree with everything else he's said tonight. I call it treason to leave the King at the mercy of advisers like Wentworth and Archbishop Laud. If the Covenanters cross into England, they will be welcomed by most of us as liberators, protecting the King against himself. And no sovereign can face an invasion without calling Parliament. It is the only possible solution. I salute you, Sir," he said to Cromwell. "You are a man of excellent sense."

Cromwell stood up and bowed and then sat down again. His heavy face had flushed; he looked almost embarrassed.

"I cannot offer more than the suggestion," he said. "I have no friends across the Scottish border. I and many like me can do nothing to remedy what is wrong with England until we sit in Parliament again. But when we do, my Lords and gentlemen, we will know how to rid the King of Wentworth and of the Archbishop."

He looked at the pale, beautiful woman sitting close to Pym and ignored the smile she gave him. He knew who she was and he had taken the trouble to find out about her reputation; her conversion to the Puritan belief made no difference to his dislike and contempt for her or to his disgust with Pym. He had no sympathy with her or with the nobles, Essex included, who hung round Whitehall as servants of the King, and sneaked into the houses of his enemies behind his back. He and his family ate and drank and dressed like the common people, and worshipped in their bare little church where a lay lecturer read the lessons and preached God's word. He did not belong to the class which was so strongly represented in that room, and if he had, he felt sure he would have served the interests of the King more loyally than they did.

Cromwell did not speak again but sat back in his chair and listened, controlling the rising impatience which resulted from these meetings when he saw the simple issues being confused in a torrent of talk. He considered himself a plain man; indeed his simplicity was his boast. His country was being badly governed by a King who had rejected the ancient laws of the Constitution and had nothing to show for his eleven years of single rule except alliances with Catholic Spain and France, a corrupt financial system and a ruinous religious policy leading in the unmistakable direction of re-union with Rome.

Cromwell had been brought up with a superstitious horror of the religion which had rent England with persecution and culminated in the Spanish Armada, long before he himself was born. For his toleration of it, if for nothing else, Cromwell abhorred and suspected the King, and he reserved his most bitter hatred for the treacherous little priest at Lambeth who was using his ecclesiastical powers to impose an English Inquisition. Cromwell had no patience for the moderates in his party, or for those like the nobles who stood with a foot in both camps. His God was Jehovah, the God of Wrath, who sent his servants into battle, and the people of God needed a Joshua to lead them. He had yet to see the prophet chosen by the Lord, but in his prayers and mediations and his reading of the fiery passages in Scripture, the call was already coming faintly through to him that the Joshua of Puritan England might turn out to be himself.

Lucy Carlisle was whispering to Pym.

"The King has appointed Sir Henry Vane as his secretary," she said. "I thought that might interest you."

"Vane?" Pym was astonished. "But his son is one of us; he defied the King in the Parliament of '29. How can he give such a confidential post to any member of that family?"

"Because the Lord always blinds those who lose his grace," she said. She had easily adopted the Biblical vernacular; it was not uncommon for her lover to express the climax of his passion with a cry of 'Hallelujah', and she had long ceased to see anything funny in it. She could not find anything to mock in Pym, because Pym had succeeded where so many other men of wit and birth and elegance had failed in the primitive essential. For the first time in her life, Lucy Carlisle was genuinely dominated, and genuinely, fiercely happy.

"The Secretary is loyal to the King," she said. "And that is all that matters to him. He punishes the son and exalts the father and sees nothing contrary to nature in it. Vane is a fool;

he leaves his papers loose and talks like an old woman. He writes down the business at the Council meetings. Would it be useful to you if the younger Vane arranged to copy them? I can find some way to help him."

"It would be invaluable! We should know everything Wentworth is planning as soon as he discloses it in Council. . . But the risk, my dear, the risk to yourself. . ."

"I take it gladly," she said. "And you needn't trouble yourself; you shall have the transcripts and Vane shall bring them to you. No one will suspect me. Shall I stay on tonight?"

He hesitated and then shook his head. He was a very logical and rather worldly man, and he had managed to manipulate his code of morals to include their relationship; he had no alternative once the first sin was committed. He had excused it to himself but he was careful to conceal it from his friends.

"It is too dangerous; it would not look well for you to linger when the rest have gone. Tomorrow. Tomorrow evening, when I will be sure to be alone."

He escorted her down to the door and helped her into her coach. She leant forward and kissed him on the mouth. The coach moved forward, rocking uncomfortably on the rough cobbled street and turned down past the river towards Whitehall. She shared the second ante-room with Lady Newport who turned over sleepily supposing that the Countess had been with a lover. Both women were roused at six o'clock the next morning to bring the Queen's chocolate and dress her for her daily Mass.

There had been a riot in the City of London. It began on May Day, the traditional feast of Spring, when the people wore their best clothes and musicians appeared in the streets and there was dancing and a good deal of horseplay and a contest of sports. The apprentices began it; they came out at Blackfriars and began streaming down towards Southwark. They were shouting and jostling and in a strangely quarrelsome mood. Many carried sticks and more were picking up stones as they went. They were soon joined by the dock workers and seamen whose ships were standing idle in the Port of London because of the disputes between the King and the City of London over a grant he demanded to finance his new army. Someone had found a drum, and the steady beat brought

132

more and more apprentices and youths out of the shops and toolyards, and the crowd became a mob and broke out suddenly in the direction of Lambeth, yelling for the blood of the Papist Laud.

The discontent and the rumours had been growing for weeks; more and more Puritan preachers spoke out against the King and the army gathering to march on Scotland, and were sent to prison. There were rumours and counter-rumours; Wentworth, now created Earl of Strafford, was throwing men into prison for refusing to join the King's army; troops were being sent by Spain to help subdue the Protestant Scots. The King had become a Catholic in return for a huge grant of money from the Pope.

The Archbishop had fled for his life through a back entrance, and eventually the mob was dispersed at the King's orders. The rioting spread to the prisons, where crowds forced the doors of Newgate and the Marshalsea and released the prisoners. By the evening the outbreak of violence had spent itself and numbers of the ringleaders were in jail; the city of London was quiet, but it was an uneasy truce rather than a victory for the authorities. The Council met hurriedly and Holland advised the King to remove the Queen and her children from Whitehall. The next demonstration might be directed against her and he was about to leave for the army headquarters at York. It was not safe, Holland said nervously, to leave her in London unprotected.

Charles took her to Oatlands the following day and wrote to Strafford that his departure for York was delayed. Nothing mattered to him at that moment except Henrietta's safety; he ordered the apprentices to be severely punished and placed a guard round Laud who had returned to Lambeth. In the peace of the country which they both loved, in the house which held such a mixture of memories, where he had taken her as the prisoner of his love when they were both in bitter conflict, Charles and Henrietta stole a few days solitude and happiness together.

They went hunting and they were defiantly gay in front of their household; when they were alone, they shared a tenderness and feverish passion which surpassed anything they had ever known in all the years of their marriage. The days fled, bringing the separation they dreaded, until he wrote to Straf-

133

ford yet again, postponing the date. She looked so pale and delicate, and he could not tear himself away from her until he felt sure that the memory of that frightful May day and the sound of the screaming mobs racing past Whitehall had left her mind

On the morning of their last day at Oatlands, he woke soon after dawn. The curtains were open, and the soft light was turning gold and pink in the spacious bedroom which was full of late spring flowers.

He looked at his wife, lying like a child curled up in the enormous ornate bed, her dark hair curling over the silk pillows, one hand under her cheek, and he bent down and kissed her. She moved and smiled, and he woke her gently with caresses on her bare arms and breasts which brought her eagerly into his arms. They did not speak; their bodies fused in the enactment of their passion, and for an instant of stolen time, they rose to the peak of ecstatic oblivion and then slowly, reluctantly, they came back to consciousness.

The room was full of sunshine and they could hear the members of the household moving in the rooms beyond.

Henrietta looked up into his face; her head was against his shoulder and her arms were round him.

"You leave today, my love." They were the first words she had spoken.

"I must," he said. "I would stay for ever but today is our last. I cannot refuse Strafford any longer."

"Why did this have to happen?" she asked. "Why has everything gone wrong when we were so happy. . . What have we done to offend God and bring this trouble on us?"

"We haven't offended, sweetheart," Charles said gently. "And you must be a good wife and not weaken now. I have my army and I have Strafford, and I thank God for both. You would not be happy with me if I were a coward. And I shouldn't love you as I do if you hadn't got a heart as brave as any man's. I am leaving, but it will not be for long. We have our troubles, my beloved, but they will be over for the rest of our lives when I come back to you again."

"You're very confident," she said slowly. She sat up, drawing the sheet round her. "Charles, how can you be so sure of victory? Strafford is a sick man—sometimes I think he's dying! How can you take an army into Scotland with all your people set against you and a commander leading his troops from a litter! Supposing he dies on the campaign. . . Supposing you are defeated!"

"If I am defeated," he said, "then I will no longer be King. And I am only a King in name while one half of my kingdom is in rebellion against me. You must not be afraid, my darling. All you must do is wait quietly here and trust in me. When this is over, we will have our old life again and it will seem like some ugly dream." He lifted her hand and kissed it.

"I make you a promise," he said. "When the war is over, I will pull down this old house and build a new Palace at Oatlands, and we will spend as many weeks here as you wish. And they will be as sweet as these few days, without any parting at the end of them."

They were silent for a moment; the King's expression was serene. She could see that he had forgotten his difficulties and was happily imagining the kind of building he would have designed at Oatlands. He had an extraordinary facility for banishing anything unpleasant in favour of some dream, whether the subject was a united Church and Kingdom on which the sun of his benevolent despotic government cast a glorious light, or a splendid Palace to commemorate his love for his wife. Or the possibility of a sweeping victory being won by a man in the throes of mortal illness. It was the romantic unrealism of his race; all the Stuarts had been visionaries, many of them poets and patrons of the arts; all had combined a fiercely material love of their power with the fantasy of the dreamer. Henrietta was half Italian and half French, but in spite of a fiery temperament, she was essentially practical. She could not share his escape into the future and talk about building a shrine to themselves at Oatlands when he was leaving that day to lead an army against the Covenanters.

"Charles," she said suddenly, "you must not leave everything to Strafford. He has performed miracles for you, but his strength is not inhuman."

"I have no intention of going to York and interfering with him." Charles said calmly. "I led one expedition alone and I haven't forgotten how it ended. As long as Strafford can direct the army, he must remain its commander. I am content to follow him into battle and to fight with him, but I am not

135

a strategist. Nor are you," he added gently. "Leave the anxieties to Strafford and to me."

She got up and wrapped her satin dressing robe round her. "It is a perfect day," she said. He was up and dressing behind her. She turned and sat on the side of the bed and watched him; he looked as calm and untroubled as if there was no parting before him, no danger and no strife. He was not afraid for himself; she knew that he had never been afraid of anything in his life. She also knew that even his loyalist supporters thought the Scottish war a dangerous enterprize which could have been settled by compromising with his principles. But Charles would never compromise. Twelve years of autocracy had divorced him from reality. His subjects were ungrateful and misguided and he was deaf to criticism and impatient of advice which was not an obedient echo.

He came and took her in his arms, and suddenly her eyes filled with tears. This was their real farewell, not the parting which would be made later that day in front of their household.

They were embracing silently, when the Comptroller of his Household rapped at the ante-room door.

"Your Majesty, a Courier from York!"

"We have not dressed or breakfasted," Charles called out irritably, "tell him to wait. It's another letter from Strafford asking me to hurry," he explained to Henrietta.

"He says it is most urgent, Sire."

"Receive him, Charles," she begged. "It must be important or they would never dare disturb you—I'll go to my ladies." She went into her retiring room, and the King told the Comptroller to send up the messenger. Then he rang for his gentlemen of the Chamber. He was washing his hands in scented water out of a silver basin when Strafford's messenger came into the room and fell on his knees. He was dusty and red-eyed, and he carried a letter rolled in oiled silk and sealed with Strafford's personal seal. Charles wiped his hands and thanked the courier, and broke the seal open. His attendants took the water away and began laying out his shirt and stockings and breeches; the King read the letter slowly, and then handed it to his valet.

"Parry, lock that in my cabinet if you please." He slipped his arms into the white lawn shirt, which was fastened by the

Lord Pembroke who had the privilege of helping the King into his under-linen. Each member of his personal household had special duties; a different nobleman handed him his shirt and breeches, a third dressed him in his coat and stockings, and a fourth gave him his Orders and put on his shoes. He said nothing, except to remark on the fine weather, and he never once looked at Parry or the cabinet where the letter had been locked away.

When he put on his rings his hands were steady; he took some time inspecting himself before his mirror, not from vanity but because a King must always look immaculate in every detail of his dress. He was deliberately silent because his voice always betrayed him. In any crisis, he betrayed himself by stammering. With an effort he turned to Lord Pembroke.

"Send for the Queen. And l—l—leave me." The peers and the valet bowed and withdrew to their ante-room, and after a few moments which seemed like years, he heard Henrietta come into the room.

"Henrietta. . ." He stumbled painfully over her name and she ran to him.

"Charles, what is it? It's the letter. . . Don't try and speak till you're calm, give it to me, where is it . . ? "

He shook his head and with an effort composed himself.

"Sweetheart—sweetheart . . . be patient with me. L-listen quietly and don't be agitated. The Scots crossed into England on August 20th."

"Sacrebleu! " The half-forgotten French oath escaped her before she could stop herself. She stared at Charles, seeing the handsome face contort in the agony of his impediment and the incredulous despair in his eyes, more eloquent than the words he was unable to speak.

"They've invaded us! Charles, it's not possible. For the love of God show me the letter."

He unlocked the cabinet and gave it to her and went to stand by the dressing table, breathing deeply to restore his power of speech.

"You waited too long! " she exclaimed, and it was not in his nature to remind her of her responsibility for the delay.

"Strafford says they met with no resistance; they crossed the Tyne in daylight and marched into England without a shot being fired at them! "

"They haven't met Strafford yet," he said at last. "I must go to York at once, as soon as we've breakfasted."

"Don't be ridiculous." Her voice was sharp. "You cannot possibly waste time being served on bended knee and losing hours over a meal you can eat on the road! You must leave now, Charles, within the hour!"

She ran to her bell rope and pulled it; the sound echoed loudly all over the outside corridors.

She cried to the Countess of Newport when she came to the door. "Send for the Comptroller! Tell him to come immediately, the King is leaving for York at once!"

"I told no one," Charles said. "There must be no panic . . . Strafford will beat them. . ."

"Strafford is a dying man," Henrietta said fiercely. "You are the King, go out and meet them with your armies. And stop trying to pretend that nothing is the matter when the whole of England will know we're invaded in a few days! Charles, Charles," she said urgently. "This is not the time to think of trifles. Get down from your pinnacle for the love of God before you're knocked down! I'm going to change into my riding clothes; I'm coming part of the way with you."

Chapter 8

STRAFFORD had been speaking for nearly an hour. He made no concessions to his health by sitting down as the King suggested, but stood supporting himself on the arms of his chair, facing the hostile faces of the Council of Peers which had been called at York. His army had met the Scots at Newbourne and been defeated, and the rebels had occupied Newcastle and were marching further into England without opposition. Strafford had got out of his bed after a terrible attack of stone and tried to rally his troops. But from that moment the war was lost and so was he; the King alone would not admit it, and he had sat through a week of bitter arguments surrounded by the nobles summoned from London, none of whom would support Strafford in his plea for a further attempt to drive the rebels out of England. The Earls of Essex, Bedford, Warwick and Bristol were sitting round the Council table, stubborn and hostile, their hatred directed against the sick and desperate man who was pleading passionately for the honour of his country and his King. But it was hopeless. England had been invaded and instead of springing forward to repel the enemy, the people were selling them supplies and the army was refusing to fight them.

Strafford looked round him. He was sick with shame and disgust, and sicker still with fear for the silent King sitting at the head of the table.

"We can still win," he protested. "I tell you, my Lords, that if a few of you will come forward and put heart into our people and support His Majesty, we can drive these Covenanters back and beat them yet: I have a loyal army across the Irish Sea which is only waiting to land here and subdue this kingdom. with their help the war could be won and Scotland pacified in a few months."

He paused, and the Secretary Vane wrote down his words in an almost illegible scribble. He was not a quick writer and, after some of the more noisy meetings, he had difficulty

139

reading his own writing and putting it into a sensible form.

"We will never sanction Irish troops landing in this country for any purpose whatsoever," Lord Warwick said coldly. "There is only one solution to this wretched situation—brought about by your ill advice to the King and your incompetence with his army, and that is to call Parliament and do what they advise."

Charles interrupted quietly and without taking his eyes away from Strafford.

"No—there will be no Parliament. Think of something else, my Lord."

"There must be," Warwick turned to him angrily. "How much longer can this illegality continue, ignoring the will of the people and bringing our trade to ruin? You cannot govern without them, Sire, and speaking for myself and the other Lords, we will not help you try! So long as you listen to Lord Strafford, our presence here is a waste of time."

"If you cannot contain your abuse of Lord Strafford, you may leave the Council," Charles remarked. "I summoned all of you because I hoped for loyalty from my nobles and I have spent the last week listening while you attack the only minister who has shown me devotion and never spared his health or his money in my service."

"Your Majesty," Strafford turned towards him, "my reputation is of no importance. You are the judge of my services and your approval is all that counts with me. I know the feelings of Lord Warwick and I am not dismayed by them—or surprised," he added contemptuously.

"But I am not so prejudiced that I cannot agree with him when he happens to be right. And now he is right. Nothing can be gained from him or anyone here. I have tried with the army and the gentry and I have failed utterly, I admit that. There is still a chance that you may find your friends in Parliament. There's still a chance that the people of England will elect loyal Englishmen to the Commons and that they will see what these surrounding you do not. You will have to call them, Sire."

Warwick and Essex exchanged a look of surprise. If Strafford advised a Parliament he must be mad. If he imagined that the body which would meet at Westminster would support him or the King, he had lost all sense of the temper of the people, and all sense of the extent to which he was hated by every section of the nation.

"I see what you are thinking," Strafford said, "and believe me, I am not thinking of myself. I'm only thinking of the King. He cannot face this invasion alone, and I cannot believe that the Commons will abandon him as you have done. I sat there for many years and there were good men among them. I beg of you to call them, Sire."

He sat down slowly and leant back, exhausted and wincing with pain.

"My answer," Charles said quietly, "is still no. The meeting is at an end, my Lords. You may withdraw. Lord Strafford, be good enough to come to my apartments, I want to speak to you privately."

He went back to his rooms and waited for Strafford. He felt cold and strangely calm; he had not lost his temper once in the last few weeks. He had been courteous and controlled and absolutely immovable in his refusal to give up the war or remove Strafford from his command. There was no alternative open to him except dishonour and retreat and he would not submit to either. He had not thought beyond it because he knew perfectly well that there was no solution.

"Thomas," he said gently, "Thomas, don't try and kneel. Sit down, my poor friend. We are quite alone."

Strafford lowered himself into a chair, and the King went to the door and closed it himself.

"Now," he said. "What is this madness you were saying in the Council?"

"It is not madness, Sire. It is the right advice. I meant what I said. You cannot go on alone, and I cannot give you the support you need. I am a sick man and I'm at the end of my strength. And of my uses," he added slowly. "I can do no more, Sire, except tell you how to save your throne."

"I couldn't believe what I heard in there and I cannot believe it now," Charles said. "You were the most insistent of all my advisers in abolishing Parliament; you've said over and over again that I must never call them. Now, when I am weaker than at any time in my reign, you change completely. I tell you I am not going to call them. What puzzles me is why you suggest that I should."

Strafford looked at him; his face was grey and his eyes were red and sunken in his face with pain.

"Because the Covenant armies will march on London if you don't, and there will be nothing left for you but abdication. They will put the Prince of Wales on the throne and imprison you. And you will not live a year after that happens."

"You are not frightening me, Thomas," Charles answered. "I know that is the alternative, and I see nothing to stop it. I would rather die than give way. I would not be the first of my race or possibly the last to meet a violent death. It has no terrors for me. I have also thought what would happen to you if I take your advice. Have you any doubt what Parliament's price would be for allowing me to keep my throne? Your life, Thomas. Your life and most likely Laud's as well. The murder of my friends and the destruction of my Church and everything that's good and wise I've tried to give my country. No, Thomas, I will not do it."

"And what will be done when you are no longer King?" Strafford countered. "How will your son protect us and protect the Church when he is only a child and the whole power of government lies with the Puritans? You talk of my life—it's ending anyway. As for Laud, no one would dare to kill him while you remain the King. And against that, have you thought what the Queen's fate would be?" He hesitated and saw Charles change colour. "What would your enemies do to her when you were gone? Would they spare her? Come, Sire, you know they would kill her for being a Papist; they'd call her a traitor and an idolatress and remove her children from her and put her to death. If you're ready to risk yourself, will you bring such a fate upon her?"

Charles faced him; he was terribly pale. That thought had been thrust upon him when it was the one fear he dared not entertain.

He was not afraid for himself; it would be easier for him to take a small company and ride out against the rebels and hope to be killed in battle than to imagine Henrietta falling into the hands of the people who had cursed and vilified her for over fifteen years, people who screamed for the blood of their fellow Englishmen and dragged them to a hideous death because they were Catholic priests.

"You should not say that," he said bitterly, and for a

moment he was almost angry. "It is unfair to put such a monstrous choice before me. I will not listen to you."

"As long as you are King, there is some safeguard for the people and the things you love," Strafford said quietly. "That is your strength, Sire, and it is greater than armies. You are the Lord's anointed and no government can exist without you. No law can be passed which anyone will obey. The Puritans cannot go beyond a certain limit and then only as far as you agree to let them. And you will have time as an ally; time to restore your power and weaken your enemies. What's done is done, there is nothing more to be got from fighting everyone alone. Parliament is not all Puritans; seek out the moderates and make them your friends. For myself, I have no fear of Parliament. I beg of you don't think of me. Think only of your duty as a King. And your duty to the Queen who loves you. She is in greater danger every moment you are out of London. Go back to her and summon Parliament."

Charles saw him leave his chair and slowly fall upon his knees.

"I beg you, with all my heart. Do it before it is too late."

The King walked away from Strafford and stood beside the fireplace, hiding his head against his arm. Every instinct warned him not to listen. Every sense told him to trust anyone, even the Scottish lords who had defied him and invaded, rather than open the door of Westminster and give back power into the hands of the Parliament. Yet calling them was the lesser of the two gigantic evils which faced him, the obvious decision in view of the threat to his wife and his own life. But he did not want to do it. For a moment he followed his instinct and turned round to refuse. As he did so, Strafford spoke.

"You must trust someone," he said. "In the end a King must trust his people. Give them another chance, and with God's grace they will not fail you."

It was a moment before Charles answered. When he did his voice was low and his words came in a wretched stammer.

"So be it. I will send word to London."

"Let me play for you, Madam. Lady Digby can sing. Sir John Suckling's verses have been set to music and they are so charming—I know it will cheer you."

The Countess of Newport looked anxiously towards the Queen who was sitting with her ladies in her Privy Chamber at Whitehall. Henrietta had tried to embroider while one of her women read aloud but after a few minutes she threw the sewing on the floor and told the reader to close her book. She looked tired and strained and she was so restless that she frequently got up and walked round the room, bringing all her ladies to their feet until she sat down again.

The poet John Suckling was a friend and a favourite of Henrietta's; she enjoyed his verses and she was passionately fond of music. The Countess was only trying to relieve her and turn her mind from her anxieties.

"Please, Madam," she repeated.

"If you like, Newport," the Queen said wearily. "Play for me and let Digby sing the words. If you can lighten my heart it will be a miracle." She sat back and closed her eyes as the clear notes of the instrument rang through the silent room, and Lady Digby's pleasant voice sang Suckling's poem to a famous beauty, Lady Catherine Howard.

> "Her feet beneath her petticoat,
> Like little mice stole in and out,
> As if they feared the light:
> But O, she dances such a way!
> No Sun upon an Easter-day
> Is half so fine a sight."

Henrietta was not listening; her thoughts were full of Charles, Charles coming back to her weary and defeated, resting his head upon her breast like a tired child. He had summoned his Parliament and there was such an atmosphere of tension and foreboding that she did not know whether to sympathize with him or lose her temper and upbraid him for the obstinacy which had ruined their peace and shattered their happiness. She had been typically feminine and done both, and then changed completely by telling him to keep his courage and wait, using Strafford's words. Wait till his enemies had weakened themselves and make as many friends among the powerful as he could.

She had received Strafford twice since his return to London, and found him strangely uncommunicative. He did not wish to discuss the war or the opening of the Commons; when she questioned him he evaded and excused himself. He was waiting for something and so was Charles, and neither of them would tell her what it was.

> "On the sudden up they rise and dance,
>   Then sit again and sigh, and glance:
>   Then dance again and kiss. . ."

The poem told of two lovers united in perfect happiness, dancing through their wedding feast. It brought unbearable memories of her life with Charles only two years before, a life when dancing and pleasure and serenity seemed to stretch before them. Suddenly her eyes filled with tears. When they came together now it was a furious escape; she could sense him burying himself in her passion, making his love a desperate act, returning unwillingly to the reality of life. The sweetness of their passion was becoming bitter with fear. Fear for her and for their children, fear for the future which had once seemed as certain as the sunrise.

"Stop! Stop the song, I've heard enough!" Lady Newport closed the instrument and got up, Lady Digby curtsied and moved away, and Henrietta found the eyes of Lucy Carlisle watching her intently.

"What is the matter, Madam? Don't you like it?"

"How can I like something which sings of peace and tenderness, when the King is so worried he cannot sleep and those wretches are sitting at Westminster, pouring out poison against him?" She turned on Lady Carlisle angrily. "Why are you wearing that plain dress?" she demanded suddenly. "Has colour and ornament gone out of fashion?"

Lucy flushed. Her dress was made of dark green silk, high collared and very simply cut; her only jewels were pearls and her face was pale. Henrietta and the other ladies glittered with gold and silver embroidery and reddened their cheeks and lips with salve.

"I thought it wiser, Madam," she answered. "It seems foolish to antagonize the people by calling attention to the rich clothes worn at Court. I did not mean to offend your Majesty."

"The people!" Henrietta snapped, her eyes bright with

145

rage. "The yelling mobs and the yapping curs at West-minster. . . Good God, how I hate them all. How I wish that this were France—we'd know how to deal with them when they dared to come round the Palace. . . If the King listened to me he'd order the guard to fire on them all."

"Why doesn't he, Madam?" the Countess asked gently. "Perhaps it would solve all our troubles. . ."

"Don't be such a fool," Lady Newport said quickly. "The King would never use force against his own. The King is the soul of justice and kindness."

"Too just and too kind," Henrietta said. "And what has he received in return? Treason! Treason from the nobles and double treason from the Commons! Not a penny of money, not a motion against the Scots—nothing but complaints and demands and open collaboration with the rebels. They have the Covenanters camped in England to protect them and they're going to harry the King to his knees if they can."

She looked round at the silent ladies, and then vented her irritation on her dearest friend, the friend who still heard her confidences but was somehow changed. Less gay and amusing, almost as if she held something of her feelings in reserve.

"Lucy, go and change that dress at once. Don't come before me again like that; you remind me of that wretched Puritan, Lady Essex."

The Countess curtsied low and backed out of the room. She went to her apartments and sent her personal servant to find Harry Vane, the son of the Royal Secretary. While she waited she hummed the tune of Suckling's poem under her breath. When Vane came through the door she sent the maid away.

"I've been waiting for a chance to speak to you since yester-day," she said. "Thank God her Majesty took offence with me this afternoon and sent me out. I persuaded your father to let me see his reports of the Council at York and I managed to copy something which might interest Mr. Pym. How long are you staying at Whitehall?"

"Only until tonight," Vane answered. They had met secretly many times in the past months. The Countess gave him the reports, explained the important parts in them and sent them direct to Pym. She had decided not to risk taking them herself.

"The King allows me to visit my father here from time to time. But he doesn't extend a long invitation," Vane added.

"Good," Lucy Carlisle found the sheet of paper in a small drawer at the back of her cabinet. "You can take this to Mr. Pym as soon as you leave. I was out of my wits keeping it here overnight. Look, I've marked what he should read first."

The paper was covered in her tidy writing; there were notes on days of debate and suddenly one sentence given in full and heavily underlined. Vane came close and read it over her shoulder.

"I have a loyal Irish Army which is only waiting to land here and subdue this Kingdom." He read it aloud in a whisper and she folded the notes and gave them to him. She was smiling.

"Lord Strafford's words," she said. "Like Judith, I give the head of Holofernes to Parliament with this single sentence. Those words alone will convict him of High Treason."

"Not if they referred to Scotland," Vane said. He was a sincere man who had ruined himself for his beliefs, and he did not like the malice of that smile. It disappeared and the Countess looked at him.

"Mr. Pym will judge which was the 'Kingdom' he meant to subdue with foreign troops. Leave at once and take care you're not seen."

With the help of her maid she took off her green gown and dressed in scarlet, the skirt and bodice sparkling with gold thread, the neck cut low over her breast. She returned to the Queen's Privy Chamber and went to Henrietta's chair and curtsied to the ground.

"Sweet Madam, do you like me better now?"

It was early in the morning of November 11th, and the House of Commons was full. There was not one vacant seat on the benches and many of the members who had arrived late were standing round the walls. The debate had been less noisy than usual; there was a sense of crisis which communicated itself to the few Royalists who had been elected; they could feel the excitement among the Puritans. There was a buzz of whispering and notes were passed between the leaders while the speeches were being made. Something was going to happen. The Speaker looked uneasy. Several times he had glanced towards the Puritan leader Pym, expecting him to enter the debate but Pym only sat with his arms folded, occasionally conferring with John Hampden who was on his right. Then at a little before noon, Pym took out his watch and at last he rose to speak. There was not a sound in the House. Everyone craned forward to watch as he stood up.

"My Lords and gentlemen, for the past eight days we have been discussing the sorry state to which our country has been brought by the mismanagement and illegality of those whom the King has entrusted with its government. We have heard of the abuses and misfortunes inflicted upon our people by a war against our Scottish brethren; we have seen our Treasury emptied, our freedom taken from us and our religion prostituted to the forms of Rome. Many of us have suffered imprisonment and confiscation, and we are but a shadow of the thousands who have cried out under tyranny for nigh on twelve years while the doors of this Chamber were locked and our voices were stilled. But now the voice of the nation cries out in protest; let those who hear it tremble!"

He paused and there were shouts of encouragement which brought the Speaker round in his Chair, calling for order. When there was silence again Pym's tone was quieter; too quiet for the comfort of the King's few supporters.

"The King's administration is on trial in this House today, and on trial before the whole of England. There was one in that administration more signal than the rest, being a man of great parts and contrivance, a man who in the memory of many present here had sat in this House as an earnest vindicator of the laws, a most zealous champion for the liberties of the people." Pym's voice rose suddenly.

"He is become the greatest enemy to his country and the greatest promoter of tyranny that any age has produced! I name the Earl of Strafford! And on these counts and others not yet set before you, I impeach him for High Treason!"

There was a tremendous shout of approval; the members sprang to their feet, cheering and stamping; the cry 'Impeachment' became a triumphant roar of hatred. Pym had promised them their victim and he had kept his word. The scattered Royalists sat in silence, too frightened to protest; one of them edged his way out of the crowd and reached the door. Pym turned and shouted after him.

"Go! Go and warn him—nothing can save him now. Tell him to come down to us before we send to Whitehall to take him. . ! "

"I second the motion, I second the motion," Sir John Clotworthy yelled at the Speaker.

He had once tried to purchase a large area of land in Derry, Northern Ireland, and Strafford, suspecting his loyalties, had advised Charles to refuse him. He was the Earl's mortal enemy for this and many other reasons; as a devout Puritan he rejoiced in the old law of an eye for an eye. For refusing him Derry, for fining and imprisoning and disregarding hundreds like him, Strafford was going to pay with his life. The motion was carried and the Impeachment was sent to the House of Lords. By the afternoon, Strafford's fellow peers, many of them friends of the King, some of them Puritans, most of them men who had hated and envied the great Minister for a dozen years, agreed with the Commons.

The Earl was to be arrested and tried for his life.

There was a large crowd in the King's ante-room and it bore a sinister resemblance to the mob which had gathered in the streets outside Whitehall and were packed round the Houses of Parliament at Westminster. The courtiers were not yelling and hooting like the common people, but they too wanted to see the mighty Earl of Strafford leave the shelter of the King's apartments and go out to meet his enemies. He had no friends among the lords and ladies and members of the Royal household. He had never tried to make any; his only loyalty had been towards the King. He had been shut up alone with Charles since the early afternoon, when the news of the Commons impeachment first reached him. Not long afterwards the Queen was seen hurrying down to them, with eyes red with weeping, and she disappeared behind the doors. The member who had been present in the Commons and brought the news to Strafford was telling his story over and over again and insisting that not even the King could protect him unless he was ready to lose his throne. There was a lot of talk and some laughter, and the sound reached Charles and Henrietta as they stood with Strafford in the inner room.

Charles was terribly pale; he had put his arm round the Earl's shoulders, and when he heard the murmurs and the laughter his eyes blazed with anger.

"How dare they! Don't they know what has happened—I'll have the ante-rooms cleared!"

"Please, Sire," Strafford begged him wearily, "ignore it. Human nature has no pity for the fallen. They know and that's why they are laughing. You cannot stop them. If you clear the rooms it will be said that I'm afraid to face them. And I'm not, believe me. I despised them from the first and I despise them now. They shall have their sight of me, and all they'll gain from it is my contempt for all of them."

"You cannot go," the King insisted. He had been arguing with the Earl for nearly two hours, forbidding him to accept Pym's challenge and surrender to arrest. "You cannot and you will not. I forbid it! You will stay at Whitehall and I shall dissolve the Parliament."

"You cannot, Charles," Henrietta said desperately. She had listened to Strafford explaining why there was no alternative, and as she listened she understood only too well that there was nothing Charles or anyone could do. Their enemies wanted a sacrifice, and if the victim hid behind the King, the King would be torn from his throne in order to get at him.

"I told you this would happen," Charles said. "I told you at York what their price would be if I summoned them!"

"I know you did, Sire," Strafford answered. "And I beg you to remember what I said would happen if you didn't."

"What is this?" Henrietta demanded. "What did you tell the King? He never said anything to me."

"He couldn't Madam, without frightening you unnecessarily. If the Parliament don't have me, they will attack the King himself. And you and your children. The King knows that. He knew it when he came to London and so did I. I must go to them; there is no choice."

He was exhausted, too tired and too ill to compete with the man he loved who was overcome by his emotions and was ready to face anything to save him. It could not be done and Strafford knew it. He had been waiting for this day since they left York, and all he wanted was to master his weakness and face his accusers with dignity. He could not bear to see Charles in his distress and he was grateful to Henrietta when she came to the King and said quietly—

"Thomas is right. He must stand his trial. He is innocent and they cannot possibly convict him."

"They will attack the King. And you and your children." She looked round at Strafford and he read the regret and the compassion in her face. But Strafford had put the choice before the King and she knew it was the right one. She turned to the Earl and gave him her hand.

"God will defend you, and the King will protect you. You need have no fear." He knelt and kissed her hand and she held his own for a moment and pressed it. "Say good-bye to the King," she said gently. "Now, Thomas."

"No," Charles made a movement to stop him, but Strafford had saluted him quickly and then stood up.

"God save Your Majesty," he said hoarsely, and turned away to hide the tears which were running down his sunken cheeks. He wiped them away with his hand, and when he paused at the door and looked back at them, both small and slight and standing close together, his face was composed and his expression strangely calm.

"My heart goes with you," Charles said, and he was weeping openly.

"Sire, you have always had mine."

The Earl made a deep bow to them both and then opened the door and went out. He could not distinguish any faces among the crowd outside; as he passed among them they moved back instinctively from long habit, and watched him go by in silence. No one spoke to him or came forward and he had reached the outer chamber when a short, stout figure rushed through the crowd towards him and he stopped, recognizing Archbishop Laud. The little priest's face was red and wrinkled, like a child that is about to cry. He came up to Strafford and threw his arms round him and for a moment they stood together, the taller man stooping towards the priest, and then at last Laud spoke.

"Thank God, thank God, I thought I was too late. . . I only heard an hour ago!"

"I am so glad to see you," Strafford said. "So very glad, my old friend. I thought we might never meet again."

"What can I say, Thomas?" Laud shook his head miserably. "How can I ask your forgiveness for all this? You left the King in my hands and I have ruined him and ruined you!"

"You did what you thought was right," Strafford said gently. "There is nothing to forgive. We both tried to serve him as well as we could."

"If I had only left well enough alone," Laud protested, "if I had never listened to you speaking in that Parliament twelve years ago and not gone meddling and recommending you to the King, you would have been living safe and well in Yorkshire now! But I did hear you and I said to myself, there's a man after mine own heart—he mustn't be wasted!"

"And so you told me, in the inner ante-chamber when I came out after seeing the King. How well I remember you then. You advanced me high, and I loved every moment of it. It's a good ending, my Lord Archbishop, that we meet here for our farewell. I'm going to the Lords to answer them."

"I'm coming with you," Laud insisted.

"Only to the Palace gates. There's a mob outside and you wouldn't be safe. But I'll be glad of one friend to go that far with me."

"I may stop at the gates today, Thomas," Laud said quietly. "But I'll follow you out of them soon. God will be with you from now onwards. When my time comes, I only pray He'll be with me. Come then, let us go."

They walked slowly down the long corridors and through the tall rooms of Whitehall, and the Earl entered his coach and drove out of the Palace. That evening, under authority from the ancient Constitution, the Gentleman Usher of the Black Rod arrested him at the doors of the House of Lords and escorted him to the Tower of London.

The trial was held in Westminster Hall. The public seats were crowded and often in the long days that followed, the spectators tired of the spectacle of the sick man who was fighting so courageously for his life and turned to stare at the grill covering a small window, behind which they knew the King and Queen were witnessing Strafford's ordeal. They came every day, two shadows behind the screen erected to preserve their privacy, and Charles refused to spare himself a moment of the agony and humiliation which was being inflicted on his Minister. He had gone in the hope that his presence might intimidate the judges; it only served to emphasize his helplessness to protect his servant and to increase that servant's pain. In denying the charges of brutality and tyranny which were poured out against him by witnesses from London and Yorkshire and Ireland, Strafford was desperately defending the King. And it was a hopeless defence. No one sitting in Westminster Hall was interested in his denials or his explanations or in the fact that those who testified against him were all personal enemies and friends of the Puritans. He was lost and he knew it, and so did Charles, listening to the vituperation and falsehood which was given against him under oath. He was there when the fatal remark about the Irish army landing to subdue Scotland was brought out with a triumphant flourish, and he started out of his chair when he heard the prosecutors say that the Kingdom referred to was the Kingdom of England.

"They're lying!" he turned to Henrietta, and she held on to his arm to keep him back. "They're lying and they know it. Strafford never meant that!"

"Of course they're lying," she whispered bitterly. "They've done nothing but lie from the beginning. Sit down, I beg of you, you will be seen if you open that screen."

"I'm going to open it," he said furiously. "I'm going to open it and denounce this evidence myself. I'll dismiss the Court if they continue with it!"

She held on to him desperately, knowing him capable of putting what was left of his power to an impossible test. He could not stop them. He could not call his own Secretary's evidence a lie without placing his personal integrity on trial. If he ordered the Court to adjourn, the Court would disregard him. He had no constitutional right to interfere, and he had no force to take the place of that right.

"If you make such a public gesture you will ruin any chance Thomas might have of being fairly judged," she insisted. "I implore you not to do it . . . you will only harm him. Please, please sit down."

He turned towards her, his face distraught with grief and

anger and for a moment he hesitated, one hand on the latch of the grill.

In the room below them he heard Strafford's voice rising, clear and firm, denying that his Irish troops were meant to do anything but fight the Scottish Covenanters.

"Listen," she said, "listen to him, Charles. If you interrupt now, no one will believe him. . ."

"No one would believe me, you mean," he said. "I am their anointed King and I am forced to sit there while they perjure my friend and faithful servant into his grave. It is not to be borne, Henrietta. I would rather die than submit to kingship at this price."

"You need not submit to it much longer," Henrietta spoke quietly. "We both know that this situation is impossible. There is only one way to save Thomas and save yourself, and I've been busy planning it while they were all occupied with this trial. Now the time has come to tell you. I've been in touch with some officers of the Army. There are half a dozen of them ready to gather their troops and occupy London and take over the Tower!"

Charles stared at her, horrified and incredulous. Henrietta smiled up at him; her eyes were bright and confident. She had kept her secret very carefully, confiding in no one except the men involved, even excluding Lucy Carlisle from the negotiations of the most deadly nature which she had conducted alone with the young Royalist officers at the Court.

"In the name of God, what have you done?" he asked her.

"I have secured George Goring, commander of the garrison at Portsmouth, Harry Percy, Northumberland's brother, Asburnham, O'Neil, and a score of lesser men. Goring is ready to garrison London and my Master of the Horse, Harry Jermyn, will lead a force to seize the Tower. Now, Charles, do you see why I would not let you open that screen and spoil everything?"

To her surprise he did not speak for a moment. He leant forward apparently listening to the proceedings in the room below; his face very pale and set. Henrietta touched his arm impatiently.

"Have you nothing to say?" she demanded. "Don't you appreciate what I have done for you?"

"I appreciate the thought, but not the method," he answered slowly. "You are my wife and the dearest person to me in the world, but I will not permit you to enter into intrigues which could result in Civil War, without consulting me. We will leave here and when we return to Whitehall I shall send for all these people and speak to them myself. Come, my dear."

He was angrier with Henrietta than he had been for many years; angry and deeply resentful because at a time when his pride and his authority was at such a pitiful level, she had taken the initiative without consulting him. And she had stopped him from making his gesture in defence of Strafford because it would have interfered with her own.

He went straight to his apartments and sent for George Goring and Harry Jermyn. George Goring was the eldest son of his old friend and Councillor, but Charles had never liked or trusted him. He was a handsome young man with a pleasing manner and a quick wit, but his morals were notorious; he drank and whored and gambled and had only showed himself to advantage when he was fighting in the Netherlands. Charles had always thought him self-seeking and deceitful and ambitious. He preferred the Queen's Horse Master, Jermyn. Jermyn had been a favourite of theirs for some years; he was a jovial, generous man and the King trusted him implicitly.

With Henrietta flushed and angry beside him, Charles received the two men and came to the point at once.

"The Queen has just told me of her dealings with you," he said coldly. "I am surprised and displeased that you should have involved her in any enterprise of this nature without consulting me. Now, be good enough to explain yourselves."

Goring came forward and bowed. His handsome face was turning slowly red, and there was a gleam of temper in his eyes which was quickly hidden when he addressed the King.

"Your pardon, Sire. The Queen herself insisted upon secrecy; she impressed it upon us and required us to take oaths. We obeyed her in belief that by doing so were we best serving you."

"You will best serve me by answering my question," Charles said coldly. "What is this talk of bringing your troops to London?"

"The garrison at Portsmouth is loyal to your Majesty," Goring answered. "They are my own men, raised and trained and equipped by me. I can vouch for all of them. My plan is to bring them to London, surround the House of Commons, arrest the members and take possession of the Arsenal and the Mint. Jermyn can take the Tower with the help of your Bodyguards. Daniel O'Neil is one of us; as the nephew of the Red O'Neil, he can rouse the whole of the Catholic Irish to your cause. That is the plan, Sire. It seemed a sensible one to us."

"It seems madness to me," Charles said shortly. "Madness and treason. Jermyn, what have you to say?"

Harry Jermyn looked towards Henrietta and received a nod of encouragement.

"I agree with Goring, Sire. You must preserve your authority by force of arms. There is no other way. There's certainly no other way to save the Earl of Strafford."

"Listen to them, Charles."

Henrietta interrupted for the first time. It was obvious to her and to men like Goring and Jermyn, that nothing was going to save Charles except the extermination of his enemies by a military coup. She sacrificed her pride, and clasping her hands, she sank down on her knees in front of them all.

"I beg of you, don't dismiss this plan of ours. Think of poor Thomas being harried to his grave—that is what you said yourself today. Think of the insults, the indignities which have been heaped upon you by these people who have dared to stand there and defy your wishes and criticize your actions! Think, Charles, and for the love of God, give Goring and Jermyn your blessing!"

George Goring had moved back a few steps; he watched the scene with a feeling of irritation which was changing to uneasiness. He saw the Queen on her knees, imploring the cold and stubborn King to act like a man, and he watched while the King's anger faded and he lifted his wife to her feet and whispered gently to her, and then kissed her tenderly on the cheek. Goring had no patience with sentiment; he had some admiration for the spirited woman who had approached him so boldly, promising all the rewards of power and wealth which his ambitious soul desired. He had almost forgotten that Charles, chilly, obstinate and hesitant, was King, and not Henrietta.

He glanced across at Jermyn, and grimaced.

"Gentlemen," Charles said at last. "I rebuked you for taking action without my consent. Now I should like to thank you for the courage and the loyalty you have shown. I must tell you honestly that the use of force against my subjects does not recommend itself to me in any circumstances, even the most extreme. What I will say to you is this: if Lord Strafford is convicted, I will think of you again. I may have need of your men and yourselves, and for the moment I should like to study this plan in more detail and possibly suggest some changes. Your oath of secrecy must be kept from everyone at Court as perfectly as you kept it from me. You may retire now."

They bowed low and backed out of the room, and Jermyn nudged Goring.

"What do you think? Will he agree? I swear the Queen will persuade him before the week is over. . ."

"Maybe," Goring shrugged. "She has the more spirit of the two. There's nothing we can do but wait and see."

He saluted Jermyn and walked away. He was frowning. Wait and see while the King vacillated, advised one way by his wife, another by that old idiot Laud, who was in hourly fear of impeachment himself, and yet again by someone else. And while they waited, the risk of discovery increased. Oaths of secrecy were only binding for a time. Inaction loosened tongues; doubt and confusion encouraged people to hint and eventually to confide. Goring looked up as the first spots of rain began to fall, and pulled his cloak round him and began to walk quickly back to the Palace. He was not going to wait till someone told Parliament, and find himself accused and arrested for the sake of a man who had not the courage to make up his mind. He went up to his rooms and sent a note to the Earl of Newport, the estranged husband of Henrietta's faithful lady-in-waiting, who had never forgiven her or the King for his wife's conversion to Rome, and was now one of Pym's most powerful supporters.

They met at Newport's house in the Strand that evening, and Goring betrayed the conspiracy to him.

A shuttered coach bumped and rattled down the cobbled road from Tower Hill and passed under the main gate of the Tower. Its escort of soldiers dismounted and the doors were unlocked; no one gave a hand to the old man who hesitated on the step; he climbed down uncertainly and nearly stumbled. Lord Newport, Governor of the Tower, came out of the Governor's house on the Inner Green and saluted him.

"My Lord Archbishop, your lodgings are ready. Be good enough to follow me."

He stared at his prisoner keenly, and there was no sympathy in his eyes. Laud hesitated and looked round him, blinking in the weak sunlight. The tall stone walls of the fortress rose like cliffs on either side of him. His round face had sunken, the ruddy skin was grey and his hands moved uncertainly as if seeking for support. He had been arrested by order of Parliament and conveyed to the Tower in the darkened coach, its windows shuttered, and he had sat in the dark listening to the ferocious yells and curses of the crowds gathered to watch him pass, the English crowds to whom he had tried to teach beauty and uniformity in worship and who would have stopped the coach and torn him to pieces if they had been allowed to see his face. He had aged in the time it took to bring him from Westminster to the Tower of London, but he was already old and beaten on the day Strafford went to the place to which he had come at last himself.

He looked into the stony face of Newport.

"Where are my lodgings?" he asked. "Are they close to my Lord Strafford?"

"As close as you're likely to be," Newport snapped at him. "I have prepared a room for you in the Beauchamp Tower. Have no fear, my Lord, it's not as dark and noisome as the cells in Newgate and the Marshalsea where you sent so many honest Churchmen!"

"They are revenged," Laud said quietly. "And they are all alive to enjoy it. They left Newgate and the Marshalsea, and if I cropped a few ears it was no more than they deserved. But no man leaves this place until they've cropped his head. Lead the way, my Lord Newport, lead the way to my resting-place. I welcome it as a refuge after that journey, believe me."

"You were lucky to survive it," Newport said angrily.

"I know," Laud answered. "I heard those gentle Christians screaming for my blood and I thank God for the silence of the Tower."

Newport turned away and Laud walked slowly after him, surrounded by soldiers on either side. He held a prayer-book in his hands pressed close against his breast, and as he walked he prayed, his grey head bent and his eyes half closed, until he passed under the narrow entrance to the Beauchamp Tower. To the annoyance of Newport and some of his escort who were Puritans, the Archbishop looked round the dismal room, lighted by one wretched window high up in the wall, furnished with a mean trestle bed, a table and a stool, and nodded as if he were pleasantly surprised. He turned to Newport whom he had known well in the old days when they had both been close to the King. There was a gentle expression on his tired face and a flickering of his old boisterous humour.

"I see no rats and fetid walls—not even an instrument of torture. You have indeed been generous, my Lord, and I am grateful. I already feel at home. If you will leave me now, I'd like to be alone and pray."

"Make particular mention of Lord Strafford," Newport said sarcastically. "Perhaps a miracle might save him yet."

Laud said clearly "His Majesty the King will save him. And all my prayers are for the King, my Lord. Strafford and I are safe in here, while he stands unprotected from such men as you."

Newport did not answer. He snapped an order to the guards and left the room. The door was closed and Laud heard the key turning and the bolts grinding into their sockets. After a moment he sat on the edge of the hard bed, and, holding his prayer-book to catch the light, he began to read.

On May 8th, Thomas Wentworth Earl of Strafford was condemned to death for Treason. The Bill of Attainder was passed in the House of Lords by thirty-seven votes to eleven, and as the count was taken a mob of yelling Londoners was beating on the doors, demanding the sentence of death. In this atmosphere of terror and coercion, it was a miracle to the distracted King that eleven nobles had been brave enough to make their protest at the sentence.

There was a reason for the mobs, a reason for the outburst of popular fury against the fallen Minister who had done so much to discredit Pym and the Commons during his trial. By sheer courage and integrity the accused had come close to being the accuser, and at the moment when the outcome was in doubt, Pym announced the existence of the Army Plot and called for an enquiry. He was never called upon to prove it, because the principals, Goring excepted, fled for their lives, leaving Charles in the frantic position of not knowing how the intrigue had been discovered or how much was known of Henrietta's part in it. Immediately, public opinion veered violently against the King and the Court and the man that the treacherous army was planning to release. There was no hope for Strafford, and on May 9th, as Charles and his Queen sat at dinner in Whitehall, the London crowds stormed the outer reaches of the Palace and clamoured round the Gatehouse leading to the royal apartments. He had stood in the room, his arms round Henrietta and his eldest son, comforting her and her trembling ladies, telling them not to be afraid, until the shouts grew less and Lord Clare reported from the window that the crowds were being driven back by his personal guards.

That same evening, he was presented with the warrant for Strafford's execution, and received a deputation of his Bishops, all trembling for their own lives and for his, begging him to sign it.

He had been sitting in his room alone for nearly two hours when Henrietta came to him.

It was quite dark, and the candles on his writing table had burnt low. The warrant was in front of him, and beside it a long letter. As she came to his side, Henrietta recognized the familiar, ugly writing.

"Why are you reading that?" she whispered. "Why do you torment yourself?"

He looked up at her; his face was pale and lined with weariness. "Thomas has my letter, giving my word of honour as a King that I will never let him suffer. And I have his, absolving me from that promise. What is my torment besides his, at this moment?"

She went on her knees and put her arms around him.

"Thomas is lost," she said. "If you do not sign that warrant Newport will execute him on his own authority—he has said so. There's nothing you can do to save him. All you can hope is to save yourself and me and all our children."

"That was the choice he put to me at York," Charles answered. "He delivered himself to his enemies for our sake and I let him go with the promise that he had nothing to fear. He believed me."

"He has exonerated you," she said, and she took the letter up, and after a moment she read a part of it aloud. "Listen, my love, for this is Thomas speaking, Thomas who loves you and knows you have done all that any man can do. *'Here are before me the many ills which may befall Your Sacred Person and the whole kingdom should yourself and Parliament part less satisfied with the one than the other. . . To set Your Majesties' conscience at liberty I beseech you to pass this Bill, and as by God's Grace I forgive all the world with calmness and meekness, so, Sir, to you I can give the life of this world with all the cheerfulness imaginable. . . To a willing man there is no injury done.'* He is willing to die, Charles, for your sake. He understands what you must do. How can you refuse his offer when all you can achieve by it is the loss of his life and probably your own?"

Charles put his hands over his face and she knew that he was weeping.

"If he dies because of my weakness, I do not want to live," he said. "If it were not for you I would have had that rabble fired upon and been glad to take the consequences."

"And surrender your rights and the rights of our son?" she demanded. The warrant was in front of him; the life of one man was the alternative to revolution.

"Sign it," she repeated. "For the love of God sign it now and have done! What are you waiting for— another demonstration like today to make you see you have no choice? What is the life of any man compared to losing your throne? Strafford has got to die now and nothing you can do can stop it. Here." She leant across and dipped the pen in the inkpot and put it into his hand. He raised his head and for a moment they looked into each other's eyes, with all the years of love and trust between them, and at that moment when he was torn by self-doubt and agony for his friend, Henrietta's will was stronger. She saw it and she made it easier.

"For my sake, Charles, I beg of you."

He signed, and as he did so Henrietta rang the little silver bell for his Gentleman in attendance. A moment later Lord Clare came in from the ante-room.

"Are the Bishops still in the Palace?" she asked. Clare

glanced at the King and saw him slowly sanding the ink on his signature. Without even seeing his face he knew what had been done.

"Yes, Madam. They were afraid to leave Whitehall, the streets are still full of people."

"Send for them. His Majesty has signed the warrant." She went back to Charles and bending down she kissed him. His cheek was cold and wet with tears.

"Come, my darling," she said, and she was as tender as if she were speaking to a child. "We will see them together and then you must rest. You haven't slept for days."

Early on the 12th of May, Thomas Wentworth, stripped of his titles and estates, left his prison in the Tower for the last time to walk in procession with the Constable, his own few friends and servants and the chaplains sent to comfort him, to die on Tower Hill in the presence of two hundred thousand hostile people. He limped painfully as he walked, a stooping grey-headed man in his last sickness, dressed in sombre black, but fortified with dignity and a peace which abashed the vindictive peers and officials who had come to see him die. At the base of the Beauchamp Tower he paused. He had not been allowed to see Laud who had gone arm in arm with him through the gardens at Whitehall and Lambeth so many times in the past, and walked with him on the final parting which ended in the Tower. Laud's prophecy had been fulfilled; he knew that Laud would take the same path for the same end, and his heart yearned for a last sign of him and a last word. The King had abandoned him and in a moment of human frailty he had cried out aloud, "Put not your trust in Princes. . ." But Laud had not failed him. They had been friends in the deepest sense of companionship and humour and genuine love, and it was Laud he looked for on that last morning of his life. In the window above him he saw the familiar figure. Before anyone could stop him, Wentworth knelt.

"Your prayers and your blessing," he called out, and the Archbishop, too far away to answer him, raised his hand and made a trembling Sign of the Cross. As he finished he fell back unconscious. Again Wentworth's voice rose strongly, unaware that Laud could not hear him.

"Farewell my Lord. God protect your innocence." He stood up and addressed the soldiers who were waiting by his side. "Proceed," he said. "My business is done on this earth." When Laud recovered consciousness his friend had been beheaded to a roar of cheering that was heard as far away as Whitehall.

Chapter 9

STRAFFORD had been dead for three months and as if the shedding of his blood had exhausted their violence and suspicion, the people of England were strangely quiet.

The crowds who had rushed the gates of the King's Palace dissipated like leaves before a squall of wind; the armies of the Covenant who had given the support of the sword to Pym and his Parliament, were persuaded to return across the border with a handsome indemnity. Parliament sat at Westminster voting away the King's powers with a succession of Bills which he made no attempt to veto. They had no fear of dissolution. Pym had presented one which deprived him of the right to dismiss them without their consent and Charles signed it without protest within days of the warrant for Strafford's death. It was a strange situation in which the King, so long the obstinate champion of his rights, and to some the trespasser on his country's ancient liberties, submitted patiently to every limitation his Parliament imposed upon him.

He was courteous to his enemies, moderate in his council to his friends, and apparently without rancour for what he had been forced to do. And a sense of shame crept over his people and with it a feeling of uneasiness. Parliament ordered arrests and conducted prosecutions and suddenly the ancient order seemed preferable with all its abuses to the innovation of a supreme power in the hands of the Commons and its leader Pym. In August, Charles left for a visit to Scotland. His intention was to restore peace and confidence in his changed policy and to unite his Scottish subjects under the Crown, bringing as he said, both countries to a firm co-operation. Parliament could not stop him; they sent commissioners to report on his proceedings because they trusted neither Charles nor the Scots. To reassure them he left the Queen and his children behind at Oatlands, and he also left a disturbing impression that he had been wiser and fairer in his rule of England than the men who had crippled his power.

In that hot summer of 1641, Oliver Cromwell was a frequent visitor at Pym's house, and he had found a friend among the landed gentry. Sir Thomas Fairfax was a very rich man, he was cultured and shy. He was a Yorkshireman, like Strafford whom he had hated with relentless bitterness and his father was a wealthy and influential peer. Fairfax was as handsome as Cromwell was uncouth and ugly, but the two men possessed the same fierce religious feeling, and a burning sense of mission. Neither liked Pym, neither liked his position of unrivalled power or trusted his dealings with the nobility. And if Pym considered the King beaten, Cromwell and Fairfax did not.

They paced up and down Pym's narrow garden on that hot afternoon and after a moment Fairfax said suddenly:

"How quiet it is, sir. Not a sound in the streets, not a voice raised. Three months ago we lived in tumult. Now the whole nation might be sleeping."

"It's an unnatural quiet," Cromwell said. "I don't like it, it's the lull before the storm and the storm is not of our making. The centre of it is in Scotland, wooing the Scots away from us. And his quietness is the worst of all."

"He hasn't changed," Fairfax said, "I hear everyone round me praising his forbearance, taking his promises as if he meant to keep them. He's submissive because he's plotting. I'd wager my life on that"

"That's what we're all wagering," Cromwell looked up at the bright sky and frowned. "No man gives up his power with a good grace. And ours is a King whose love of it brought the whole country to the edge of ruin. Why does he go to Scotland, Sir Thomas, answer me that? It is for love of them? Why, God's life, they were the first to defy him with armed force! He's set out against them twice with an army and now he goes full of fair words of friendship, calling himself King of Scotland and taking his worst enemies into his Scottish Council, flattering and ennobling right and left. He's trying to win them over so that when he returns he can strike against us! I've said this again and again to Pym but he won't listen. He thinks the King is defeated and he's bent on humiliating and breaking him still further."

"Pym goes too fast," Fairfax said slowly. "Even some of my friends are changing. Three months ago they were set against the King, ready to kill Strafford with their own hands if he refused consent, but now they're murmuring and its not a murmuring I like to hear. All the blame is laid on Strafford. See, they say, now that the tyrant is dead, how sweetly reasonable the King's become! And what are these powers the Commons take to themselves without any right or precedent when they first proclaimed themselves the guardians of the ancient law? I cannot talk to Pym. I try but he smiled and shrugs and turns my arguments against me."

"Lawyers' tricks," Cromwell said angrily. "His tongue is smooth enough but his sense is another matter. He's only a common man, Sir Thomas, dealing with common men, and in the end the commonalty prefer to bend their knees to Kings! If he doesn't turn away from taxes and legislation and look to the true point, we'll be helpless when the time of testing comes. And it is coming, Sir, it's coming as surely as the night will follow this day! "

"I believe that," Fairfax said. "But what is the true point? In all this welter of debate and law making, which is it? "

Cromwell stopped and faced him, his small eyes were smaller still under their heavy lids and there was a piercing light in them.

"The army—the army is the ultimate of all power, greater than tradition, greater than law! And the right to command the army and the right to levy troops is still the King's right. It is the only one left to him, but by Heaven it's the only one that will count in the end! And that's what Pym will not see! Times have changed; the nobles who followed him unwillingly to Scotland see that not only his authority but theirs is being taken by Parliament. I tell you, Sir Thomas, if the King made a call to arms, he'd find a strong and willing support among the nobles *and* the gentry. They wanted to be rid of Strafford and limit the King's power, and now they find they cannot halt what they began."

Fairfax put his hand upon his shoulder and the two men stood still.

"Do you think it should be halted? "

Cromwell looked at him and again the fanaticism blazed in his pale eyes.

"No, I do not. I think it should go further even than Pym dreams. I think the chance has come to sweep away all the privilege and abuse which has bedevilled our country for centuries. At last we are in a position to keep faith with our ancestors and bring the Reformation to reality. We can abolish the Bishops and destroy the last vestige of Romanism. We can give every man the right to worship according to his conscience and the right to live under just laws, free from the caprices of a King. Parliament can be the saviour of England and England can save the Protestant world if we accept our destiny with courage. And Pym is no longer the man to do that. God knows who is," he added slowly.

"God knows and he will direct him," Fairfax said quietly. "Let us go in now, Oliver."

Charles was in Scotland, making friends with his old enemies, and Henrietta was at Oatlands secretly negotiating with every peer and landowner who could supply the King with troops and money. Both of them were tireless, both of them sacrificed their pride and exerted their charm, so different and yet so appealing, in the cause of winning allies and infusing loyalty into those who had wavered and even those who had actually betrayed them in the past. In Scotland, Charles tried to make amends to his tough, independent nobles by giving them positions in his Government, promising them the religious reforms they wanted and attaching them to himself personally.

Henrietta's letters assured him that at home their friends were growing in numbers and importance. The nobility resented Pym and the Parliament, and the moderates in both Houses longed for a return to stable government, headed by a wise and tolerant King. All was going well at Oatlands and all was going well in Edinburgh, and then suddenly, with the speed and fury of a volcanic eruption, rebellion blazed out in Ireland.

It was a rebellion for the King. It was the rebellion of the Irish Catholics, nobles and peasants alike who saw their rights threatened by the power of the Puritans across the Channel. All Strafford's work had been undone, all his attempts at justice for the native population and tolerance for their religion were reversed by his triumphant enemies and to the minds of the Irish worse was to come. The nation rose in arms, with the King and the Church as their battle cry, and soon the refugees were streaming into England, telling tales of horror and atrocity, lucky to escape the vengeance of the rebels who were burning and killing in a terrible retribution for the wrongs inflicted on them over the last hundred years. From that moment the issue Cromwell raised in the Commons became the only one that mattered. Parliament and not the King must raise the army to crush the Irish revolt.

Henrietta met Charles at Theobalds, the magnificent Elizabethan country mansion built by the old Queen's great Minister Burleigh and, forgetting all protocol, they ran into each other's arms, surrounded by their children.

Tenderly he kissed her cheeks and lips, and stroked her hair, and held her away from him to see how she looked. Still pretty, still as sparkling and vivacious as ever, but there were fine lines under her eyes and grey lights in her hair.

" My love," Charles whispered, " my own darling love, thank God to see you."

" And you," she said, clinging to him. For some moments they stayed in each other's arms, ignoring the young Prince of Wales and his brothers and sisters who stood shyly in the background, waiting to greet their father. They loved their children, but that love came far behind the intense passion they felt for each other. At last Charles broke away from her and kissed his eldest son. Their eldest daughter Mary was already married to the Protestant Prince of Orange. It was a poor match for such an illustrious Princess, but her parents had more need of the Dutch Prince's money than time to search for a suitable bridegroom. The bride was only ten and her husband twelve, and Henrietta had delayed sending her to join him for a very pressing reason. When the King went to war, and they both knew that now there was no alternative, she needed an excuse to leave the country and raise money and support for him abroad. So Mary came forward and curtsied and kissed her father's hand, and then he hurried his wife away to their apartments and the children returned to their own quarters.

" What has been happening? " Henrietta asked him, " Tell me, tell me everything! "

" I wrote as much as I dared," Charles said. She was sitting on his knee with her arms round his neck, and he interrupted her questions to kiss her repeatedly.

" I've won over the Scots," he announced. " Rothes, Montrose, even Argyle. I've made Argyle's kinsman, Loudon, my Chancellor, and Argyle himself a Marquess. I've even given General Leslie the Earldom of Leven!"

"Leslie, who led the Covenanters against you?" she exclaimed. "Charles, how could you!"

"Easily. I went to make friends, my love, and I succeeded. I cannot hope to fight here with the Scots at my back unless they can be trusted. And now I feel certain of them. I've drawn my worst enemies into my government and made them my friends. We've nothing to fear from Scotland. . . What news from you?"

"Good news," she said happily. "I've talked to so many people I can hardly remember them all. I saw them all at Oatlands and I can promise you money and men from Lord Herbert, Bristol and of course his son Digby, George Goring, Newcastle and Falkland and Sir Ralph Hopton, to name only a few! Half the Lords are ready to side with you and abandon Parliament, and I hear news from some of my people in Ireland that the Irish rebels are only waiting to march into England if you will give the word."

"You've performed miracles," he said gently. "Those names alone mean millions of pounds and thousands of men. God bless you, sweetheart." He hesitated, hating to rebuke her when she had accomplished so much. "But what do you mean by some of my people in Ireland? How have you communicated with the rebels?"

"Oh, by word of mouth and by letter—other people's letters," she added quickly. "I hear news through the priests here at the embassies. The rebellion is for you, my darling. For once in their history these people have given an example of loyalty to the world."

"An example of treason," Charles said slowly. "Treason and horror, without my consent and using my name. I forbid you to involve yourself by word or letter with anything or anyone connected with it. The revolt must be put down. If I need Irish troops I'll send for them in my own time."

"That's what you said to Jermyn and Goring," Henrietta retorted. "And you never did use them because Pym found the plot out somehow and the whole thing miscarried. Why will you never act without troubling about all these scruples and niceties like what is treason, when a whole race is fighting your enemies and offering to support you, and these Puritan wretches are levelling your power with every day that passes. Now they want command of the army and the Militia! Will you give them that, before you fight?"

She got down from his knee and faced him angrily.

"I will never give them that," he said quietly, and reaching out he took her hand and brought her close to him. "Don't flay me, sweetheart, I couldn't bear to quarrel with you. Come here and sit with me again."

"I'm not flaying you," Henrietta said. "I love you more than anything in the world, but there are times when you frighten me more than the people who are fighting against us. You are a good man, my love," she touched his face and looked into it sadly. "A good man and a kind one, always trying to do what is right and hoping that by doing so you'll turn away the wrath and wickedness of men who could never be like you. In my heart I know you're nearer to God than I shall ever be."

"A King should be in His Image," Charles said. "I cannot compromise with what is right and still claim to be a King in the true sense. I have only done that once, and I shall never know peace of mind again."

"Thomas had to die," she whispered. She had heard him say again and again that he had perjured his soul by condemning Strafford. He had turned to her and to many witnesses on the morning of the execution and said simply, 'I owe a life,' and then walked out of his room and spent the rest of the day on his knees in the Chapel at Whitehall.

"You must not blame yourself, blame me if you like. It was I who persuaded you."

"I shall always blame myself," Charles answered. "Thomas was not your responsibility. Yours was my safety and the safety of our children. You were right in your way, my darling, but I was eternally wrong in mine. I compromised once and all I know is that I will never compromise again with anything I know is wrong. The Irish rebellion is wrong, and I will not make use of it."

"What will you do then?" Henrietta asked him.

"I shall refuse to surrender my power over the army. If Parliament persists I shall send you to Holland with our daughter and raise my standard for war."

The following day he made a state entry into London, and the fickle London crowds pressed round his horse and cheered him loudly. And now there were two rival mobs, prowling the London streets. Charles was not alone as he had been a few short months ago. When the King had found friends among the young gentry and nobility, and army officers began returning from the Continent, hoping for action in England; and they filled Whitehall, talking and boasting and wandering out in search of Puritans distinguished by their sober clothes and close cropped hair. And some wit among the Royalists nicknamed them Roundheads, to the amusement of the Queen and her ladies.

Roundheads. The apprentices and sailors and dock-workers took up the name with pride, and shouted the insult Cavaliero, at the elegant gallants with their flowing hair who surrounded the King with swords at their sides, hoping for trouble. Cavaliero. It was a foreign word, and therefore doubly insulting, connoting Spain and Popery and oppression of the people. English tongues shortened and Anglicized it until it became a round gracious word and not an epithet. At Whitehall and in Royalist society throughout England, it became the fashion to rejoice in the description Cavalier.

Puritans and Cavaliers insulted each other in the streets and sometimes came to blows, and in the last few weeks of the year 1641 families were already dividing in loyalty to the King or Parliament. Fathers and sons quarrelled bitterly and brothers ranged against each other and went off to train with rival bands. War was coming and Christmas was celebrated sadly in the homes of Royalists and Puritans alike. Charles and Parliament were irreconcilable; he would not surrender his right to command the army and Pym would not put such a weapon into his hands on the pretext of subduing Ireland. And then, in the first week of January, the end came. It came as Charles returned from a hunting expedition at Greenwich. As he crossed the Great Hall to go upstairs to his apartments and change for dinner with the Queen, Lord Falkland, his new Secretary of State, hurried across to him and stopped him.

"Forgive me, Sire, I must see you immediately. I've had a message from Lord Holland."

Charles hesitated for a moment, frowning. Holland, once his

old friend and Henrietta's favourite, had voted against him in the Lords and expressed his sympathy with Pym. He had been bitterly angry with Holland, who he now saw as a spineless opportunist, hoping to come out on the winning side.

"No message from Holland is of interest to me," he said curtly. "I cannot see you now, sir, or I shall keep Her Majesty waiting."

"You must see me," Falkland went so far in his agitation that he caught the King's arm. "It is desperately urgent, Sire. It concerns the Queen. I beg of you, let me come to your rooms now. I can speak to you while you're dressing."

"Very well." Charles looked down at the hand which was laid on his sleeve and Falkland stepped back in confusion.

"Be good enough never to do that again. You may follow me."

In his own rooms he stood while Parry took off his hunting coat, and one of his grooms of the Chamber brought him a bowl of water and a napkin in which he leisurely washed his hands. Falkland stood watching him, not daring to speak first. Charles sat down in his shirt and breeches and glanced up at him.

"Well, what is it?"

"I must see you alone, Sire," Falkland said. "I told you it was desperately important, I cannot discuss it with you in front of witnesses."

"I have no secrets from Parry, the rest of you gentlemen may leave for the moment." His three attendants bowed and backed out of the room. He turned to Falkland. "Proceed, my Lord. What is this message from Holland that's so secret and so vital it cannot wait for half an hour?"

"Holland was at Pym's house this afternoon," Falkland said. "He heard something that horrified him so much that he sent a message to me at once, begging me to warn you."

He saw the King looking up at him with surprise and he paused. For a moment he did not know how to put it into words.

"They are going to impeach the Queen for Treason," he said at last.

For a moment Charles stared at him without speaking or moving. During that minute he thought quite seriously that he had misheard. His mind refused to register, he saw Falkland standing in front of him, his usually remote face pale and contorted with anxiety, and very slowly, Charles got up and came close to him.

"Repeat that, if you please," he said.

"They are going to impeach the Queen," Falkland said again. The King had changed colour, he was so white that the Secretary of State was alarmed, and a curious light flickered in his eyes, a flash that reminded the unimaginative peer of lightning. There was not a sound in the room. Out of the corner of his eye he saw the valet Parry standing with the King's velvet coat in his hand, his mouth slightly open.

"Impeach the Queen. . ." Charles spoke very slowly and carefully. And then suddenly his voice rose as Falkland had never heard it in his life.

"Impeach my wife! Good Christ above, Falkland, are you standing there and telling me this thing and expecting me to believe it? "

"It is the truth, Sire. Holland wouldn't lie. Whatever he is, he wouldn't say such a thing unless it was true. He always loved the Queen and he risked his own life sending me the message. He knows she is in mortal danger."

"Don't you dare say that! Don't dare speak of the Queen in such a way." Charles stepped very close to Falkland and he reached out and caught him by both arms. "No man in England can touch my wife, do you hear? No man in the world, without answering for it with his life. . ."

"It is the Queen's life which is at stake, Sire," Falkland's voice was low. "They are going to charge her with inspiring the Army Plot and encouraging the rebellion in Ireland. If they can find one witness to testify against her on either count, they can do to her what they did to Strafford. She is only the Consort, she hasn't the Sovereign's immunity from English law."

Slowly Charles released him; his hands were trembling. The Army plot. He could remember Goring and Jermyn standing side by side in Henrietta's Privy Chamber at Whitehall, explaining the details of the intrigue she had instigated, and then her answer to his question when he returned from Scotland and asked her if she had communicated with the Irish rebels . . . 'By word of mouth and by letter . . . other people's letters of course. . .'

She had committed herself so deeply that if the evidence came to light, Parliament would have a better case in law against her than anything on which they had convicted Strafford. He could think no further and he closed his eyes. They knew what she had done; Pym had spies everywhere, spies in the Army, spies at Whitehall, spies even in his Council. Someone had betrayed Henrietta, and if she were ever to face a public accusation, witnesses would be found to come forward and condemn her. It was still inconceivable to Charles—a part of his mind, the part which regarded himself and all connected with him as beyond the reach of any law but his own will, refused and rejected the possibility with outraged scorn. Three years ago he would have dismissed Falkland and ordered the arrest and execution of every man responsible for the idea, but now he knew it was beyond his power. Parliament had taken his judicial rights, dissolved his Courts, imprisoned his judges. Parliament commanded troops who would come to Whitehall and take the Queen by force, and he knew with absolute certainty that the time had come when they would not hesitate to demand her life of him as they had demanded Strafford's. In moments of crisis he had always been calm, and at that moment when everything he loved better than life itself was threatened, he mastered his anger and his panic and confounded Falkland by saying quite quietly, " Very well, my Lord. Let us discuss this as calmly as we can. What must be done? "

" Strike first, Sire ! Impeach the impeachers. . . Accuse them of Treason. They've been constantly treating with the Covenanters all during the late war—we can find dozens of witnesses to prove it. On no account have the Queen's name mentioned in any of it, or she and you will be lost. Accuse them and arrest them before they can bring their motion against her in the House."

Charles looked at him coldly. He had once liked Falkland. It was unjust, but human, that he would never like him again because he had not sprung to Henrietta's defence and echoed the cry of rage and anguish in Charles' own heart by calling for war against her enemies on her account alone. As if Falkland had seen into his thoughts, he added, " You must believe this, Sire. You cannot make Her Majesty the issue. The Consort is not sacred in law, as I told you. Two Queens were

executed in the reign of Henry VIII, and your own grandmother the Queen of Scots was beheaded on a charge of
Treason against the State, and she was an anointed Sovereign.
Your only plan is to strike at Pym and his fellows with their
own weapon. Otherwise you will bring Civil War upon your
country for the sake of your wife, and however much you love
her, I tell you truly, it's not a cause which will make Englishmen unsheathe their swords against each other."

Charles was looking at him with obvious anger and he
stopped. His conscience was clear. Nonetheless, he went down
on his knees in front of him.

"I beg of you to listen to me," he said. "It is the only
way."

"Do they imagine," Charles said slowly, "that I would
deliver my wife to them to be tried like a common criminal?
Don't they know I will defend her honour and her safety with
my own body?"

"Of course they know that," Falkland said. "They know
that such an attempt will mean war and that is obviously what
Pym wants. He wants you to defend the Queen by force
against the laws of England. Then he will have the right on
his side and rally the people to him. Then he will destroy you
as well as her."

"You're very shrewd, my Lord," Charles answered. "Take
aim at what a man loves most and he will stand in front of it
and make himself the target. So be it. This has been coming
for many years, and I tried to avoid it by every means in my
power. Now I have no scruples. In attacking my wife, who is
blameless and absolutely sacred to me—they have relieved
me of all responsibility for what must happen now."

"If you succeed in seizing them," Falkland said earnestly,
"if you can prove them traitors and discredit them all, you can
behead your enemies and cripple Parliament with the same
blow. And now is the time to do it. London is against you, but
most of England is sick to death of Pym and Parliamentary
tyranny. They will support you, so will three quarters of the
House of Lords, I swear to it! If you act quickly, you will be
King again and there will be an end of all your troubles!"

"I will act quickly," Charles promised. "Parry, my coat!
And not one word of this must reach the Queen—I won't have
her distressed."

For the first time his voice shook.

If he arrested Pym and the others, Falkland thought he might succeed without a national conflict. In Charles's opinion he misjudged. He misjudged the temper of the bitter London crowds and the antagonism of the Puritans whose creed had widely infected even the educated and aristocratic classes. If he imprisoned and executed their leaders they would still not be leaderless, Charles did not believe that for a moment. It would still be war.

He turned to the silent Secretary of State.

"We will draw up a list of names this evening," he said. "I will have Edward Herbert move the impeachment in the Lords tomorrow and I will go down and arrest them myself."

Chapter 10

To the surprise of the Countess of Carlisle, the Queen suddenly decided to change her dress. She had dined with the King early that afternoon, and the Countess had noticed how tense and preoccupied he looked through the long formal meal. At the end he took Henrietta into his Privy Chamber without any attendants and they remained shut up alone for nearly an hour. Something had happened or was about to happen and the Countess could not discover what it was. She presumed it was detrimental to the King until she met the Queen outside his door and saw Henrietta suddenly transformed. She had been listless and irritable all that day, but when she came into the ante-chamber, the Countess saw that she was smiling and animated; there was a flush of excitement in her thin face and she turned to them all and said gaily, "Come, ladies, the sun is shining. We will go for a walk this afternoon."

And then when they returned to her apartments she decided to change from the pale pink dress she wore, into a new gown, lately arrived from her favourite dressmaker in France. It was yellow satin, encrusted with pearls and green tourmalines, a rich and splendid dress which she had never had occasion to wear.

The Countess helped to undress her and while Henrietta stood in her petticoats, she said lightly, "You must be feeling better, Madam. You certainly look better than I've seen you for a month or more."

Henrietta smiled; it was a dazzling smile full of triumph and it made Lucy Carlisle freeze with suspicion.

"Better? I never felt so well in my life."

"Is that why you wish to wear your best gown?" Lucy questioned. "Is it a celebration, Madam?"

"It is indeed," the Queen said. "Newport, fetch me some fresh slippers, I'm tired of these."

Lady Newport went to the shoe closet and the Countess said gently, "If you're celebrating, Madam, won't you tell us what it is and let us join in it too?"

"Dear Lucy, if only I could. . ." Henrietta held her breath while the Countess and a tirewoman laced in the bright golden dress at the back. She longed to confide in her friend, she was so excited that she could hardly contain the news. When Charles told her what he was going to do that afternoon, she had thrown her arms round his neck and kissed him and told him to go down and pull the rogues out by the ears. All her doubts and frustrations were gone. At last, at last he had stopped waiting and temporizing and shown himself capable of the kind of action she would have taken in his place. She had always loved him and now her resolute spirit rejoiced in being able to admire him wholeheartedly.

"What is the time?" she asked suddenly, and Lady Newport put down three pairs of green and yellow shoes and looked at the little watch hanging from her waist.

"It is almost three o'clock, Madam."

"How slowly the time goes!" The Queen moved impatiently and Lucy Carlisle came round to her and pulled out the skirt of her dress so that it hung in straight folds to the ground.

"If you are going to walk in the grounds, Madam, you should wear stronger shoes than these. It rained early today and the grass is still damp." Something was terribly wrong. The King was plotting and he had told his wife the secret; her work might be useless unless she could persuade the Queen to betray it to her. She stepped back and gave Henrietta a smile which was warm with friendliness and admiration.

"You look magnificent," she said. "I've never seen any gown that suited you better."

"It isn't the gown, Lucy," the Queen said. "What you see is a happy woman, happy for the first time in months—no, years! Those shoes will do, Newport, I've changed my mind. I shan't go out today. We'll stay here and wait."

"Wait for what, Madam?" Lady Newport asked innocently.

"I can't tell you, but you will see. . ."

She loved Lady Newport, who attended Mass with her and had been cast off by her Puritan husband. She was a gentle, faithful creature and Charles's favourite among her women.

It was a pity that she was not as gay and quick-witted as Lucy. She was glad to see her old friend sharing her happiness. The compliment had touched her and she felt as if the slight strain which had grown up between them in the past year were entirely her fault. She held out her hand to the Countess and walked with her to the window where she sat down, turning to look into the gardens below. Lucy saw her start, and the natural colour left her face, emphasizing the bright patch of rouge on both cheeks. The Queen painted very heavily to hide her sallow skin and the unsightly blotches caused by intense nervous strain. Under the make-up, she was grey and the hand holding Lucy's was trembling. The Countess leaned forward and looked down from the window and there she saw the King with a gathering of armed Cavaliers leaving the gates of White-hall.

This was the moment; she tightened her fingers round Henrietta's hand and squeezed them hard.

"Madam, what is it?" she spoke in a whisper, "You're as white as death. Where is the King going with an escort of that size. . . . For God's sake trust me and tell me what's happening!"

"I cannot, I cannot say a word," Henrietta whispered back. "Oh, Lucy, pray for him! You don't know what this means. . ."

"Is he in danger?" the Countess asked quickly. She could have taken Henrietta by the shoulders and shaken her.

"No," Henrietta turned from the window and leant back. For a moment she closed her eyes. Charles had gone, taking his company of two hundred courtiers with him. When she opened them again and looked into Lucy Carlisle's face she saw nothing in it but anxiety for his safety. "No, he's not in danger. But his enemies are. I promised to say nothing, but I know I can tell you. The King has gone down to Westminster to arrest them!"

"Arrest whom?" There was not a flicker on the beautiful face, not a shadow in the bright blue eyes.

"Pym," Henrietta said, "And Hampden, Mandeville, Holles and Strode. They're accused of Treason and he's gone to seize them himself. He only told me this afternoon."

"Thank God," the Countess said piously. "Thank God,

Madam. You will be rid of all your enemies with those five men under guard."

"The King will serve them as they served Strafford," Henrietta stood up and the Countess followed, still holding her hand. They came back into the centre of the room.

"What is the time, Newport?"

"Close to four, Madam."

The Queen sat down again, releasing the Countess and looked up at her.

"They will be there very soon now. Dear God, what an eternity it seems. . ."

"I have a book in my room, Madam," Lucy Carlisle said quickly. "It's a collection of French poetry, I know you'd like it. I'll read it aloud and it'll help to pass the time."

She almost ran to the door and was gone without waiting for the Queen's permission. Outside she did run, holding her long skirt in one hand till she reached the apartments of the ladies-in-waiting. They were empty, everyone was on duty with the Queen or outside in the winter sunshine. She found paper and pen and ink in her private cabinet and wrote a few words. 'Fly at once. The King is coming to arrest you.' She scrawled the other four names the Queen had mentioned and then rang the bell for her personal page. While she waited she swore. Her hands were trembling as she folded the message into a tidy square, small enough to be hidden in the palm of the boy's hand. He had been dozing in the pages' room down the corridor, he came into the room rubbing his eyes and the Countess sprang forward and gave vent to her terror and anxiety by shaking him violently.

"How dare you dally when I ring for you! Come to your senses you fool or I'll have you whipped for idleness. Take this to the House of Commons. Give it to John Pym and no one else. Go down to the stables and take one of my horses, and may God help you if you arrive too late!"

"Yes, my Lady," the boy stuttered. He was afraid of his mistress who bullied him and boxed his ears and had had him beaten several times.

"Go!" The Countess pushed him. "Don't lose a moment. If you find Pym in time I'll give you a gold piece!"

She listened, hearing him run down the corridor and down the back stairs and then she composed herself. She smoothed her dress and arranged her hair in the mirror. Five minutes later she was back in the Queen's room, serenely reading aloud to her.

At five that afternoon the King returned. He dismissed his Cavaliers and walked slowly up the main staircase of the Palace, his eyes fixed on the figure of the Queen who was waiting at the head of them, her yellow dress shining in the dim light, surrounded by a crowd of her ladies. They drew back, curtseying as he approached, and the Queen ran forward holding out her hands. She stopped, gazing into his face—it was pale and distracted, and without asking a question, she knew that he had failed.

"Charles," she said uncertainly, "Oh, Charles. . ."

"They had gone," he said slowly. "Someone warned them and when I reached the Commons they were leaving on the tide for the City of London. The City gave them refuge and has refused to deliver them."

"Oh, God," Henrietta whispered. "What did you do?"

"Saved what was left of my dignity and came home," he said, wearily. "God knows how they were warned."

Henrietta swung round suddenly—the Countess of Carlisle was standing just behind her.

"I told you!" she exclaimed. "I told you where the King was going! Come here, come here and get down on your knees and swear that you spoke to no one when you left my room!"

Lucy Carlisle knelt. She saw the King looking at her, hatred and suspicion in his eyes and for a moment she was terribly afraid. But her exultation was greater than her fear. Pym had received her message. He and the rest were safe and now the King was really lost. She faced them both without flinching and said clearly—"Before God, I swear to Your Majesties that I am no traitor."

Charles put his arm round Henrietta; he did not believe the woman, but he doubted if the charge could be proved without a scandal which would apportion the blame on his wife. She had suffered enough.

He looked down at the Countess with disgust. "Get up," he said. "No false oaths are required of you. The Queen relieves you of your duties. If you have betrayed her confidence, I am content to leave you to the judgment of God." With his arm still round the Queen who was weeping and leaning on him, he walked past them all and went into their private apartments. For some moments there was silence. No one moved, and the Countess rose from her knees and looked round at the women who had lived in daily contact with her for nearly fifteen years. The first to speak was Lady Newport.

"You sent the warning," she accused. "You left the Queen for more than ten minutes . . . fetching that book. May God forgive you! "

Lucy Carlisle looked at her contemptuously.

"I should guard your tongue if I were you. Nothing is proved against me. Nothing will ever be proved. If the Queen blabbed to me, no doubt she blabbed to others. She is the guilty one, not I." She turned her back on them all and walked away to the waiting women's quarters. Late that night her carriage and a wagon full of luggage left Whitehall for ever.

On February 23rd, 1642, Charles said good-bye to his wife at Dover. They stayed in the same bleak Castle where they had first met seventeen years ago, and now she was leaving for Holland with her daughter Mary, ostensibly bringing the child to her husband, but carrying the Crown jewels in her baggage with a commission to pawn them and raise money for her husband's war with his people. They had left Whitehall on January 10th, driven out by crowds of rioters, who were screaming for revenge on the persecutor of their hero Pym, still safely hidden behind the walls of the City of London. Catholics were being hunted through the streets and the embassy Churches in London were invaded and desecrated and the priests dragged out and thrown into prison. Henrietta was in hourly danger, and the King fled with her as if they were fugitives, followed by his Courtiers for whom there was no longer any place in the hostile capital. From Windsor they travelled to Dover, and on a cold day with a sharp wind blowing in from the sea, they gathered at the quayside, the King and the Queen and the little Princess, with the young Prince of Wales and the Duke of York beside them.

A fleet of fifteen Dutch ships were anchored outside the harbour to escort the Queen's ship, the *Lion*.

Henrietta was wrapped in a velvet cloak lined with sables,

and she reminded Charles so much of the tiny childish bride who had greeted him in Dover Castle all those years ago. In his eyes she was as pretty as she had ever been, the lines of fatigue and worry, the streaks of grey in her hair seemed to vanish. He gathered her in his arms and his cheeks were wet with tears.

"Farewell my love, my darling. God give you a safe journey and bring you safely back to me."

For a moment she clung to him and hiding her face she wept. Her tears were bitter with grief for him and fear for the uncertain future she was forced to let him face alone. In the shadow of war, with their security gone and their lives in danger, nothing remained but the durability of their love for one another, and it was deeper and more selfless than at any time in their lives.

At last she raised her wet and drawn face to his and wiped her eyes. Out of the tears a little spark of spirit shone at him.

"Have courage, my darling," she said. "I am going where I can be of the best use to you. I'll raise all the money you need and I'll send you arms and ammunition and men too, if I can recruit them. I shall be thinking of you and praying for you every moment. And I'll come back to you the moment you send word. Say good-bye to Mary, now."

Charles turned to his daughter and bending down, embraced the solemn little girl, who would one day be Queen of Holland.

"Farewell, my child. Take care of your mother and remember me. God bless you."

"I must go," Henrietta said desperately. "I must go now or I shall never have the courage. . . Farewell my son. . ."

She kissed the Prince of Wales, and then the little Duke of York.

"Obey your father in all things. Pray to God we will soon be re-united."

For the last time Charles embraced her, and then she walked slowly down towards the ship, holding the Princess Mary by the hand. He waited in the biting wind until they reached the decks and then he saw Henrietta turn and wave. The ship began to move out on the tide.

"Come, Sire. It's freezing and you will catch cold." The Duke of Newcastle had approached him.

"I think I can still see them," Charles answered. "If I were higher up . . . Newcastle, order my horse. I'll ride along the cliff."

In the years to come, when he had spent his great fortune and risked his life a dozen times in defence of the King and was living in unhappy exile, Newcastle spoke of that ride along the towering cliffs of Dover, following the King who galloped for miles to keep the ship in view. The following day, looking as if he had not slept at all, Charles left Dover and turned his train northwards towards the old city of York.

In London the city militia were drilling, and in the King's absence, Pym and his four friends left their hiding-place and made a triumphal return to Westminster, surrounded by cheering crowds. They found a depleted Commons and a House of Lords from which three-quarters of the peers had fled and joined the King. War had not yet been formally declared but fighting was breaking out in parts of England as far apart as Cornwall and the Midlands, and both sides were recruiting men and seizing supplies. The last of the King's powers were claimed by Parliament, including Cromwell's Bill for control of the armed forces of the Kingdom. The farce of negotiation between the King and his rebellious subjects broke down finally in July, and on August 22nd, 1642, Charles raised the Royal Standard at Nottingham and called his people to arms.

That night he was writing to Henrietta with the news, that war had broken out, and Hull, the vitally important port and Arsenal, had shut its gates on him and declared for Parliament when Lord Digby came into his room.

"Your pardon, Sire! Forgive me for intruding but you have a visitor!" Charles looked up irritably, he was not yet used to being disturbed. He was surprised to see Digby's excited face.

"What visitor? I'm not expecting anyone tonight."

"He forbade me to tell you, Sire. He wants to surprise you himself. He's outside." A man was standing in the shadows beyond the open door and as Digby spoke he walked into the room.

For a moment Charles stared at the immensely tall figure and then jumped to his feet with a cry of amazement and joy.

184

"Rupert!"

"Uncle!" The Prince rushed to him and caught both his outstretched hands, then he fell on his knees and kissed them.

"I wouldn't let Digby announce me—I knew you'd be surprised."

"Surprised and delighted," Charles said unsteadily. "My dear boy—I had no idea you were coming! When did you get here?"

"An hour ago. I had the devil of a time passing the sentries outside the city—they didn't know me and they wouldn't believe me when I said who I was."

"You've changed," Charles said. "You've grown. God, Rupert, how tall are you, you look like a giant!"

"I'm touching six feet six inches," Rupert laughed. "I left you a boy, uncle, and I'm returned a man."

"You are indeed," the King looked at him in wonder. He could hardly recognize the lanky youth in this tough, confident young soldier. And he was a soldier. He moved and spoke with the confidence of a campaigner and his sword was a heavy, practical weapon, not a Court ornament. He had always been handsome—now his nose was broken and it gave a sinister look to the dark face, already furrowed with experience far beyond his years.

"I'm so happy to see you I can hardly speak," the King said at last, and Rupert smiled at him tenderly and led him back to his chair.

"I left Holland three days ago and those scum at Westminster sent ships to intercept me. I evaded them easily enough but that's why I was delayed."

Charles caught hold of his sleeve.

"How was the Queen when you left?" he begged. "I haven't heard from her for ten days and I was just writing to her when you came. . . Is she well, Rupert? Had she any message for me?"

"Many messages, much love and much encouragement. Don't fret, uncle, she's in excellent health and working as hard as ten men to raise money and get help from France and Holland and anywhere she can. She has a wonderful spirit."

"She has indeed," Charles agreed wistfully. "I only wish that she were here to bolster mine."

"I'll try and do it for her," the Prince said gently. "I've

185

come to help you; uncle. My life and every talent I possess is at your sole command."

"You're generous, my dear Rupert," the King said. "But this is not your quarrel. It weighs heavily enough on me that I must ask their lives of strangers. I shall certainly not put you in danger on my account."

"Uncle, when I was a boy without a penny in my pocket and hardly a spare pair of breeches, you took me in and treated me like your own son. For all these years, when I've been fighting all over Europe, even while I was a prisoner of the Austrians, I've dreamed of repaying you and showing my gratitude. I'm only your nephew but I *feel* like your son. And you cannot deny me. You need me—you need someone with experience of war, and by God I'm not boasting when I say that I'm the best cavalry general in Europe!"

"I know that," Charles could not help smiling at him. "Your mother wrote to me that your exploits were taking years from her life."

"My mother only says that because she would rather be proud of my brother Carl than of me." His face grew sullen. He had always been second in his mother's affection and at that moment he looked like a sulky boy again.

"I told her I was coming to England to fight for you. If you refuse me, it will break my heart."

Charles put his arm round the broad shoulders.

"How can I refuse you Rupert? I never could, even when you were a boy. And how," he added gently, "could I refuse the best cavalry general in Europe?"

Immediately Rupert's face grew light and he smiled again. His very dark eyes shone with what Charles could only describe as expectation of a fight.

"In that case, uncle, let us begin at the beginning. What is our strength? Who are your commanders and what men can they muster?"

"I've made Lord Lindsey General-in-Chief; he has worked so hard in the Northern Midlands, raising men and money. Harry Wilmot is Commissary General. He's full of fighting spirit and he knows how to organize."

Rupert said nothing—Wilmot was not a bad choice but Lindsey was sixty years old and had last seen action in 1597. The King continued.

186

"Forty of my peers have agreed to maintain a troop of horse each for the next three months; Sir Richard Lloyd has promised ten thousand men from the North of Wales."

"And the Navy?" Rupert asked. Money and men and the support of the Northern nobility might satisfy the King at the moment but they would soon be exhausted without the protection of the Fleet for fresh supplies from abroad.

"The Navy has declared for Parliament," Charles answered slowly. "A few ships remained loyal but the rest joined the rebels."

"The Queen told me before I left that you could expect no help from Scotland," his nephew said after a moment.

"No help, but no hindrance either. The Covenanters will mediate between Parliament and myself, but they will not send support to either."

"Thank God for that," Rupert was relieved. "At the moment, uncle, you are in no position to fight on two fronts." In his opinion Charles was not particularly well equipped to fight at all. He had lost his Navy, and the South and the City of London were staunchly Puritan.

"Uncle," he said, "I want you to give me the command of your cavalry. Mounted troops are in the heart of a modern army—speed, manœuvre-ability and co-ordination—that's what wins battles! And by God, I'll give you a cavalry force will sweep the Puritans down to the beaches and into the sea!"

"The Command is yours," Charles said. "Your opponent will be Sir Thomas Fairfax who leads the rebel horse."

"I've never heard of him," Rupert said contemptuously. "But before the month is out, he'll hear of me. Who commands their main army?"

"Essex," the King answered. "He and Warwick and Brooke and all that miserable coterie have joined with Parliament. Wharton, Willoughby and Manchester are with him, to name the most important. That's all I can tell you, Rupert."

"At the moment, it's an even match," his nephew said at last.

"If we can get money and munitions through from the Queen in Holland and keep the Scots neutral, we can change the balance in our favour." His hard young face softened in a smile as he looked at Charles.

187

"Trust in me, uncle, and above all trust in yourself."

"I trust in God," the King said simply. "With a right cause and His Blessing, I shall win." He stood up and made one of the few gestures of affection he had ever shown anyone except his wife. He put his hand on Rupert's shoulder and kissed his forehead.

"My trust is in God and my cavalry. God bless you, my dear boy. Now I must finish my letter to your aunt."

Henrietta had arranged one of the rooms in the New Palace on the Staedt-Straat as a Presence Chamber, and most of that morning she and her ladies had been arranging a magnificent collection of jewellery on a long table against one wall under a window, where the stones would show to their best advantage in the light.

This was not her first interview with the Dutch merchants. She had received them soon after her arrival, and they had shown surprising reluctance to buy and absolute determination not to pay what the Queen of England asked. Henrietta had dismissed them in disgust, and then recalled them on advice from the Prince of Orange. Charles was desperately in need of money and she could not afford to be proud. Later that morning the Dutch and Jewish merchants came to the New Palace again—small men, some of them very dark with the sad, self-effacing air of their race, and bowed low before the little woman in the bright green satin gown.

On the table by the window the sun was shining on a blazing treasure of diamonds, rubies, emeralds and pearls. One by one the merchants examined the pieces; there was a collar of rubies, each stone enormous and perfectly matched, and another of diamonds, part of the regalia of the English Crown and of such quality and rarity that they lingered over them, whispering and admiring and holding them up to the light. There was the necklace of pink pearls and diamonds that Charles had given her one New Year's day, and a massive emerald brooch which had belonged to her own mother, the Queen of France. There were rings and chains inset with precious stones, even the smallest personal trinkets were laid out for inspection. Henrietta had nothing left but the pearls round her neck and one fine corsage ornament which she had brought as a bride from France.

She watched them anxiously for some moments, wishing she could understand what they were saying; she knew only a few words of Dutch and not a word of Hebrew.

"Well, gentlemen? Have you decided?"

They turned and moved away from the table. The richest merchant in Amsterdam, with the improbable name of Webster, came up to her holding the gorgeous ruby collar and bowed very low.

"We have examined the jewels, Your Majesty, and we must agree that we have never seen the like of some of them. This collar"—he held up the ornament which Charles had worn at his coronation—"this collar is unique. There is not another like it in the world."

"In that case," Henrietta said impatiently, "I hope you are prepared to pay what it is worth."

The merchant shrugged.

"Unfortunately Madam, you have misunderstood me. A piece like this is beyond price in one sense, and in another it suffers from too much excellence. If I buy it from Your Majesty, there are few indeed who could afford to buy it afterwards from me. It is a King's ornament, magnificent, superb—but not very saleable. Out of consideration for Your Majesty and because you have done me the honour to approach me, I can offer you 100,000 guilders. Believe me, I am robbing myself at such a price."

Henrietta flushed with anger.

"On the contrary Sir, you are trying to rob me! That collar is worth a half a million, that is the value of it. I will not consider what you offer."

Webster bowed again. "I ask you to have patience, Madam," he said gently. "Not only is the collar impossible to sell, but word has reached all of us in Amsterdam that the Parliament of England denies your right to dispose of it or of any of these things belonging to the English Crown. What would my position be if I were made to give it back after buying it from you?"

"Everything here is the King's property and mine," she said angrily. "You will never be asked to return anything you buy unless His Majesty redeems it from you himself after his victory. If you have nothing else to add, Sir, let someone else examine the collar."

"It has been examined," Webster answered, "and I am the only merchant here prepared to offer for it."

Henrietta stared at them one by one. There was nothing to be seen on any face but respectful deprecation. Only the night before she had received a long letter from Charles, asking her anxiously for news of the sale. Rupert was raising an army, training and equipping them and co-ordinating all the disordered elements of his supporters into a fighting force. Within days, the King said, his troops would meet the Parliamentary army outside Oxford.

She put one hand to her aching head, and for a moment she faced Webster as a desperate, helpless woman. Her voice was trembling.

"I beg of you, I appeal to any chivalry you may have for the distress of a noble King, at this moment fighting for his life—raise your offer. On my word as Queen of England, you will not regret it."

The merchant held the great collar up and looked at it again, turning the stones round and round.

"140,000 guilders, as a tribute to you, Madam."

Henrietta nodded, it was useless to argue.

"Agreed. Now gentlemen, what of the rest?"

For the next hour she bargained and promised and one by one her treasures were sold and the merchants left her to make out deeds of sale with Harry Jermyn whom Charles had sent to Holland to help her with her financial dealings. Fletchers of The Hague—she could hardly help smiling at the incongruity of the plain English names on such un-English faces—paid out 129,000 for some choice diamond and emerald ornaments worth twice as much, and the representative of the Rotterdam burgomasters allowed her 40,000 guilders on some of her personal jewels including a beautiful set of pearl buttons which had belonged to Charles. She watched them pack the jewels away without regret; only the loss of his pearls upset her and suddenly her eyes filled with tears and she hurried out of the room. She was surprised and irritated to find Charles' sister, the widowed Elizabeth of Bohemia waiting for her.

"I heard you were entertaining the merchants again," her sister-in-law said. She was a tall woman with a stern, beautiful face; she was oddly like her son Rupert—they shared the same imperious expression and the same direct stare. Henrietta found her critical and selfish and resented her habit of giving advice.

"I have," she said, "and to some purpose this time. I sold everything."

"At far less than their value, I've no doubt," Elizabeth said. "All merchants are nothing but a pack of thieves. I hope you told them so!"

"No, I did not!" Henrietta snapped at her suddenly. "I drove the best bargain possible and I must remind you, sister, that my need of them was greater than their need of what I had to sell them. I took their price and I thank God for it. At least I have something to send back to the King."

"And what will he do when that's gone?" his sister demanded. She had been fighting for a throne for nearly twenty years and she had bitter experience of the way in which wars devoured seemingly huge sums of money with little or no return. "Really, my dear Henrietta, if you loved Charles and wanted to save him from this disastrous war, you'd tell him to make peace before it's too late and remain in exile yourself. How can you urge him on to fight? What will you feel if he's defeated—haven't you seen what happened to me and my sons after we lost our throne? I know you're proud, my dear, and everyone knows you're obstinate, but surely there's a limit to this stupidity!"

"You call it stupidity," Henrietta said fiercely, "you talk about making peace and staying in exile as if he would be safe by giving in and trusting to the mercies of his enemies. How dare you say that! How dare you advise me to discourage him when he's on the eve of a major battle!"

Her tears began to overflow and she stopped, she put her hands to her eyes and sobbed and as she looked at her, Elizabeth first shook her head and then shrugged.

"What battle?" she asked quietly. "You never told me. I should like to know—my son Rupert is with him."

"A place outside Oxford," Henrietta said at last. "I received a letter yesterday. He says Essex and the Parliament army are gathering outside Oxford on the way to London. Rupert has advised him to march on the capital and they should meet at a point in between called Edgehill.

"God help them," Elizabeth said slowly. "I should try and

calm yourself; weeping will not do any good. I'm afraid you are just at the beginning of your tears."

As the door closed behind her, Henrietta went quickly into her oratory. Her religion was as unpopular in Holland as it had been in England; that was another complaint Elizabeth made against her. But her faith and her letters from Charles were all the comfort she had left. Edgehill. She fell on her knees in front of the tiny altar and prayed desperately for her husband and her nephew and all their friends and for the outcome of the battle outside Oxford.

The King rose before dawn on October 22nd, 1642. Parry dressed him in the tent which had been set up on the higher slope of the escarpment at Edgehill, surrounded by his personal guards wearing scarlet, which was known as the Royal colour. Three thousand cavalry and dragoons and nine thousand infantry were deployed over the high ground in the rough shape of a half moon. Prince Rupert's four cavalry regiments and Charles' own lifeguards were placed on the right flank, the infantry in the centre and five regiments of horse under the command of Harry Wilmot were on the left. Charles's army had overtaken Essex and the Parliament troops and at Rupert's insistence, they had turned to meet them at Edgehill. It had been a long and weary march through hostile country, where the villagers hid their food and closed their houses, and the Royalists had eaten little during the past two days. They were hungry and tired but their morale was high, and when the King came out of his tent into the early autumn sunshine, he was greeted by a roar of cheering. He wore black velvet, his short cloak lined with ermine, and he mounted a pure white horse. He had spent some time praying quietly in his tent before going out to encourage his troops, and his spirit was composed and confident. He turned as Rupert came riding up towards him on a big bay, the scarlet sash blazing across his breastplate, with half a dozen of his chosen officers close behind him. Rupert raised his sword in salute.

"The army is ready for inspection, Sire."

"I'm ready," Charles answered him. "Come with me, Rupert." He spurred his horse and began to move down among the ranks of infantry. There were tenant farmers from York and the Midlands, labourers and townsmen, bearing arms for the first time in their lives, and for many it was their first close view of the King for whom they were going to fight that day. What they saw was a personification of the ancient sovereigns of England, handsome, grave, supremely dignified in his rich dress with the Royal ermine on his shoulders, riding the magnificent white horse, and when he stopped to speak to them they broke their ranks and crowded round his stirrup, cheering and waving their hats. He waited for some moments, the colour coming into his face and such a mixture of emotions overwhelming him that he did not trust himself to speak. The sun was high above their heads and down below him Charles could see the bright green Avon valley, marked with darker lines of hedges and a few clumps of trees and further still, the mass of Essex's infantry. The light caught flashes of steel among them; from that distance they looked like toys rather than men. On the right a slight ground mist was gathering.

"Silence! Silence for His Majesty the King!" The officers were shouting and he could hear Rupert's voice above them all. He noticed a small man standing a few feet away from him, the red cockade blowing in his hat, and gave him a special smile of recognition. He remembered the man's name was Shuckburgh. He was a local squire who had met the King's army coming through as he was on his way to hunt; after kneeling at the King's feet, he had gone back to fetch his tenants and rejoined the army outside Rawdon. It was the first he had heard of the war. There were many like him.

"Gentlemen!" As Charles spoke, the last cheer died away and there was silence.

"I come among you on this day to tell you that your King is both your cause, your quarrel and your captain; come life or death your King will bear you company, and ever keep this field, this place and this day's service in his grateful remembrance. God bless you all!"

"God Save The King!"

That shout and the tremendous cheer that followed it were clearly heard in the furthest ranks of Essex's army down the hill.

The army of Parliament numbered nearly thirteen thousand; eleven thousand foot and two thousand horse, with dragoons, musketeers and artillery. The Earl of Essex had great confidence in his ability to blow the Royalists off the field with his superior cannon, but to his chagrin, less than half the artillery trains had caught up with his main force. He placed what guns he had between his infantry brigades and moved his cavalry regiments under the commands of Sir William Balfour, Sir Philip Stapleton and Sir James Ramsay forward to repel the Royalist foot.

Essex had also reviewed his troops that morning, and one of the minor officers in the cavalry was Oliver Cromwell, having his first major experience of combat. The Puritan preachers had travelled with them, and they passed among the men exhorting them to fight in the name of religion and the ancient laws of England and praying for a signal victory over the unbelievers. The Royalists cheered the King and the Parliamentarians retaliated with psalms. Through his spyglass Essex glimpsed the King on his white horse riding up the high edges of the escarpment, followed by his Standard Bearer carrying the flag with the Royal Arms of England. That would be the core of the battle, that spot where the slight figure in black stood, with his Standard blowing out in a stiff breeze above his head.

Essex called a hurried conference with his officers, and decided not to wait any longer in the hope of his artillery arriving in time. At two in the afternoon, Essex's guns opened fire.

The first cannonade struck a crowded infantry encampment. The Royalists were sitting down, their swords and muskets on the ground beside them, making a wretched meal of coarse bread and a ration of ale and the balls crashed in among them with terrible effect. The screams of the wounded mingled with the noise of gunfire as battery after battery opened up on the Royalist forces, and with the shouts and curses of the officers who ran in and out of the shattered ranks, trying to calm their men and have the injured dragged out of range.

Charles himself started to spur down towards them.

"Order our guns to open fire," he shouted to Sir Jacob Astley, the general in command of the foot. "Stop those cannons!"

Astley passed on the order and held on to the rein of Charles' horse to stop him going into danger.

"Hold on, Sire, hold on a moment! Our guns will silence them. . . If you go any further you'll come within range!

"If your batteries don't come into action in another minute, Astley, I'll order the advance and stop them." Charles said angrily. "What are we supposed to do, stay here and be shot to pieces?"

"There's our reply, Sire," Astley shouted; he had to shout to be heard at all, for the few Royalists' guns began a thunderous cannonade at the enemy.

"Thank God," Charles pulled his horse's head round. "Astley, we seem to be missing—we haven't touched a man in that battery on the left! Tell them they're aiming too high, the balls are going above them!"

"The guns are on high ground, Sire," a perspiring officer from the batteries ran up to him, "we can't deflect the muzzles and we can't get a true aim. Their aim is right on us, we've had heavy casualties among the dragoons in the van."

Charles swung round on him, "Where is Prince Rupert?"

"Coming now, Sire."

Rupert was riding towards him, scattering men on either side. His face was dark with rage, and an old sword scar which ran across his forehead was livid. He looked like an incarnation of the devil as he pulled his horse up within a few feet of the King.

"This is madness," he yelled. "Those fools placed their guns too high up to hit anything but the birds, and they're up there pouring out our ammunition to no purpose! Uncle, for God's sake have them stopped." He turned savagely on Astley. Already his temper was proverbial. He had quarrelled violently with the senior officers, insisting on the importance of his cavalry in the strategic plan.

"What the devil are you doing, man, to let the artillery waste its fire and get in the way of my horse! Stop them at once or I'll ride down on them and spike those guns myself!"

"When His Majesty commands," Astley shouted back. "I take my orders from him, not from you!"

Charles turned quickly on them both.

"Enough, enough, gentlemen," he said angrily. "Astley, the Prince is right. I gave the order, now I rescind it. Cease firing!" With a furious glance at Rupert, Astley rode down towards the artillery and Charles said, "It was my mistake, Rupert, not his. Don't make any more enemies, for God's sake. What is the next move?"

"The cavalry," his nephew answered. "They're ready to charge now. Give me the word, Uncle, and I'll take my four regiments out and sweep these scum off the face of the earth!"

"Charge then, and God go with you!" the King called out and as he spoke the Royalist guns ceased firing. He watched Rupert riding headlong down through the ranks of foot soldiers and he pulled his horse round and urged it to higher ground. From there he heard a ringing shout, surely given by Rupert in his powerful voice. And from there he saw the first wave of troopers leave the escarpment and begin their head-long gallop down the slope, their swords glittering in the sunshine, led by that towering figure on the big bay horse. The single cry, "For England and the King," became a roar from fifteen hundred throats and they swept down and forward across the bright green ground below, gathering speed until they met the outposts of Essex's troops.

As Charles watched, he saw the first shock of impact as the mass of horsemen collided with the enemy foot-soldiers; the cries and shouts and the thunder of hooves came clearly to him and then saw the Roundhead lines divide and scatter. The men were running like insects before the terrible onrush of that charge and as they ran they fell and the victorious cavalry rode over them and beyond into the second line and in a matter of moments the right flank of Essex's army was disintegrating, flying for their lives. More horse were following Rupert, and Charles saw that they were the reserve, under Sir John Byron, following that magnificent charge in spite of orders to remain behind. His cavalry overran the enemy guns and the cannonades were silenced; a wild cheer broke out from the Royalist army and at the same moment Wilmot's cavalry descended on the left, and the battlefield became a mass of men and horses, shrouded in dust and smoke.

Then the Roundhead infantry advanced from the centre. They should have been unprotected by cavalry, for Rupert had routed the Parliament horse on the right and Wilmot must surely have attacked the troopers of Stapleton and Balfour. But in the confusion, blinded by the speed of their advance and the treacherous ground mist which had remained since early morning, Wilmot's charge had missed them, and as Charles watched, he saw the regiments of mounted soldiers wheel and charge his infantry who had not a single horse left to protect them.

What followed was a nightmare. The armies fought hand to hand and slowly, with terrible losses, the Royalist infantry gave ground. Someone seized the King's bridle and forced him further back out of danger. He saw his Standard surrounded, and Sir Ralph Verney into whose charge he had given it that morning, fighting with sword and fist to protect it. It was surrounded and it was overwhelmed. As Verney fell dying from a dozen wounds, a Roundhead soldier hacked the hand grasping the Standard from his arm. Out of Charles' sight the gallant Lord Lindsey received a pike thrust through the chest, and round him the remnants of the Royal footguards fought the levies of the Parliamentarian Brooke, neither side yielding a yard. It was the bitterest fight between Englishmen that had taken place since the Wars of the Roses two centuries before, and there was no sign of Rupert and his cavalry returning to change what seemed a certain defeat into a victory.

But if Charles had no reserves, neither had Essex. Both sides had exhausted themselves in a tumultuous and bloody mêlée which lasted until dusk, and as the darkness fell, the sounds of fighting died away, leaving only the thin cries of the wounded and dying and the eternal silence of five thousand dead upon the battlefield.

At eight o'clock that night, Charles sat once more in his tent. The twelve-year-old Prince of Wales and the nine-year-old Duke of York were with him. The little boys' faces were pale; they sat beside their silent father not daring to speak. When Parry served some food and wine the King sent it away untasted. No one knew whether it was victory or defeat, and the young Prince of Wales had spent the day hidden on the top of the escarpment in a ditch with his brother and his tutor, Doctor Harvey. He watched his father closely; from the expression on his face the boy decided that the battle must be lost. He felt very lonely and afraid and wished that his mother were with them. He might have questioned her, or approached his cousin Rupert who was always kind and treated him as an equal instead of a child, but he dared not speak to Charles.

When Lord Bristol came into the tent, Charles looked up

at him, his face weary and drawn, and spoke with a visible effort.

"What is the news, Bristol? Is there any sign of Prince Rupert?"

"A messenger has just arrived, Sire. The Prince and his men are returning now. They found Essex's baggage train outside Kineton village and looted it. He should be here within a few moments."

"Does he know how the battle went in his absence?"

"No more than we, Sire," Bristol answered with some bitterness. "If he hadn't taken all the horse with him, we'd have gained a certain victory. As it is, we've lost more than the enemy and gained nothing."

"Nothing!" No one had heard Rupert come through the flap-door. He stood in the flickering candlelight like a giant, covered with dust and blood, and the Prince of Wales jumped up with a cry of relief and ran to him.

"Cousin! Oh, cousin, we thought you were dead."

"Dead?" He laughed and put his arm round the boy's shoulders and together they came up to the King's chair, and Rupert knelt to him and lifted his hand to his lips.

"Greetings, uncle. I return with hardly a man lost and most of my Lord Essex's ammunition, guns and supplies. I hear the infantry did not fare quite so well."

"They fared better than anyone had a right to hope," Charles said. "On your way here, you must have seen how dearly they yielded every foot of ground. It's been a massacre, Rupert. A massacre on both sides."

Rupert stood up and looked suspiciously at Bristol. After three months with the King's army, he had hardly a friend left among his officers or the Councillors. To Bristol he looked like nothing so much as a swaggering mercenary as he stood there, one hand on his sword hilt.

"If a battle has been a massacre for both, then it's achieved its purpose," he said curtly. "Who been whimpering about losses into the King's ear? Was it you, my Lord? As I came in I heard you say we had gained nothing!"

"I'll say to your face what I said behind your back," Bristol replied coldly. "We've suffered terrible casualties and there's been no victory. You must forgive us, Highness, if we don't take the loss of life as lightly as you seem to do. We haven't

198

your long experience of bloody wars. . . As I said, we have gained nothing from today."

"Nothing but the open road to London!" Rupert swung round on his uncle in amazement. "Has no one thought of that? Essex is crippled, mutilated, exhausted. And we are in front of him! All we need do is gather our forces tomorrow and march on the capital, and it's ours! The war will be over, Sire, over with one battle! And you say we have gained nothing . . ." He glared at Bristol and turned his back on him.

"Rupert," the King spoke very quietly. "Sit down. Lord Bristol, send for Lord Digby and Sir Jacob Astley. My sons, say goodnight to your cousin and retire. You must take what rest you can before morning."

The young Princes kissed their father's cheek and were embraced by Rupert, as they left the rest of the King's Council of War came one by one into the tent, and sat down to discuss what should be done.

"Go on to London," Rupert insisted. "We'll never have such an opportunity again." He did not address the other lords; his eyes were fixed on his uncle who seemed so pale and distracted that he doubted if he were even listening.

"Verney is dead," Charles said in a low voice, "and Lindsey and my kinsman D'Aubigny. Willoughby was captured."

"All the more reason not to waste their lives," was Rupert's answer. He had always loved and admired his uncle, but he found his sentimentality infuriating. He had no sympathy with shaken nerves; he had been risking his own life since he was fifteen and when his enemies said that he loved fighting and sought out trouble, they were telling the truth. There was an instinct for killing in Rupert, but it found no counterpart in Charles's nature on that evening in October after he had witnessed the slaughter of five thousand of his subjects, loyal and rebel alike. Charles was sickened by it, grieving for the loss of men he had liked, pitying even those who had fought against him and were lying stark under the evening sky.

"What do you suggest, Highness," Bristol demanded. "Taking the King on to London with an exhausted army to lay siege to his own City without even giving them to chance to negotiate? I for one am utterly opposed to it. Have you forgotten that they hold two of his children as hostages there?"

"I have forgotten nothing," Rupert said savagely. "Even Pym won't harm the King's children, it's madness to put that forward as an excuse. If we stop now, we lose an opportunity that may never come again."

"If we go on, we risk another frightful battle," Charles said slowly. "If London does not submit I shall have to lay it waste or retreat. Bristol is right."

"Then lay it waste!" Rupert sprang up, unable to contain himself. "Destroy its defences and occupy it. Good God, uncle, this is a war, not a game of chivalry . . ."

"This is a war between rebels and their King," Charles spoke with a sharpness that surprised him. "I am not an invader, ravaging and burning . . . I will not march an army against my capital without putting my case to my people once again. If they refuse to submit we will have all the bloodshed you could wish. But it is my duty to give them that chance. We will not march on London, my Lords. I have decided. We will go to Oxford and establish ourselves there and I will make a last appeal to Parliament." He stood up.

"Nephew, and my Lords and gentlemen, my thanks for what you did today. Please God, it won't have to be repeated. I bid all of you goodnight."

In February 1643, a Parliament force under the command of Oliver Cromwell occupied the university city of Cambridge. Five troops of cavalry came riding through the quiet streets, watched by a crowd which was curious and apprehensive. War had not touched the University; though its sympathies were with Parliament, it had not yet been infected with the fever of partisanship which raged in Oxford where the King had made his headquarters and established his Court. Cromwell's was an orderly occupation; the men kept to themselves, there was no drunkenness or rioting, no repetition of the unruly high spirits associated with the Cavaliers who frequented the Oxford taverns, brawling and baiting the citizens.

Cromwell began fortifying the city. He never seemed to tire. He spent hours drilling his men in the fields outside Cambridge, and more hours inspecting the horses and equipment and talking to the officers and troopers individually. His business was war and war was his only occupation. His critics at Cambridge were aware that he would blow the Colleges to pieces rather than let the city fall into the hands of the King's army. By the end of the month he was satisfied that Cambridge was properly fortified against siege or attack, and he entertained his cousin John Hampden and his officers to dinner in his lodgings.

Eight officers were seated at a long table, with Cromwell at the head and Hampden on his right hand. It was a plain table set with plain food in wooden dishes; there was no wine and the spoons and mugs were country pewter and the drink was local beer. Tallow candles burnt round the walls, smoking and spluttering and dripping their strong-smelling grease and some of the officers were men of such rough manners that they ate with their hands and threw their leavings on the floor. It was not a hilarious meal, the only laughter came from Cromwell who was in a boisterous humour, talking across his neighbours and thumping Hampden playfully on the back. Hampden had seen him in many moods; he had seen him sunk in apathetic depression from which nothing could rouse him, sometimes angry, at other times humble and quiet, but never noisy and confident and loquacious, dominating and overbearing with the sheer force of a personality which had suddenly found release. Cromwell was happy for the first time in his life; he was at ease and at home in the shabby lodgings surrounded by his dour soldiers, with the whole of the university city under his command.

Hampden was a Puritan, but he was also a gentleman, accustomed to refinement and good manners. He had never thought of his cousin as a boor before, but there was no other way to describe him—or to describe his officers. Four of his captains were relatives, including his own son; of the rest, Henry Ireton was gentle born, and his immediate neighbours were a former clerk in an iron foundry and a yeoman farmer who had obviously never used a knife and fork.

"Eat heartily," Cromwell said to him, "and fill your tankard." He looked at him slyly and grinned. "I daresay it's a change from the dainty fare you've had in London, but it's wholesome and the beer's good."

"No more, thank you, cousin," Hampden protested, but Cromwell filled his tankard just the same.

"And how is London?" he demanded suddenly. "While we've been putting Cambridge in good order for them, what has Parliament been doing for the Cause?"

"Arguing," Hampden said wearily. "Quarrelling among themselves, pretending to negotiate with the King just as he's pretending to negotiate with us. And accomplishing little in the process."

"They talk while we fight," Cromwell said contemptuously. "How does Pym fare? He was ill when I was last in London, and made iller still by that fool Essex bringing his rag and bobtail troopers back from Edgehill as if it were a victory. Is he worse then?"

"Much worse. He's so thin you'd hardly recognize him and I've seen him sit down after a speech and double up with pain. When he dies, Oliver, I dread to think what the confusion will be."

"No man is indispensable," Cromwell mumbled with his mouth full. "Certainly no politician sitting at Westminster, while the real business of victory or defeat lies with the army." He brought one hand down on the table. "The army is what matters, cousin, and not the kind of army we saw running for its life at Edgehill!"

"No one could have withstood that charge," Hampden had flushed. "I fought in the rearguard and I came up against Rupert and I know!"

"I'm not impugning your courage," Oliver laughed and put his arm round Hampden's shoulders like an affectionate bear. His small eyes were bright, flickering along the lines of faces down the table.

"No one could have withstood it, you say? Well, I saw your troopers . . . old decayed serving-men and tapsters and fellows of that kind, while *their* troopers were gentlemen's sons and persons of quality. . . Do you think that mean, base fellows like those will ever be able to encounter gentlemen who have honour and courage and resolution in them?" He took his arm away from Hampden and spoke to them all, his son and his brother-in-law and his nephew, and the illiterate artisans he had made officers because he saw in them the quality he wanted in his soldiers.

"You must get men of a spirit that is likely to go on as far as gentlemen will go, or you will be beaten still. Men like these, cousin. Captain Berry, for what Cause do you fight? Stand up and tell us!"

James Berry, the former clerk, rose to his feet. He was a thin, slight man with a pale face, his light hair cut close to his head. He faced Hampden, and his eyes were bright and burning. He was not drunk, but there was a strange intoxication in his manner.

"I fight for God and the true religion," he said. "I fight to cleanse my countrymen's souls of Popish practises and to save them from the rule of an ungodly King. I fight for that and I will die for it. You know this, Colonel, for your Cause and mine are the same."

Cromwell turned slowly to his cousin and said gently,

"That is the spirit you need. That is the spirit which will withstand the cavalry of Rupert. It's the spirit you'll find in every man of my regiment. I refuse the others. I want only those men who know that they are fighting for God—not for pay or for Kings or Parliaments, but for the Cause of the Divine. Such men will never lose a battle, cousin. Where even gentlemen will run, my men will stand. Sit down, Captain Berry. If all our soldiers had your mettle, the King would be defeated in six months. And that," he said in a low voice, "is what we must have, if we are going to win. Cousin, listen to me. Pym is holding Parliament, but Pym is dying. Very well, that must be the will of God. And when he dies, what protection will we have from all the little men, full of fear and indecision and self-interest? Only the army! The soldiers who have fought and know what they are fighting for! Myself and others like me, men sitting round a humble board together, joined in loyalty to the cause of freedom, living and working and training as one. . . Tell me this," he demanded, "what brought the King down? Taxes, loss of liberties, unpopularity? I tell you none of these alone would have brought men out to fight against their King, none of these would send sons into battle against their own fathers!

"We are not at war for any of them. We are at war for religion, cousin! Berry here has told you. Berry is fighting for the voice of truth in his conscience and that voice tells him that the children of Israel are in peril of their souls, that God's

Holy Word is profaned and the Devil speaks from the King's pulpits. That is his Cause, and it is the only Cause for which we have a right to fight our own flesh and shed our brothers' blood."

His voice rose to a shout. "If thine eye offend thee, pluck it out! That is God's command, Cousin. That is our Cause and that will be our victory."

For some moments there was silence. Cromwell took a deep breath as if he were suddenly tired out. He was right and he knew it. In the confusion of his personal life, tortured by doubts of his own way of salvation, clever, ambitious, super-stitious and supremely practical, at last he had managed to fuse all these separate conflicts into a single purpose, pitiless as fire and strong as steel. His path to God was the one he had ridden at Edgehill.

"What do you want me to do?" Hampden said simply.

"I want you to get me the authority to recruit as many men in East Anglia as I can get and to train them in my own way. I want absolute freedom to choose my own officers, equip and maintain my troops as I think fit. Do that for me, Cousin, and I promise you you won't regret it."

"I will do it," Hampden promised, " and I will begin training my own men on your model."

"Discipline," Cromwell said slowly. "Discipline and more discipline still. The best soldier in the world is more afraid of God and his Commander than the enemy."

By the middle of the Spring, Cromwell had begun the formation of his own force, a force composed of cavalry armed with pistol and sword and wearing back and breastplates which earned them the nickname of Ironsides. Their discipline was a phenomenon in any army of that age and wherever they met the King's forces in skirmishes through the countryside, they cut them to pieces. Cromwell was soon famous for win-ning every fight he engaged in, and infamous for being the first on either side to refuse quarter to the wounded. It was disturbing and the cruelty revolted Charles, but he could not think about it seriously because he was waiting at Oxford for news that concerned him more deeply than the outcome of any battle. After months of delay, Henrietta had set sail for England, bringing eleven transports packed with men and ammunition with her. There was no port in Royalist hands on the South or East Coast where she could land, and there was nothing Charles could do but entrust her reception to Newcastle in the North and wait for her to join him with her army.

Chapter 11

THE little Yorkshire fishing village of Bridlington, with its thatched cottages and its small quay, was the place where Henrietta landed in England after an absence of a year. One of the worst storms in living memory had battered her fleet, driving it back upon the coasts of Holland, and only her indomitable courage and inflexible will to rejoin her husband had made her set out again on a second voyage. At last she landed, and slept her first night in a humble cottage at Bridlington, exhausted and exhilarated by a reception from the people such as she had never experienced in her life. A thousand cavaliers crowded into the village, cheering and singing and besieging her lodgings and the ordinary people hurried in from miles outside, carrying food and clothing and provisions. They brought tears to her eyes and she shed them freely, thanking them all for their loyalty in her faltering English, promising to reward every sacrifice made for the King, when the King had won his final victory.

She fell asleep worn out with emotion and excitement, and woke at five in the morning with cannon smashing over the roof of her house and shot peppering the streets. Four Parliamentary ships were bombarding the helpless village in an attempt to kill the Queen it sheltered and Henrietta fled in her nightdress at the height of the bombardment. It was snowing and she lay in a ditch outside for two hours in the freezing cold, covered in dirt and blood from a man who had been killed a few feet away from her. The enemy ships ceased fire only after the neutral Dutch ships which had accompanied her, threatened to blow them out of the water. She had come to Bridlington as the King's emissary and she left it in triumph as a heroine in her own right. The little village lay in ruins and one of the saddest of the many casualties she left behind her was a lady-in-waiting who had gone out of her mind from shock.

At the head of a brilliant procession, riding a fine chestnut mare, the tiny figure of the Queen of England drew the loyalists to her like a magnet. When she arrived at York, where Newcastle and a company of the greatest landowners of the North received her, Henrietta entered the city with three thousand foot soldiers and thirty companies of horse and dragoons.

And at York she met the King's old adversary in the Scottish wars for the first time. The Earl of Montrose was only thirty-one; when he came to her presence chamber in St. Mary's Abbey, Henrietta was surprised to see that the famous soldier and poet was so young. For a moment they looked at each other without speaking. He too was surprised by what he saw. She was so small, and painfully thin and her little pointed face was lined with worry and fatigue, as if a pretty child had grown suddenly old. There was nothing to suggest the militant Papist, the immoral devotee of wicked pleasures that her enemies described. Montrose saw courage and spirit and perhaps a sign of wilfulness in the bright dark eyes and the determined chin, and then she smiled at him, and her face looked young and bright as if the sun were shining on it.

"Welcome, my Lord. Rise, if you please."

"I am your servant, Madam. I should like to thank you for receiving me."

Henrietta watched him cautiously. "You may sit down my Lord. Now tell me, why have you come to me?"

"I've come to you for two reasons, Madam. Firstly, to beg you to believe when when I fought against His Majesty I did so from motives which seemed right enough at the time. Now I would give my life to undo what I have done: even if you and the King can find it in your hearts to forgive me, believe me, I can never forgive myself."

Henrietta knew as she looked at him that he was telling her the truth or he would never have come to York at all.

"You have my pardon," she said gently, "And I can vouch for the King, he always spoke well of you after his last visit to Edinburgh. What is the second reason?"

"The King's cause is in the greatest peril, Madam. When I left Scotland, commissioners from the English Parliament were trying to persuade Argyle to send an army over the border to attack the King. Argyle would do anything to force England into accepting the Covenanter's religious settlement," Montrose said gravely. "If they make a treaty, His Majesty will be fighting a fresh army of Scots as well as the rebels here! "

Henrietta got up and stood in front of him, clasping her hands in agitation. She looked very pale and her voice trembled.

"God help us—we cannot fight on two fronts—we will be crushed to pieces! What can we do, my Lord? For the love of God, tell me what can we do? "

"Send warning to the King and let me go back and raise a loyal army." Montrose stood with her, and on an impulse he caught her hands and held them. "There are thousands of Scots who are true to the King! All they need is a leader. Write to him, Madam, tell him what threatens him and beg him to accept my offer."

"Better still tell him yourself," she answered. "You must come with me to Oxford. Will you do that, Montrose? "

"With all my heart," he said.

"You'll find more enemies than friends at Oxford," Henrietta said suddenly. "But be sure of one thing. I am your friend for ever. God bless you for coming."

She slept badly that night and woke before dawn, irritable and unrefreshed, and in no mood for the complacency of the nobles and Cavaliers who talked as if the war were won already and their progress to the King would end with a triumphant entry into London. And there were mutterings and sidelong, jealous looks when Henrietta announced that Montrose was going to Oxford with her. As soon as the cumbrous baggage trains and the troops of her army could be organized, she set out from York on her way through Yorkshire to the Midlands. It was a slow progress, because of the presence of Parliamentary troops in her way, and when she received Charles's loving letters, full of comfort and tenderness, minimizing everything of which she warned him, Henrietta raged at the delay. At Stratford-upon-Avon she was met by Rupert, a Rupert so changed from the buoyant nephew who had cheered her loneliness in Holland that she hardly recognized him.

He was weatherbeaten, his great height accentuated by the flamboyant dress of the English cavaliers, and yet he looked so much a foreigner. . . There was a peremptory note in his voice and a tough, determined expression in his eyes when he spoke of Edgehill, describing the famous charge of his cavalry. And she detected a strange bitterness in his references to the King. Charles had refused to march on London; he was full of scruples and he detested the war he was fighting, talking of peace and negotiating while his enemies organized into a formidable striking force. He had no stomach for it, Rupert said harshly; when he heard of the death of men he knew, he was depressed for days.

"And they call him the Man of Blood," Henrietta exclaimed. "Good God, Rupert, does he expect to win without losing lives? What is he doing at Oxford?"

"Living in a dream," her nephew said. "Listening to a pack of fools who flatter him and tell him he is winning without effort. . . All he cares about is seeing you again. . . Forgive me, Madam, but I'm a professional soldier, not a gentleman amateur and I find it hard to stomach sometimes. If he had your spirit, the war would be over in a matter of months!"

She had worked miracles and Rupert knew it. The evidence of her energy was all around them in munitions, money and volunteers drawn from every country through which the Queen had passed. She lacked his uncle's gentleness of spirit, and he had never loved her as he loved Charles, still loved him in spite of what he regarded as his weakness, but Rupert shared Henrietta's suspicion of the English; he had been forced to fight against their jealousy and their inertia and their dislike of his rough, drunken troopers and their rowdy officers. They criticized him for pillaging their enemies as if he were a common mercenary, they criticized his tactics, accusing him of seeking his own glory, and most of all they hated him because he was successful.

"You must make the King listen," he urged her. "You must make him believe in Montrose and send him back to Scotland before it is too late. These Puritans have good generals too; Fairfax and Cromwell are the equal, if not better, than anyone we've got, except myself. If Scotland attacks us, we're lost!"

"Will he accept Montrose?" she asked him.

Rupert shrugged. "I doubt it. He's put his trust in the Covenanters and I doubt if he'll take Montrose's word. But he's mad if he doesn't. *I* trust Montrose and I'm a fair judge of men."

They left Stratford early in July, and on the thirteenth of the month the Queen and her army rode down into the leafy vale of Kineton, within clear view of the high ground of Edgehill which was pited with graves after the famous battle, and riding his splendid horse at the gallop to meet her, she recognized the figure of the King at the head of a brilliant escort which stretched as far as the eye could see.

Oxford was decorated like a fairy city, the beauty of the lovely old grey colleges, the bright green lawns and gardens made Henrietta feel as if she had passed from reality into a dream. A dream which was full of the sound of cheers and music, with flowers spread under their horses' feet, garlands hanging from the houses, flags and draperies and loyal addresses. The sun was shining and the swords and breast-plates of the King's lifeguards blazed and glittered as if they were on fire. They rode at the head of the procession, the King's white horse and her bay mare walking side by side, with the King's hand on her bridle, and hundreds of happy faces, full of affection and enthusiasm surrounding them, wishing them well.

She had not forgotten that she loved him, she had perhaps forgotten how much he loved her until she came face to face with him and saw his eyes and felt his hands tremble when he touched her, lifting her down from the saddle for a brief embrace before they formed up for the state entry into Oxford. A few words had passed between them, a quick whispering, confused and as unsteady as their hold upon each other, and in both of them, their senses leapt at the contact of hands and lips, and Charles brought her to his Royalist capital as if she were a bride. And like a bride she was conducted to her lodgings in the Wardens' House at Merton, and then at last she was alone with him with the sounds of the cheering crowds outside her windows and the sun streaming through the mullioned windows into the lovely old room.

For some moments he held her to him without speaking. His embrace was so hard that it hurt her and she rejoiced in the pain. She felt the tenseness in his muscles and the passion of his longing for her swept over him, denying him words, making his hands rough and impatient as they stripped off her green velvet cloak and broke the fastenings of her dress.

When he laid his head upon her shoulder she put her arms around him and began to kiss him.

"We should not," he whispered, "My darling love, my life . . . this is no time to give you a child. . . Send me away, before it's too late."

She did not answer, and he did not ask again. The empty chill which had settled on his heart from the moment they separated, the months of loneliness, the sleepless nights when he could not escape the anxieties of war—everything melted in that moment like snow in sunlight. His passion was a return to life, a reawakening as if for long months he had been dead.

Later they slept like children and the shadows in the room grew longer and the bed became a pool of darkness.

"I am disturbed, but not alarmed," Charles said firmly. His expression as he looked at Montrose was not hostile, he had been urged by Henrietta to receive the young man and listen to him and after hearing all he had to tell him of the negotiations between Parliament's agents and the Scottish Covenanters, the King merely shook his head and refused to be panicked.

"I am well aware that Parliament has sent Commissioners to Edinburgh," he continued. "I am also aware that their object is to persuade the Scottish people to join them in this rebellion. But I am perfectly sure they won't succeed."

"But why, Sire?" Montrose said. "How can you trust Argyle and the others when I have just come from them and I tell you that I *know* they will turn on you if they can get their price from your Parliament? And it's not a price that you would ever be willing to pay them."

"They gave their word to me," Charles insisted. "I spent months in Edinburgh and I came to know them all well. I honoured them and granted their wishes for a Scottish Parliament and a Scottish Kirk Settlement. I left them content, my Lord, and I left them bound to me by their word of honour. I am a Scot myself, I must remind you, and I know they will not break it."

"Saving the Earl of Montrose," Rupert interrupted fiercely. "I can't see your reasons for trusting them, Sire. They began this rebellion when they first marched into England five years ago! They set themselves and their damned religion above any oaths of fealty to you . . . And they're not over-careful of their Kings, if I remember the history of your house—my house—for my mother's a Stuart. Is that not true, Montrose?"

"True beyond doubt," was the answer. "They are not King's men, any of them. Argyle, Leslie, Leven, none of them have any love for your Majesty or what your Majesty represents. We're an ancient people, Sire, and, as Prince Rupert says, not over careful of our Kings. Where the clans flourish, no one man can hold any man's heart. They are set upon spreading their version of the Word of God and spreading the glory of Scotland with it at the expanse of England. There's nought to be got from you now, and they know it. Argyle will sell you, Sire, and the Parliament will pay his price. On my knees," he said desperately, "I beg of you to let me go home and rouse the loyalists and have an army there, ready to fight the Covenant and keep them occupied in Scotland."

Charles shook his head. "Nothing would bring them over the Border quicker than any such attempt," he said. "They would feel that I had betrayed them and they would be right. My Lord, come closer, please."

Montrose advanced to the steps of the dais where Charles was sitting in the room in Christ Church College which he used for audiences. Henrietta was right, he liked and trusted the young Scottish peer, and he gave him his hand and smiled at him with kindness.

"You are a soldier," he said gently, "Your fame has spread before you, and as a fellow Scot I know the strain. But I cannot let you be both brave and rash on my account. Not till I see the need more clearly than I do today. But this I promise you—if the time comes when I must send a general into Scotland, it will be Montrose."

"I thank you, Sire," Montrose said quietly. "With your permission I'll remain with you until that time."

The King dismissed him and Rupert followed and ran after him, his steps echoing down the quiet stone corridor.

"I knew you'd fail," he said, "I told the Queen he wouldn't listen. Great God, what are we to do?"

"Wait," Montrose answered him. The two young men had fallen into step. "There's nothing else to do. When the Covenanters cross the border, I shall at least be ready to return and stir up what trouble I can against them."

Rupert looked at him. "And you've no word of complaint," he said slowly. "You make yourself an outlaw and come all the way across Scotland and England to warn the King and he won't listen, and you are content?"

"Years ago," Montrose said to him, "when I was scarcely twenty, I heard the King called a tyrant and a liar, and a servant of the Pope. I listened and I fought against him because of what I heard. And then I met him in Edinburgh, after the Covenant War was over. Can you imagine how I felt, Prince, when I saw the King and spoke to him for the first time, and knew that every word spoken against him was a lie? Argyle and the rest promised loyalty with their hands upon their hearts and he believed them. He believes them still."

"But why," Rupert raged, "why can't he realize that all men have a price if only you can find it out?"

"Because he hasn't one himself," Montrose replied. "He is the gentlest and noblest man that I have ever met, and whether he wins or loses, he is a King worth fighting for. I am content, Prince Rupert."

The summer days passed quickly. The queen arranged masques and theatricals and spent her time walking in the lovely gardens with the King. While the summer sun shone and the gallant soldiers left for a week or more to skirmish with the enemy, the King and his War Council formed a plan formulated by Rupert which seemed certain to bring him final victory before the end of the year. Three Royalist armies were to march upon London. Sir Ralph Hopton, leader of the Cavaliers in the West Country, was to come up through Hampshire, Newcastle would march down the Great North Road, and Rupert himself would join them through the Thames Valley.

When they met and surrounded London, Parliament would be cut off from all help and supplies. Gaiety and optimism infected the courtiers and the soldiers, and for the first time in countless months Charles found happiness again. He often marvelled at Henrietta's capacity for loving, and it was a love in which there was no thought for herself or for her children or for anything in the world but him. He lay in her arms night after night, sometimes talking until the dawn came, watching her sleep beside him, touching her face with grati-

tude and awe, wishing that there were anything worthy of
her devotion that he could give her. Often he found himself
brooding upon Henrietta's wrongs as a reason for continuing
the war which had become so abhorrent to him; he had
ceased to resent insults to himself. Even the cruel name his
enemies had given him, doubly cruel because it was so patently
unjust, the Man of Blood, became a joke between them, and
lost its bitterness.

In the autumn he rode out at the head of his army with
Rupert to intercept the Earl of Essex and his troops who were
marching towards London. He met them at Newbury and
among the leafy lanes, under trees turning gold and brown,
through hedges and ditches and across fields where the summer
crops had been harvested, he fought in what was the bloodiest
battle of the war, more bitter than the fierce cut and thrust
of Edgehill. Again Rupert's cavalry came sweeping down upon
the enemy. And at the end, when what was left of Essex's army
struggled on to London, unhindered by the Royalist troops who
were without the ammunition or the energy to fight, Charles
sat in an inn outside the town, watching one of his own commanders, Lord Caernarvon, dying from many wounds. Falkland, his Secretary of State and wisest friend, had died as a
prisoner of the enemy; the Earl of Sunderland, a brave and
gallant nobleman whom the King knew well, had fallen with
Caernarvon. And all around him yeomen and artisans, farm
boys and clerks, lay still and silent, bodies across bodies, some
wearing the scarlet Royalist scarf, others the orange sashes of
the Parliament. He sat by Caernarvon's bedside, watching the
fair young face contort with pain, and wiped the sweat away
from it with his own handkerchief. In the groans of a single
man, born to a life of power and riches, it seemed to Charles
that all those humble thousands who had died at Edgehill,
at Gloucester, Bristol, Hull and Newbury, called out to him
in their last agonies. They had given all they had for him
and there was nothing he could do for any of them except try
to ease the discomfort of one dying man. He closed Caernarvon's eyes himself and covered his face with his own handkerchief.

When he returned to Oxford, he found the city and the
Court rejoicing as if he had won a great victory, and Rupert
met him with the news that he had killed John Hampden in

a foray not far from Newbury. And in December, while Charles was preparing for Christmas with the Queen and his children, he heard that Pym, his greatest enemy, had died in London of a malignant tumour. Pym was dead, and the Cavaliers drank toasts to his eternal damnation and the confusion of the Parliament which they boasted would be suing for peace within the month now that they were leaderless. Hopes of a settlement rose high at Oxford, and Charles celebrated the great Christian feast of peace and joy in an atmosphere which was full of optimism.

But by the end of January all hope was gone. Parliament had found new leaders, and in that same month of January, a Scottish army of 20,000 men crossed into England to fight on the side of Parliament.

Charles was alone in his apartment at Christchurch College, sitting in front of the fire, with one of Henrietta's little dogs sleeping beside his chair. It was bitterly cold and the rain spattered against his windows and blew down the chimney on to the burning logs. It had rained for a week and he knew from despatches that his armies were bogged down in mud. The plan for a triple advance against London had failed. Hopton's West country troops had been diverted to help in the siege of Bristol and Gloucester, and Newcastle was blocked by the forces of Cromwell in the North and hurled back in Lincolnshire. The advance was halted and then abandoned, as Rupert pressed on to take Newark and join Newcastle in meeting the Scots invaders.

Montrose had warned him, and Montrose had been proved right. The men he had trusted and honoured in Edinburgh had betrayed him and ruined his chances of victory. And when at last he sent Montrose to Scotland to raise a Royalist army, he knew in his heart that it was already too late. He had been sitting in his chair, staring at the fire, absently leaning down to stroke the spaniel's head and feeling as if he were living in an evil dream. All he wanted was peace—not because he feared war or was afraid to die himself, but because the ruin and bloodshed was abhorrent to him and the loss of his friends was a personal blow which poisoned even the victories they won for him. He was brave, but his courage could not overcome a growing presentiment of defeat, and that presentiment never left him. It shadowed him night and day, making a mockery of his plans for the future, and he could see it reflected in the faces of his advisers. For the past two hours he had been thinking quietly, examining his conscience for any means by which he could avert final disaster without sacrificing his honour as a King. Then at last he rose and stretched wearily—he rang his bell for Parry.

He picked up the spaniel and stroked it gently.

"Mutz," he said, "Mutz, there is no way out. A King cannot turn back. I was a fool to think of it. Ah, Parry, be good enough to ask Her Majesty to come to me."

The valet bowed. "Will you have supper served here, Sire? The Queen has already eaten."

"I had forgotten how late it was," the King said. "But I'm not hungry. Bring some wine."

Parry hesitated. "You should eat, Sire," he said, "you've scarcely touched anything all day."

"Hunger is not what ails me," Charles kissed the dog, which whimpered excitedly and nuzzled his cheek. "Tell the Queen that Mutzi and I are lonely and low-spirited, we need her company."

He listened for Henrietta's step and hurried to open the door for her himself. They kissed without speaking and with his arm round her shoulders Charles led her to his chair and settled her into it, placing the dog on her lap, and lifted her feet on to a little stool. Henrietta was nearly five months pregnant.

"How are you feeling?" he asked her. She had begun to be sick and listless and complained of pains in her side.

"Better this evening," she smiled at him, forgetting her own discomfort. He looked so pale and tired, and they had received nothing but bad news for days.

"I wanted to be alone with you," he said. "That's why I asked you to come to me. Parry said you'd eaten already, my love, so I thought you must be feeling better. Is Mutz too heavy for you? Here, let me put him down . . ."

"What have you been doing, shut up here alone? You look so weary, my beloved. . ."

"Talking to Mutz, and thinking, sweetheart. Thinking what must be done for you."

"Nothing can be done for me," Henrietta said. "The doctor's say I shan't miscarry, and that staying in bed only

216

lowers my spirits. Don't worry about me, I'm well enough . . .
after all, dear heart, this child will be my ninth! "

"This is no time to have a child," he told her. "What happened was my fault. What you are suffering is the result of my
selfishness. I should never have touched you, rather than risk
giving you a child at such a time. If you had reproached me
afterwards I couldn't have borne it, but believe me, I never
cease reproaching myself! " She took his hands and held them
against her cheek.

"How could I reproach you? " she said softly. "These
months have been so happy—all the time I felt as if we had
somehow turned back time and were living again at Whitehall."

"What wonderful days those were," Charles said. "Four
months ago we seemed likely to win, and now——" he did not
finish the sentence and Henrietta held on tightly to his hands
and closed her eyes. She felt so weak and ill that her hopes
were sinking as low as his. She did not believe that Rupert
could win an impossible victory in the North, fighting both
Scots and Parliamentarians, or that Montrose could raise an
army in the Highlands and bring them sweeping down into
England in support of Charles. Defeat was in the air they
breathed—the shadowy room was heavy with it.

"I shall have to leave Oxford," Charles said at last. "Hopton
can't reach me, and Essex's army is re-forming. I daren't risk
an attack here."

"Where will we go? " she asked him.

"I shall take my forces and march to Rupert and Newcastle to engage the Scots. We must destroy Cromwell's
cavalry before they join with them."

The name of one obscure Roundhead general was on everyone's lips at Oxford. Essex was still the commander-in-chief but
the troopers who shattered Charles' forces, the strategist who
had hurled Newcastle's army back and turned them from
their advance on London, was Lieutenant-General Cromwell.

"That brute," Henrietta said. "They're all brutes, these
people, singing psalms and reading their bibles, and killing
wounded men. . . When must we leave here? Oh, Charles,"
she said suddenly, her eyes filling with tears, "I feel so safe
here, so protected . . . must we really leave? I don't know
how I am going to bear the travelling at the moment. . ."

"I know my darling," he said gently, "but its better for you now than later. And now you must listen to me and promise to be patient while I explain something. We cannot go together."

He put his finger to her lips. "No, do not interrupt me, sweetheart. You cannot possibly face a series of long marches through the country at this time of year, and I haven't enough men to leave you here in safety. I have thought very carefully, and I've decided to send you to Exeter with an escort. You must stay there until the child is born."

"But Exeter is almost the other end of England," Henrietta protested. "Charles, how can I make such a frightful journey in my present state? I'm hardly able to walk! Why can't you take me with you—I'll bear anything if only we can be together!"

"Because I am going to fight, and I shan't know where my next night's lodgings will be, or whether I'll have any lodging at all. Exeter is the safest place in England, guarded by Hopton's army and staunchly loyal. You'll be comfortable and safe there my darling, and if my cause is going well we can be reunited as soon as you're able to come to me."

She looked at him, the colour fading from her face, and after a moment she asked him, "And if things are worse, where must I go then?"

"You must go to France," Charles said gently. "You must go where I know you will be safe and cared for and beyond the reach of our enemies."

"No," Henrietta said suddenly. "No, I am not going to France or anywhere else and leaving you again. Very well, Charles, I will go to Exeter though I think it's unnecessary, and have the child, and then I insist on rejoining you *whatever* the situation—you must promise me that. I am not going to take refuge abroad and leave you to fight on alone. If anything happened to you I would rather die with you than live without you. . ."

Charles drew her close into his arms; he sensed the hysteria in her voice. It was too shrill and emphatic to be normal. He decided not to argue with her. He had no illusions about the length of the separation which was in front of them, or even that eventually it would take Henrietta across the Channel. He was in desperate straits, short of ammunition and supplies, his funds swallowed by the expenses of his army and his court. And he was facing the fresh Scottish troops, fully armed and equipped, and the well disciplined forces raised and trained by Cromwell, and these numbered many thousands.

As he comforted her, stroking her hair and agreeing that Exeter was the furthest she should go from him, Charles knew that Sir Ralph Hopton could not protect her for ever. His troops would be needed, and there were too few to spare an adequate force for the defence of a sick and pregnant woman who would make a most valuable hostage if she were captured. She was infinitely more precious to him than his eldest son and heir or his other sons and daughters—the most precious human being in the world, without whom he would lose his will to fight and live. Looking at her tenderly, smoothing the dark soft hair away from her face, Charles thought in agony how inexpressibly he loved her. Everything in that face, small and pointed, with the determined little chin and the big luminous eyes, now red and shining with tears, the generous mouth, the delicate bones and fine brow, everything he saw and touched was as familiar to him as his own reflection in a glass. And his knowledge of her, physical and mental and emotional, only increased the enormous satisfaction of his love.

For a moment, tortured beyond bearing by the coming separation, he hid his face in her hair and wept silently.

"No further than Exeter," she insisted, "promise me. . ."

"No further than Exeter," he whispered, his face averted from her. They spent the evening quietly by the fire, his arms round her shoulders and their hands entwined, talking of their daughter Mary, who was quite at home in Holland, though still too young to consummate her marriage, reminding each other of things in the past which were sweet and gay to remember. He talked of the wonderful masques she had given each New Year's Eve, staged in the Banqueting Hall at Whitehall until he decided the smoke of the torches would spoil his splendid Rubens ceiling. And so he had built a pavilion for her instead and hung the walls with cloth of gold and priceless tapestries. They talked of visits to the theatre, of concerts and receptions and picnics at Hampton Court and Oatlands after a morning's hunting. The past came back and sheltered them, and for those few hours they hid behind their memories.

When they talked of Rupert, it was of the gangling youth of sixteen who had come for a few weeks' visit and stayed for two years. They even talked of Buckingham, and laughed over their old quarrels.

That night Henrietta stayed in the King's apartments, and for the fourteen days that followed before she left him, neither she nor Charles mentioned Exeter again.

Chapter 12

APRIL the 18th was a beautiful day; the sun, which had hidden behind massed clouds of low driven rain for so many weary months, blazed down upon the little town of Abingdon, a few miles beyond Oxford, and the air was full of the bright scent of an English Spring. On the outskirts of the town, a train of carriages was moving slowly down the road to the Vale of the White Horse, escorted by a company of armed men under the command of Harry Jermyn, the Queen's staunch friend.

Jermyn was taking her first to Bath, where it was hoped that the curative waters would help her health, and then to the stronghold of Exeter, where her child would be born. Charles had said good-bye to her in private, wrapping rugs round her in the heavy coach because she complained of the cold, settling the cushions behind her head, kissing her limp hands and trying to warm them between his own.

She was so ill that he hoped the full significance of their parting had escaped her; she was wracked with pain, her limbs were swollen, and she cried continually. For a moment he held her and said the word which he had dreaded saying for so long, and when he said it, he stammered pitifully.

"Farewell, farewell, my dearest love . . ."

Her hands clung to him, suddenly strong, and twisted round his neck, and he heard her sobbing and felt her tears wet on his face.

"Farewell . . ."

Her ladies came crowding round the carriage and Charles stepped back, holding his head down to hide the anguish which reflected the hysterical cries coming from the coach. He spoke to Lady Newport as she climbed into it.

"If you love me, care for the Queen."

He went back to the small company of Cavaliers who waited a little distance from the procession, and mounted his horse. His two sons, the Prince of Wales and the Duke of York, had come with him from Oxford; they had said good-bye to their mother the evening before. Charles had wanted to part with her in a privacy that excluded even their children. As he watched, the carriages and their escorts began to move forward down the westward road, raising a screen of dust. He had seen her for the first time on a Spring morning nineteen years ago, a little, dark, pretty child of fifteen who was already his wife by proxy, and now, with a lifetime of experience and a family of children he had taken leave of her, and he watched the procession growing smaller until all trace of it was lost down the long road and nothing but the settling dust remained.

He turned his horse's head, and without speaking, rode slowly back to threatened Oxford.

On July 2nd, the two largest armies to be seen in England since the days of the Wars of the Roses, faced each other outside the City of York at a place called Marston Moor. Twenty-seven thousand Parliament troops, of which fourteen thousand were Scots Covenanters, confronted the eighteen thousand men who fought for the King that day, and by the end of it, when a full moon rose over the battlefield, four thousand of the King's men had fallen and the rest had fled or been taken prisoner. Oliver Cromwell's cavalry had charged headlong against Rupert, and for the first and last time in the war, Rupert had met his master. Nothing held before that charge; the Royalist horsemen wheeled and galloped back in hopeless confusion, and nothing Rupert could do by personal example rallied them again. By ten o'clock that night, the sound of a great hymn of thanksgiving rose over the silent ground, and from his tent at the rear, Oliver Cromwell stood up and sang in triumph with his men.

He had been shot in the neck, and the dirty bandage round his throat was soaked with blood; he seemed unconscious of pain, his heavy face was streaked with grime and sweat, and there were powder burns above his eyes where the shot which had wounded him had exploded within inches of his face. His Commander, the Earl of Manchester, was with him, so was the Covenant Commander, David Leslie, and they sang with him. God had smitten the unbeliever; Jehovah's wrath had levelled them like chaff, and lo—how were the mighty fallen! Thou-

sands of fanatics sang the victorious psalm of the armies of
Israel, and the powerful voice of Cromwell filled the tent.
Manchester did not finish the hymn. He was an obstinate and
rather stupid man and displaying his emotions embarrassed
him. He admired Cromwell, and secretly feared him; but in
moments like this, when the great General roared out his
vulgar hymns, he felt able to despise him a little. Gentlemen
did not behave like that. Gentlemen did not rejoice so crudely
over the defeat of a brave enemy, Manchester had seen their
bravery close to that day, and whatever he thought of Rupert,
the Prince had fought like a madman among his flying cavalry,
barely escaping capture.

There was something a little indecent about the ugly,
dishevelled man, with his bloody neck and scorched face, exult-
ing over the fallen at the top of his voice. And it was not a
musical voice either; Manchester had an appreciative ear,
and he winced. He glanced at Leslie who grimaced in sympathy.

"See how our armies rejoice!" Cromwell exclaimed. "Did
you ever hear soldiers show such a spirit at the end of such
fighting? By God, my Lord, if we gave the word now, they'd
march on to Worcester and rout the King himself."

"Let us hope that won't be necessary," Manchester said.
"After this defeat, with the North of England lost to him, the
King will undoubtedly negotiate for peace."

"Negotiate!" Cromwell's face darkened, and he pulled at
the sodden rag round his neck. "Negotiate on what grounds?
After a victory like this, are we going to waste time making
proposals to a defeated man, instead of pushing forward to
annihilate what forces he has left and insisting on complete
surrender! Come now, my Lord, you'll discourage Leslie here
with such talk as this . . . Tapworth," he shouted, "Tapworth,
we're thirsty, bring some beer! His personal servant came into
the tent with a jug and some mugs and Cromwell took
the first one and drank it down. In moments of excitement, he showed very bad manners towards his superiors in
rank.

"The King will never surrender unconditionally," Leslie
spoke for the first time. "And we in Scotland would not wish
to see him do so. We have always said, sir, that misguided as
he is, he's still the King. If he were killed or forced to flee

abroad, there could be no government without him, only anarchy. We have joined you to secure a right settlement, but that settlement includes King Charles."

"Your settlement includes much else that makes a mockery of what my men have done today," Cromwell said angrily. "We are fighting the King for liberty and freedom of conscience. There are many in this camp tonight who neither want his Church nor the Church as it stands in Scotland . . . what of them, what place is there for them in your scheme of governing with the King after he's been defeated?"

"No place," Manchester said curtly. "Whatever we make of this kingdom, there is no place for these sectaries and independants of yours, General, preaching every man's right to worship as he pleases. That is anarchy, and it's as unthinkable as the King's Roman leanings at their worst."

"I heartily agree with Manchester," Leslie said. "We came into this war to force the King to govern justly, and establish the true form of worship, under Parliament's control. You speak as if you hoped to destroy the King completely. That is not our wish."

"It is not the wish of the English people either," Manchester added. "You talk of the King's surrender as if he were an ordinary foe in battle. Let me tell you this, sir, if we beat the King ninety and nine times, he is still the King and so will his posterity be after him. If he beats us, we will all be hanged and our posterity will be slaves. That is the difference!"

For a moment Cromwell did not answer either of them. He poured out another mug of beer, and for the first time that day, his hand shook. When he did speak, his voice was very quiet.

"If this is so, my Lord, why did we ever take up arms? This is against fighting ever hereafter. If the King remains the King, in victory or defeat, what have we gained from fighting him?"

"A right settlement," Leslie answered.

"A monarchy under the guidance of Parliament," Manchester insisted. "And after today, we may see it before the year is out."

"We may," Cromwell said; his back was turned to them,

and he began unwinding the bandage from his neck. "We may, but I doubt it. If you'll excuse me now, I'll have this dressing changed."

They left him, and for a moment he stood with the bloody bandage in his hands. The tray with the jug of beer and the empty cups was on a stool in front of him, and suddenly he kicked it over.

A Monarchy: the King they had fought so bitterly for two years, would remain King at the end of it, even though he had been beaten to his knees. A King under the control of Parliament. And Cromwell lifted his head and laughed aloud. Parliament; he had sat in Parliament and listened to the clever talkers, and been duped into thinking that here was the means of saving England. But now, after two years' service in the army, after living and fighting with men who were ready to die for what they believed, Cromwell saw Parliament at its real value. Without realizing the transition, he had begun to think as a soldier and to adopt the contempt of the soldier for the civilian who talks while he fights.

If Parliament faltered and muddled and tried negotiating with the King, the tremendous victory he had won at Marston Moor would be cast away, like Rupert's triumph at Newark and the feats of his own cavalry in every past engagement. Neither side had won because they lost their opportunities. The King lost because he was poorer and facing armies twice his strength, because he had no Navy, and no central organization to weld his scattered forces into a fighting whole. And his army, the magnificent, fanatical machine he had made out of the few regiments given to him after Edgehill, would have won the battles only to have men like Manchester and that pompous Scot lose the peace.

He called out for his servant, and sat down to wait for the army surgeon to come and wash and dress his neck. Parliament must give up its control of his army. He used the word 'his' in his mind, and he meant it. The first thing to do was to oust Manchester and all the members of the Lords from any military command. The army could dispense with the noble Lords who treated the war as if it were some kind of gentlemanly game and came to the battlefield with their carriages and servants and installed themselves in the houses of the local gentry. But it could not dispense with him. And, in the end, the Generals and the army who had won the victory would be the force which dictated the peace.

When the surgeon had bathed his wound and re-bandaged it, Cromwell sat down to write an account of the battle to his brother-in-law; afterwards he knelt for an hour in concentrated prayer. He was up before dawn inspecting his troops.

On June 16th, the Queen gave birth to a daughter at Bedford House in Exeter. Her doctors were not concerned with the baby; it was surprisingly healthy. They gave it into the care of the midwife who had been sent over from France by Henrietta's sister-in-law, Queen Anne, and did what they could for the mother.

Henrietta was desperately ill; she was feverish and tortured with pains and swellings all over her body, and the doctors were already discussing who should send the King the news that his wife was dead. Even the old English doctor Mayerne, who had travelled all the way from London after a personal letter from the King, thought it unlikely that Henrietta would live for more than a few days. At first most of her symptoms were hysterical; he had written to reassure Charles that there was no need to worry, and at the time he had felt greater pity for the harrassed King fighting his enemies outside Oxford, than for the weeping, ailing woman. He was an old man who seldom practised, but he had fond memories of the King in the brilliant days of Whitehall, and the tragic cry of that letter, "Mayerne, if you have ever loved me, go to my wife," had brought him out of his retirement and sent him on the long and dangerous journey to the West Country.

But now, five days after the birth, he noted the signs of temperature and the racing pulse, and revised his opinion. By the end of the week it was common knowledge all over the city that Essex was marching on them with a large army to raze Exeter and capture the Queen.

She was propped up on a heap of pillows with a thin covering over her, for she complained of the heat and weight of the bedclothes and her face was flushed and damp with fever. It was a miracle to them all that she was still alive. She looked at the anxious faces round her, and dragged herself upright, catching hold of Mayerne's sleeve.

"What is it? Has something happened to the King? Mayerne, for the love of God, tell me!"

"Nothing has happened to His Majesty," the old man said gently. "All the news of him is good, Madam. He has evaded the enemy, and is bringing his army Westwards, towards Exeter."

"Thank God," Henrietta leant back and closed her eyes. "All that matters to me is his safety. Why are you all here, Mayerne? Have you come to tell me that I am going to die? I have known it for days and I am not afraid."

"Madam," he said at last, "you must prepare yourself. Your health is better than we hoped a few days past and now we cannot keep the news from you a moment longer. The Earl of Essex is marching on Exeter. The City Commander says he cannot hold it against such a force. You must decide what you are going to do, Madam, while there is still time. If you stay here, Exeter will fall and you will be captured. If you fly, you will almost certainly die on the way."

She did not answer for a moment. Essex was marching on Exeter, where Charles had assured her she would be safe . . .

"But you said the King was coming?" her voice quivered.

"And so he is, Madam; he knows what is threatening you and he has turned his army to the West to try and head them off. But he won't be in time. There is no doubt, no doubt at all. Essex will reach you first."

She lay very still, with her eyes closed, almost as if she were sleeping, and for a few moments they stood round the bed, looking uncomfortably at one another, watched by the sturdy French midwife who did not understand a word of English.

At last Henrietta opened her eyes, and Mayerne was surprised to see them flash with something like her old fiery spirit.

"I will never be captured. I will never live to be held hostage against the King. I will ask that wretch for a safe conduct and if he refuses, I will go without it. How long can I wait?"

"One week, Madam, and not a day longer. Agreed, gentlemen?" The two doctors nodded.

"Then we have a week to prepare. You needn't warn me that Essex will refuse, Mayerne, I know that already. I'm not counting on anything but flight."

"You realize what it may mean for you," he reminded her gently.

"I do. I have no illusions."

"And you cannot take the child. You will have to travel by night and run the risk of their advance patrols. A new-born baby would betray you. The Princess must be left behind."

"I know that too;" she turned away, biting at her lips to stop a fresh outburst of tears.

"The child can be hidden here; no one will denounce her. And what happens to me is not important. I would rather die a thousand times than live and be used to harm His Majesty. Thank you, gentlemen. Will you be good enough to leave me for a little while. I'm very tired. . ."

When they had gone, the midwife came to her; she was a plump, cheerful woman, the most skilled in her profession in the whole of France, and she was shocked by the plight of the Queen of England, who had borne her child in such uncomfortable conditions, with her husband and children far away. She bathed Henrietta's face with rose water, and gently brushed back the damp hair.

"Bring me the baby," Henrietta said.

"Not now, Madame," the midwife protested. "You are exhausted with all these people talking. You must sleep first."

"I can sleep later. Bring the baby here."

It was a small child, but the weight of it made her arms ache, she was so weak. She held it, moving the embroidered satin shawl away from its face, and kissed it.

"The King named her Henriette, even before she was born," she said. "She's a beautiful child, Péronne, and so healthy, isn't she? Look at her skin, it's like a rose. . ."

"Beautiful indeed, Madame," Madame Péronne smiled at them both. Few of her noble patients showed as much interest in their children as the Queen of England.

"And exactly like the King," Henrietta whispered. "Her hair has red lights, and her eyes are the same blue as his. They won't change, will they. . . They're too bright to change. . ."

The baby kicked in its coverings and began to cry. It was a loud and lusty cry. Henrietta held her tightly for a moment, and when she raised her head the midwife saw that she was crying bitterly.

"Take her," she said. "And don't let me see her again. In

a week from now I shall be leaving Exeter without her. If I see her or even hear her cry before I go, my heart will break."

Essex refused a safe conduct. If the Queen fell into his hands, he retorted, he would send her under guard to London to stand trial, where she would be in good company, for the vindictive and victorious Parliament had dragged the ageing and enfeebled Laud out of his prison in the Tower and arraigned him on a charge of treason.

Fifteen days after her child was born, Henrietta gave it into the care of Lady Dalkeith and escaped from Exeter in disguise. She was hardly well enough to walk; her fever continued and she hid for two days without food in a peasant's hut, under a heap of refuse, while the soldiers of Essex's army marched down the road outside. A week later she reached Falmouth on the Devon coast, carried in a. litter with a little company of faithful ladies and gentlemen who had met her on the way, and on July 14th she embarked on a Dutch ship and sailed through a bombardment of Parliament ships to the safety of France.

Those who had made that frightful journey with her spoke of her survival as a miracle. She had not died on the road, or in the wretched hovels which sheltered her, but her spirit was broken and her health was gone for ever. Her last letter to Charles, explaining why she had left him, reached him at Dartmoor a week later.

The words swam in front of him, distorted by the tears which filled his eyes and fell in drops upon the paper.

"I am giving you the strongest proof of my love that I can give. I am risking my life so that I may not hinder your affairs or prejudice your victory. If I die, believe that you will lose a person who has never been other than entirely yours——" The pen had trembled, blotting the last letters, and then been taken up again in an unsteady hand. "And who by her affection deserves that you should not forget her . . . Adieu, my love, may God protect you always, ever your faithful and devoted wife. . ."

Charles folded the letter and put it away in his coat. The Battle of Marston Moor had been lost; Newcastle's men had been annihilated, and Newcastle himself had fled to Holland. Rupert had been defeated, and his defeat was like an omen. He had marched his weary army into Devonshire in a desperate attempt to save Henrietta, but he had not been in time and she had gone. She had gone to France where she would be safe and well, and now he was free to continue the war without the fear of her death or capture to impede him. His mind was light of that insupportable burden, but now that she had truly left him, his heart was as heavy as if he had suffered the final defeat.

In November of that year, Cromwell rose in the House of Commons, in the place where he had sat silent for so many sessions while the great orators like Pym and Hampden spoke. The atmosphere was hostile, for the members were suspicious of the insignificant squire who had returned as a famous General. His voice filled the Chamber, resonant and full of fire and authority, and it was the voice of a preacher with an inflammatory power that made his words sweep over them like the exhortations of the ancient prophets. He denounced Manchester, and until that moment Manchester had been their favourite. He denounced the muddle and delay which had squandered the victories bought with the blood of thousands of honest men. Let those who sat in Lords and Commons prove their good faith, he demanded, as he was ready to do, and disarm all criticism of the army and the Commons, by resigning their commands. When he had finished, the Self-Denying-Ordinance was passed by a triumphant majority and the career of Manchester and all the moderates was in ruins.

The army was voted an independent force, generalled and officered by men outside the power of Parliament, guaranteed regular pay and identical training. By popular demand, Cromwell was pressed to defer his resignation, and with suitable humility he allowed them to persuade him to keep the power he had wrested from his rivals. Essex had been defeated by the King in Devonshire, and Essex had failed to seize the Queen. Essex retired into the shadows with Manchester and all those who might have wanted to keep the King in power after his defeat. And now the defeat was only a matter of months.

And in his dwindling Court at Oxford Charles waited for the final battle. The West of England still held out for him, and Rupert was in the North, gathering recruits and forming an army to replace the scattered hosts of Marston Moor. The months passed and the new year opened with preparations on both sides for what each knew would be the end for one and the beginning for the other. And in January, 1645, four years after the death of his friend Strafford, the seventy-year-old Archbishop Laud went out alone to die on the scaffold on Tower Hill.

" Your Majesty, Her Majesty the Queen and His Eminence the Cardinal will see you now. If you will be gracious enough to follow me. . ."

Madame La Flotte was a personal friend of the Queen of France, and she curtsied very low before the Queen of England who had come to beg an audience at the Louvre.

Henrietta was unable to walk without a stick; her spine had been wrenched in childbirth and her shoulders were not quite straight; she was haggard and haunted-looking, with prematurely grey hair. She had once been high-spirited and decidedly frivolous; now she was never seen to smile.

"I hope your health is better, Madam," the lady-in-waiting ventured to speak to her, presuming on her singular friendship with Queen Anne of France.

"I am as well as I shall ever be," Henrietta answered. "I owe my life to the care Queen Anne has taken of me since I came here as a miserable fugitive. She has a noble heart."

" She has suffered a great deal herself," La Flotte said under her breath. "Only now at last she is finding a little happiness. Two years ago she could not have succoured you, Madam. She had scarcely the right to order a few necessities for herself."

"I know how my sister-in-law was persecuted by my brother King Louis and by Cardinal Richelieu. She has survived her trials with fortitude and now fortune smiles on her as brightly as it once shone on me."

And not only fortune, but another Cardinal, and a very different Cardinal from the implacable genius who had ruled France for over twenty years until his death. Richelieu was dead, and his successor as Minister and confidant of the Crown was an Italian, Giulio Mazarin. But where Richelieu had been the King's man, Mazarin was the Queen's.

And Anne was Regent for her son, Louis XIV, and in a position to alter the outcome of the war which was blazing across the Channel. Kind, generous Anne, who had sent her money and a midwife when she was in such straits at Exeter. As she approached the entrance to Anne's private apartments Henrietta began to hope as she had not dared to do for months.

The French Queen's Cabinet was in fact a large room with a high frescoed ceiling, and an abundance of splendid furniture and hangings, and Queen Anne herself was sitting in a velvet chair under a canopy at the far end of it when Henrietta came into the room.

She rose and walked forward to meet her sister-in-law; the two women kissed, and Anne led her by the hand back to the chair. The figure of a man detached itself from the shadow behind that chair and moved down towards Henrietta, his scarlet robes sweeping the floor; they hid his feet and she thought suddenly that he moved as if he were gliding. It was not a man's approach; it was as smooth as the dark handsome face which bowed over her hand. He had very black eyes and they shone at her with velvety softness. There was no reason in the world why that look should make Henrietta feel suddenly very tired and weak and unsupported, and wish that her green velvet dress were not three seasons out of fashion.

By contrast, the Queen of France was almost too effusive. She held her sister-in-law at arm's length and exclaimed indignantly at the ravages of travelling and worry that she saw. And under Anne's examination, Henrietta looked at her with envy. She had always been beautiful; she could remember Buckingham standing rooted in front of Anne at a reception in Paris, and saying out loud that he beheld a goddess rather than a mortal woman. It was a fiery beauty, full of colour and statuesque proportions, and there was not a grey light in her red hair or a line on her smooth and handsome face. And yet she was a cold woman, cold and strained and lacking in natural charm. Henrietta felt grateful to her for her kindnesses, and they were many, but she also sensed reserve. She also imagined that while they were exchanging trivialities about their health and Henrietta's dreadful experience and escape, that the Queen glanced once or twice towards the Cardinal who stood a few paces behind them and did not speak a word.

"My poor sister," Anne said, "How terribly you've suffered. I can't bear to think of it. Come, Cardinal, doesn't it horrify you?" He moved beside her, and to Henrietta's surprise he put his hand on top of the Queen's chair. His enormous ruby ring shone in the candlelight.

"Thank God your trials are over, Madam," he said gently. His French was heavily accented. Henrietta stiffened; this was her opportunity, and she knew by instinct that unless she came to the point, her interview would be over and she would not have been encouraged to say anything. Neither Anne nor the Cardinal had asked for news of Charles.

"My trials have just begun, Eminence," she said. "I may be safe under your kind protection, but my heart and soul are with my husband. And you must believe me when I say that only my love for him brings me to beg still greater favours from you."

"My dear sister," Anne said uncertainly, "what can we do?"

"Send money and men to England!" Henrietta begged her. "The King is in desperate need of help. In his last letter he told me that the rebels have reorganized their army, and that it outnumbers him by two or three to one. He has no resources left, he has pawned and borrowed on everything he possessed and I haven't a jewel left to sell for him. Madam, I beg of you, think of his position! How can he arm and feed and pay his troops without money."

"Has no one subscribed for him?" Mazarin asked gently.

"Everyone," Henrietta spoke up sharply in defence of the hundreds of loyal peers and gentlemen who had beggared themselves to help the King.

"Everyone has given to him with the utmost generosity. Lord Newcastle alone gave him three million pounds since the beginning of the war. There's nothing left to give."

"Wars are expensive," the Cardinal remarked. "As we know to our cost, having just fought one with Spain. Our own finances are sadly low. I cannot help feeling that the King of England would be wise to treat with his Parliament if he is really as hard pressed as you say."

"That's good advice," Queen Anne interrupted quickly before Henrietta had time to answer. "After three years of war, both sides must be ready to compromise."

"The King will never compromise," Henrietta's voice trembled; she was afraid that she was going to demean herself by bursting into tears in front of them. "If he loses, God only knows what will be done with him. . . Madam, Madam, I beseech you, think if your own son were in peril from a treacherous revolt, bereft of men and money, separated even from those who love him best in the world—think if it were him and yourself, and give me one word of hope to send to my husband!"

"What use are words?" Anne said slowly.

She avoided the strained and desperate face of the unhappy woman and looked up at Mazarin for guidance. He had warned her to delay seeing Henrietta, impressing upon her in his gentle yet insistent way how awkward it would be to refuse her pleas for help. Because she was certain to make them, and it was cruel to disillusion her by explaining that France had no intention of wasting men and money to put back on his throne a King who was incapable of keeping it— as incapable as he was of winning this extremely foolish war. He had made Charles seem so inept and ridiculous that she had lost her sympathy for him; now it had returned and to her miserable embarrassment, the proud and noble Henrietta, daughter of Henri le Grand, Princess of the Blood and Queen of the three Kingdoms over the Channel, left her chair and fell on her knees in front of her and Mazarin.

"I kneel and implore you both," Henrietta was weeping as she tried to speak. "Send help to my husband before it is too late. If he is defeated he will never run away. And if they capture him, they will kill him. I ask you, my Lord Cardinal, use your influence with the Queen and her Council, in the name of a brave and noble King!"

Anne rose from her chair and whispered quickly to him. "Giulio, Giulio, can't we do something. . ." Out of sight of the Queen of England, who remained on her knees, Mazarin put out his hand and pressed Anne's shoulder. "No," he murmured. "You have promised to trust me. . . I know what is best. . ."

Courteously he lifted Henrietta to her feet.

"Hope, Madam, and pray to the Almighty Power. It is unfortunate that you come to France at a time when we are in no position to help you or the King of England. France is impoverished by many wars and unstable after the misgovernment of the late Cardinal. Believe me, my heart bleeds for you and his Majesty King Charles. And now, if you will pardon us, Her Majesty is expected in Council."

Henrietta stood in front of them, and her sad pinched face was suddenly hard. She glanced at the tall, handsome woman in her rich blue dress, diamonds worth millions of livres sparkling round her neck and wrists, and, as she looked at her, the Queen of France avoided her eyes and turned away. She was ashamed and embarrassed, but there was nothing she could do. It was suddenly obvious to Henrietta that Mazarin and not Anne had been conducting the audience. And as she looked at them both, her instincts, sharpened by suffering and anxiety to an abnormal pitch of sensitivity, told her that they were lovers. She straightened, and without speaking to Mazarin she turned to her sister-in-law. The reproach and the contempt in her eyes made Queen Anne flush to the roots of her fiery hair.

"I understand, Madam," Henrietta said. "I thank you for the shelter you have given me and all the proofs of your kindness. Forgive me for asking that you should extend your generosity to the person who is dearest to me in the whole world. I will take the Cardinal's advice and go and pray that God may help him in his mortal need. I see only too plainly that he has nothing to expect from France."

It was a very hot day. a heat haze shimmered over the flat plain of Broad Moor which stretched below the Royalist Army, and further still, drawn up in order of battle on rising ground, the sun set the armoured hosts of Parliament on fire. Seven thousand troops, mounted and on foot were waiting to fight for the King on that boiling June day in 1645, and fourteen thousand soldiers of Cromwell's New Model Army prepared to meet them across the baked and dusty plain.

Charles, mounted on his white horse, wiped the sweat from his face and stood in his saddle to watch Rupert's cavalry on his left flank, for Rupert was about to lead the attack.

The King had dined with his nephew the night before, after leaving Market Harborough with only a few hours to spare before the enemy caught up with them, and Rupert had chosen this spot, a few miles beyond the little town of Naseby, to halt and accept Cromwell's challenge. In spite of everything, Charles felt a resurgence of hope that morning. No aid was coming from France; Henrietta had admitted that, in a letter full of anguished apologies, but he had not expected any. His armies were depleted and undisciplined, but the hard core of loyalists and officers were with him still, and over the border Montrose had at last raised the Royal Standard in the Highlands and was routing the Covenanters of Argyll. If he could win today, with the genius of Rupert to help him, all was not yet lost. And now the battle was beginning. A shout rose, as it had done at Edgehill and Marston Moor and many other places where Englishmen had shed their blood over the past three years, and the word of command was taken up and passed down the troops of cavalry, and though there were only two thousand of them left, Rupert's horsemen stood in the saddle and yelled their battle-cry, and the roll and rumble of hundreds of horses hooves made the ground tremble.

Charles had chosen the word for the day, the day on which he knew he would either be finally defeated or restored to power. And because his rough Englishmen could not pronounce Henrietta's name in full, he had shortened and anglicized the last part of it. His army advanced upon Cromwell with the battle cry " Queen Mary! "

Rupert's big black horse was galloping ahead, flying over the rough ground, and behind him, racing in line abreast, the famous Cavalry rode down into the hollow of Broad Moor and passed up the hill like a wave. And like a wave, with the shocking impact of a mighty tide of steel and muscle, they smashed into Ireton's horses on the brow of the hill. Rupert himself killed and ran down so many men that he reined in to wait for the rest of his forces, and recognizing the commander of the retreating enemy, yelled to his men to capture and not kill him. For a moment Rupert paused, looking down on the dishevelled soldier in his breastplate and scarlet coat. Blood was seeping from beneath his steel helmet, and two of Rupert's cavalrymen were binding his arms behind his back.

" Your name," the Prince shouted at him.

" Colonel Ireton, Commander in the Parliament Army," the prisoner answered. Rupert levelled his sabre and brought it against the man's throat; Ireton remained standing where he was, and Rupert surprised him by laughing and putting his weapon up.

" I know your name and your fame," he said. " You're also

a brave man, sir, and for that reason I'll not cut you down as you have done to prisoners taken from me. Content yourself; you'll see your general before the day is out, and in the same sorry case as yourself. Unless he meets with me, because I'll surely kill him." He spurred his horse and in leaping forward, it knocked the helpless Ireton to the ground.

"Forward," Rupert's shout rallied his men from their business of riding down the fleeing stragglers. "Forward to Naseby!"

As the King's cavalry chased down the hidden side of the hill in pursuit of the enemy's baggage train, the Royalist infantry locked in a fierce struggle with the foot-soldiers of Thomas Fairfax. Sir Jacob Astley, the veteran of Edgehill, had been made a peer by Charles, and he fought the last battle of his life with the tactics used at Leipzig so many years ago, his pikemen in the centre, his musketeers supporting them on either side. He was sixty-six, and he led his forces into battle, crying the name of the Queen he had never liked, and by the miracle of courage and example, he thrust Fairfax back on his reserves. From his place on the hilltop, Charles turned excitedly to Lord Carnworth, a Scot and a professional soldier, and pointed to the wavering, retreating line of the enemy.

"God be praised," he said, and he thrust his glasses on him. "Look for yourself! Rupert has broken through, and Astley is pushing their infantry back. We're going to win, Carnworth, we're going to win the battle and the war!"

As he spoke, and the Scot focused the glass upon the confusion below them, the dark and glittering mass of Cromwell's cavalry detached itself from the right flank of the enemy, and began to trot down the hill. The trot became a canter, and as they approached the rise behind which the Royalist, Sir Marmaduke Langdale, and his horses waited, the canter broke into a furious gallop. It was a terrifying sight. They were not scattered or uneven like the best of Rupert's horses. They rode side by side in unbroken lines, perfectly disciplined, the sun blazing down upon their polished breastplates, racing across the uneven ground and breasting the hill in a most unnerving silence, and from that distance it was impossible to see if the great General Cromwell was riding in the first line of them or not. As Charles snatched the viewing glass back and strained to see through the thick dust, Cromwell's Ironsides met with Langdale's men, and broke through them as if they had burst a paper hoop. The sounds of fighting were all about Charles; his horse began to tremble and curvet nervously from side to side; he calmed it gently.

" Who is it, Sire? " Carnworth demanded. " Who's leading them? They've ridden Langdale into the ground. . ."

" General Cromwell," the King said, but the noise of shouts and firing was so close that the Scot could not hear him. " Cromwell," he repeated. " For the moment I had forgotten he was here in person."

There was no doubt about it now; officers passed him running for their lives, and as they passed, they shouted to him to ride off. Rupert had won, and old Lord Astley had driven Fairfax back, but Cromwell had driven his men down upon the cavalry protecting the King and his reserves, and having scattered them, he wheeled his troops and fell upon the infantry. The Royal Horseguards surrounded Charles; they were picked and seasoned cavalry, every man of whom was trained to fight to the death for the King. He turned to the commanders of the troop.

" There is the enemy! Follow me! " Carnworth heard him, and as Charles called out, he sprang forward and pulled his horse's head round.

" Will you go to your death? " he shouted. " Ride back, Sire, ride for your life! " He lashed the white horse with his own crop and the animal sprang forward away from Cromwell's advancing troopers, and as the King turned, struggling with his frantic mount, the Horseguards wheeled and followed him into retreat.

When Rupert returned with his cavalry, he found the Royalist army broken and fleeing, and the King carried away into the rear. Astley was captured and his infantry, including Rupert's famous Bluecoats, perished as bravely as the vanished host at Marston Moor. By the afternoon five thousand men were prisoners of the Parliament, and the King and what was left of his officers were fugitives. Cromwell declared that God's triumph was complete when he welcomed his friend Ireton back into his camp.

The King's camp was at their mercy, and Cromwell and Fairfax led their men in to take possession of it. It was deserted except for a few sentries who were quickly taken, and

Cromwell stood in the middle of the King's tent, watching Ireton and two other officers opening the boxes of letters and secret correspondence which the King had left behind. Colonel John Oakey, who had commanded the dragoons that morning, interrupted the General to tell him that numbers of women had been discovered in the camp and waiting in carriages outside it.

"We have no orders, General. What is to be done with them?"

Cromwell looked up at him and frowned. "Make haste with those boxes," he told Ireton. "They must be sent back to London for examination. Of what degree are these women, Oakey?"

"Prostitutes mostly. I think they must be Irish, General; no one can understand a word they speak. There are some Englishwomen of the same sort, and others are gentlewomen—wives and daughters of the officers. What must we do with them?"

"What is it Oliver?" Fairfax looked up from some of the papers he was reading and putting in order.

"Camp-followers," Cromwell explained. "We might have expected something of this sort in such a place. I'll deal with it; there's no need to disturb yourself."

Fairfax went back to his reading without further interest. He had found a letter from Henrietta to the King promising to ask for French troops. He did not even trouble to listen to Cromwell's orders concerning a few hundred useless women.

Cromwell turned to Oakey.

"This was the Lord's victory, and it must not be profaned by tolerating evil, in whatever shape it dwells. Have the Irish whores put to the sword and cut the noses off the rest. Then turn them loose. We've no provisions to waste on them."

For several hours on that bright afternoon Cromwell and Fairfax and their officers were disturbed at their business of collecting the King's private papers by the shrieks of the women their men were killing and mutilating with Godly fervour. The wretched Irishwomen, among whom were many Welsh, were murdered without exception, and by the evening the English whores and the ladies of rank who had followed their husbands to the battle were driven out into the empty countryside to die of their frightful wounds. Contented, exalted by the customary prayers and psalms of thanksgiving, Cromwell and his Commanding General Fairfax dined quietly and soberly in their quarters that evening.

Naseby had been the King's last battle. That little village in the heart of Midland England had given its name to the final encounter between Charles and his Parliament, and Charles had lost for ever. They stood and drank a toast to their victory, and Cromwell said slowly, "When I saw the enemy draw up and march in gallant order towards us today, and we a company of poor ignorant men . . ." He paused and his eyes shone with holy joy, fanatical, triumphant, prouder in its humility than the unforgivable sin of Lucifer. "Then," he went on, "then I had a great assurance of victory, because God would, by things which are not, bring to naught things that are. And God did it."

The Louvre was unoccupied that hot and baking summer a year after Naseby; the French Court had left Paris and gone to St. Germain to escape the heat, leaving behind them the Queen of England with a diminishing retinue of friends and refugees from England. Her quarters were sumptuous, but the splendid rooms were bare of furniture and the sound of her footsteps echoing in the vast Palace drove her to hide in a small portion of it where the sense of isolation was less painful. Her allowance was considered generous by the Cardinal, who frequently remarked that it would have to be cut down. France could not afford to support the homeless, bickering English nobility who came crowding across the Channel to live off the bounty of their exiled Queen. It was difficult enough to meet the expenses of Henrietta herself, without encouraging a tribe of foreign beggars. For a few months she had lived in the style due to her rank, with footmen and servants and lords and ladies in attendance, but now her household was a miserable collection of those who were too loyal to leave her and those who had no better place to go.

It was a sad little gathering in the middle of so much splendour and security, and the French nobility avoided it. And then, during the endless stifling weeks, made more unbearable by the total absence of news from England, Henrietta heard that her son, the Prince of Wales, had escaped and was on his way to join her in Paris.

It was nearly three years since she had seen him; when he came into the room, she hardly recognized the lank, sallow boy who hesitated shyly, staring at his mother as if she were a stranger. She had aged and she seemed even smaller than his memory of her; a little, thin woman in a bright red dress that was as old as their last meeting.

"My son!"

She ran to him with a cry, and falling on his knees he put his arms around her, and for a moment they embraced and Henrietta felt him tremble.

"You are not to do that," she said quickly, as if he were still the child she had left behind. "Princes do not weep. Get up, my son, and let me look at you."

He was very tall, and she searched in vain for anything that reminded her of Charles. It was difficult to believe that this dark-skinned, black-eyed youth with his irregular features and silent air was the son of the being she loved best in all the world. She had waited for him in a fever of excitement, imagining that some part of Charles would be restored to her through their eldest son, and she stepped back from him in disappointment.

"You have grown," she said. "You are a man now. Come and sit with me and let me present my household to you."

Harry Jermyn, the faithful steward, still as fat and cheerful as ever, and Mademoiselle Orpe, a new confidante whom the Prince had never seen before, saluted him and then withdrew. Mother and son were alone.

"Where is your father? I have been without news for nearly two months and I am almost out of my mind with anxiety!"

She had not asked him anything about himself; his news, his journey, even the dangers which might have threatened his escape to France—none of these things interested his mother, and he had not expected that they would. She had always loved his father best, and his father had always loved her. Their children had grown up with the feeling that their presence was almost accidental.

"He is in Newcastle," the Prince said. "He asked refuge of the Scottish army." He saw his mother's face flush and an expression of incredulous alarm crossed it, turning quickly to suspicion that her son must be mistaken.

"Refuge with the Scots! Refuge from what, in the name of God! I wish you wouldn't talk so wildly, Charles. Make yourself plain and don't distress me. . ."

"Refuge from the Army of the Parliament, Madam. After Naseby, Oxford was surrounded—our forces were defeated and scattered—all our strongholds reduced or surrendered. The King escaped from Oxford disguised as a servant with Ashburnham and Ollens to accompany him. He was fortunate to reach Newcastle and the Scots army, rather than fall into the hands of Cromwell. I myself left England for the same reason, at his express command."

For a moment Henrietta did not answer him; she was unaware of the dark, unhappy eyes of her son, or of the slight movement he made to take her trembling hands in his own and try and comfort her. He did not exist for her as a personality, only as a messenger of her beloved's shattering misfortune and increasing danger.

"What will they do with him," she said at last. "Is he a prisoner? Who is with him? Oh, my God, my God, why must we be separated now. . ?"

She walked up and down, weeping and exclaiming to herself, and her son sat with his head bent, unwilling to watch her futile, lonely grief, suffering himself because he had never been allowed to come close enough to her to offer what help and sympathy he could. He would have been just as useless to his father.

"What was the last you heard?" she said at last.

"I had a message from Ashburnham," the Prince answered. "He assured me that the King was well and treated with all honour by the Scots, and that he would soon be able to write to you direct as the Lords of the Commission were coming straight from Edinburgh to negotiate with him. Ashburnham said they'd ask him to swear to the Covenant, and if he did that, he'd be allowed to return with them to Scotland as a King in his full power again."

Henrietta came to him and stopped in front of his chair. "If your father takes their miserable Covenant oath, they will restore him? Is that what Ashburnham thinks?"

"Yes, Madam. And he must know; he was with the King day and night at Newcastle when some of the first of the Commissioners arrived."

242

"Then all is not lost!" she exclaimed. "Thank God, he has this chance at least!"

"Mother——" He came towards her and Henrietta looked at him in surprise.

"Mother, listen to me before you raise your hopes too high. Ashburnham said all that and more, but he also said my father had refused."

She stared at him and she seemed to shrink before his eyes; she looked so white and haggard that he pulled a chair up and put her into it.

"Refused?" It was a whisper, and the Prince knelt beside her and took one of her hands in his; in her confusion and collapse she felt a clumsy kiss upon it.

"He won't abandon the English Church and make it Presbyterian," the boy said. "That's what he told Lord Lothian who came to see him first. He'll do anything they wish except deny his faith. You know the King, you know he will never betray his religion, even to save himself. . ."

"Betray his religion!"

From agony she turned suddenly to blind and shaking rage; rage with the man she loved so desperately who was throwing his life and freedom away for what seemed to her a worthless quibble. "Religion! One form of heresy against another, that's all it is! And he sacrifices everything for that! His throne, our re-union, *your* inheritance. . . Merciful God, is there not one honest friend to tell him what he's doing?"

The Prince released her and said slowly, "It's not heresy to him, Madam. The King believes in his Church as strongly as you do in yours. He will not abandon it."

"And you," Henrietta said fiercely, "does it mean so much to you, that you can talk so glibly while your father puts himself in mortal danger!"

"No," her son answered. "I believe in nothing; not even God, when I think of how some men interpret Him. But I am not my father. I only wish I were."

"Oh, what is the use of talking to you," Henrietta turned away from him in despair. "You're only a child, how can you judge. . . I must talk to Jermyn; I must write to the King at once. . . Ring for Jermyn and go to your rooms. You must be tired, my son. Orpe will take you and see that you have everything you need. I will send for you later."

The Prince bowed and she kissed him absently on the cheek; he could sense that she was impatient at his presence in the room. And suddenly he was impatient too; so impatient and so hurt and angry that he could not wait to get away from her. She loved his father but she did not understand him in that fundamental which was obvious even to his children, with whom he had never been intimate. She would sit down and write a long impassioned letter, urging him to do the one thing of which he was incapable, as she had urged him years ago to sacrifice Strafford to his enemies.

But this time, Charles would not yield. He was alone and defeated. He was a prisoner of the Covenanters without any resource but the bargaining power of his own person, and without any strength but the strength of his own convictions. Henrietta had overcome them once when she persuaded him to abandon Strafford. She would not prevail again, though the consequence was the loss of his own life. His son knew it, though she did not, and when they met again that evening, there was a coolness between them which was to last for the rest of their lives.

"It is not our intention to force Your Majesty." The Earls of Lauderdale, Lothian and Hamilton were standing in the King's presence in the old City fortress at Newcastle. They had made many visits to that room in the months which had passed since he first came among them, and not one of them had ever seen him less serene than he was then. Lothian was their spokesman; he was a cold, aggressive man who had begun the negotiation with a violent prejudice against the King whose form of religion he detested and whose word he regarded as worthless. He was less arrogant and less hostile now in the face of that gentle, yet unswerving resistance to the demands he had made day after day without success. The King had never lost his temper or his patience; if Lothian had been less convinced of his sovereign's religious heresy, he would have described him as sustained by truly Christian fortitude.

"I repeat," he said, "that the Commissioners are not trying to force you. But if you refuse to sign the Covenant and declare yourself in agreement with the faith of your Scottish people, there is nothing we can do to help you."

"I understand your difficulty," Charles said quietly. "But

you must also appreciate mine. I have no wish to dictate the terms of conscience to any man, but I reserve the right of freedom for my own."

"And what of the Prayer Book," Lauderdale interrupted angrily. "What was that, Sire, but an attempt to interfere with the conscience of the nation!"

"I recognize that," the King answered. "And if it was a mistake, and I admit it, then you must also grant that I have paid for it. Paid dearly, if you consider my position now."

"Recriminations are no use at this time," Hamilton said quickly. "You put yourself under our protection, Sire, and we have given it. Now the time has come when that protection can't continue. The English Parliament has paid us the subsidy they promised for our troops and they are demanding our withdrawal. Our armies cannot stay another day on English soil without the risk of war. And they are demanding *you*, Sire, with the same threat."

"And you are going to give me to them, are you not?"

"No!" Lothian exploded, stung by the truth in that question. "No, never! Sign the Covenant—promise to establish the Presbyterian worship in all your kingdoms and you shall come back with us in triumph. And return with us at the head of an army before the year is out! That is all we ask of you!"

"And all I ask," Charles said, "is that you will trust me. I cannot sign that Oath without breaking a trust which is not mine to break. I will not promise to enforce upon my people something which I believe to be wrong. But I will promise to allow those who want to worship in this way full freedom to do so without hindrance from their King. And in return I ask of you that you will honour the trust I placed in you when I came here as a fugitive, and not sell me to men who are my enemies and will soon be yours. Cromwell does not want your Church in England, any more than he wants mine. He wants neither Bishops nor Church Assemblies, but licence for all his free thinkers to interpret the Bible as they think fit. You do not want that, my Lords, and nor do I. Nor, I suspect, do most of the people in England at this moment. But I have discussed this with you over and over again, and you must know your own peril as well as you seem to know mine."

"Your peril has been coming closer every day," Lothian said. "And now it is upon you. This will be our last meeting before an English garrison enters Newcastle, and then we cannot take you with us even if we would. When we leave, Sire, you will be left behind. That is not a threat, though you have accused me of making it before now. It is a fact. You cannot come back to Scotland with us unless you come on the terms I have laid before you. You cannot expect to come, and have every Catholic rebel in the Highlands marching on Edinburgh to release you."

"What Catholic rebels?" Charles asked quietly. "I ordered Montrose to disband and exile himself to please you, and he obeyed me. Huntly is in arms, but that is a private quarrel between Catholics and yourselves. I am not a Catholic. I am the Head of the Church of England, and what you are asking is what my Parliament asked before this war began. I give you the same answer as I gave them. I will never abandon my Church or my friends."

Charles stood up.

"That is your last word, Sire?" Lauderdale asked him.

"It is," the King said. "Except for one thing. How much are the English paying you?"

In spite of himself, Lauderdale, his implacable enemy and the rudest of his interrogators, hesitated and his heavy face flushed.

"Four hundred thousand pounds, Sire."

Charles smiled at them; it was a slight, wry smile, and for the first time he permitted his disgust and contempt to show in his eyes as he looked at them one after the other.

"As one Scotsman to another, my Lords, you've made a poor bargain. You sold me far too cheap."

They came and kissed his hand, Lauderdale, Lothian and Hamilton, who had been his friend, indeed his intimate in early years, and he said farewell to them with dignity. It was a dignity that brought tears to Hamilton's eyes; he tried to stammer an excuse, but Charles merely shook his head and repeated his dismissal. When the door closed, he heard the sentries posted outside saluting the Lords and then the metallic sound of their crossed pikes as they barred the entrance again. The light was fading fast, and he hesitated, wondering whether to ring for Parry, who had followed him to Newcastle, or draw the curtains himself. He went to the window and looked out on to the courtyard below. The rooms allotted to him were high up; too high for anything but a suicidal jump, and the troops marshalling below looked very small, as small as the men he had seen running and falling in battle. And now there would be no more battles.

Oxford had surrendered, and his nephew Rupert, the invincible General with whom he had felt such a sense of love and union, had laid down his arms and been permitted by the enemy to march out of the City with all the honours of war. He had sailed for France, and with him one of the saddest of Charles' memories, for in the stress and agony of that last year of conflict, he and Rupert had quarrelled, and it was a quarrel which had not really healed. He had quarrelled with Rupert because Rupert had surrendered Bristol, and Bristol was his only seaport and his last remaining stronghold of importance.

The breach which had opened between them had caused him bitter regret and self-reproach, but now they were separated, and it was unlikely that they would ever meet again.

Down below he watched the preparations for the Scots' departure. They had been taking place for the past week, all during the Christmas celebrations, when a horrible, forced atmosphere of gaiety among his attendants and his captors placed an intolerable strain upon his self-control. But greatest of all was the burden of Henrietta's letters to him.

For the first time in twenty years he had begun to dread the couriers who carried news from her, because the content of her letters was an unvarying demand that he should perjure himself and take the Covenant oath.

He could not make her understand that what she asked of him was quite impossible, and just before Christmas he had written her an angry, bitter letter, begging her to stop tormenting him. The Prince of Wales was with her, and Rupert had joined her too, and was adding his advice to hers. There was not one person to sustain him, even among those he loved most in the world. And by tomorrow, January 28th of the year 1647, the English troops would enter Newcastle and he would be in the hands of his mortal enemies.

'He pulled the curtains, closing out the last of the fading winter daylight, and rang his bell for Parry. When the valet came into the room, he found the King sitting by the fire; his eyes were closed and he was so quiet that Parry thought he was asleep. He began to light the candles, and the room filled with a soft light, a light that threw his moving shadow on the tapestried wall as he removed the King's papers and set out the table for his supper.

When he turned, Charles was sitting up and smiling at him.

"I thought you were resting, Sire. Forgive me, did I wake you?"

"No, Parry, I was not asleep. What time is it?"

"Almost five o'clock, Sire."

"It grows dark so early now," the King said. "When I have supped, I think I'll go to bed. The nights are cold here. Thank God we will be moving soon."

"Where will we go, Sire," Parry asked him.

"Somewhere in England, God knows where. We'll know more tomorrow when the Parliament garrison arrives."

Parry came to him, and going down upon one knee he knelt beside his master's chair.

"Then they are not taking you to Scotland?"

"No," Charles answered. "Four hunded thousand pounds is worth more to them than the person of their King. By tomorrow the last of them will be gone, and we will have new captors. They tell me Colonel Skippon will be in command."

"Who is Colonel Skippon?" Parry asked; "do you know him, Sire?"

"I know of him," Charles said quietly. "He is a personal friend of General Cromwell. Are you afraid, Parry?"

"Only for you," the valet answered, and his voice quavered. "Oh, God, Sire, if only there was anything that I could do to help you—I'd gladly give my life!"

"I know that," Charles said gently. "I'm very fortunate to have you Parry; whatever befalls, I know I have one friend. Will you stay with me to the end?"

The valet took his hand and kissed it.

"To the end of my life, Your Majesty!"

"Say rather," the King said, "To the end of mine. That is enough."

Chapter 13

T H E spring months of 1647 had been mild and by August the summer had come with a long spell of hot, dry weather which turned the roads to baking dust. It was so hot for the rest of that month that Cromwell gave orders to leave London at dawn to avoid travelling in the full heat of the July day. He rode out towards Hampton Court, taking the route worn flat by generations of courtiers who had gone seeking favours of the Kings of England and a troop of a hundred and fifty horsemen escorted him. Colonel Ireton, who had married his daughter Bridget, and was the General's closest friend, rode at his right.

The Army had won the war, but the reward it demanded was not one which the English people or the English Parliament sitting at Westminster felt inclined to grant. They wanted their pay, and they wanted it before disbandment. They also wanted laws passed guaranteeing the right of all the free-thinkers among them to worship God in their own way. They wanted yearly Parliaments elected by the people, and full voting rights for every adult male. They wanted liberties and innovations which were as abhorrent to the middle classes as the restrictions once imposed upon them by the defeated King. And when they were refused and ordered to disband, they mutinied and Cromwell had taken the King into Army custody. He was then on his way to Hampton Court to offer him a separate peace.

His mood was optimistic that morning: Ireton heard him humming as they rode up to the splendid gates of Hampton Court, and the soldiers on guard swung back the heavy wrought-iron gates and let the cavalcade pass.

They crossed the stone bridge over the moat and Cromwell came out into the bright sunshine of the outer Base Court, walking his horse carefully over the cobbled ground. Colonel Skippon met him at the entrance to the Palace and saluted.

"Your servant, General. Yours, Colonel Ireton. The King is expecting you."

Cromwell dismounted and wiped the sweat from his face with his sleeve.

"Have the men water their horses and see that they are given food and drink. Colonel Ireton and I are in need of a wash and something to take the dust out of our mouths before we see anybody. Tell the King I will wait on him in an hour. Come, Ireton."

They looked round their quarters in the Palace with interest; the lofty rooms with their magnificent painted ceilings and delicate furniture were very different from the rough bivouacs of the battlefield and the homely house at Ely where Cromwell had spent the years before the war.

"So this is how Princes live," Ireton remarked, sitting on a spindle-legged chair with a bump that nearly broke it under him. "There's enough of value in this room alone to give my troop six months' back pay!"

"Hampton Court was built by a Cardinal," Cromwell reminded him, "and a King took it from him as we have taken it from the King. Don't lose your common sense, my son. A few chairs and a bed with hangings on it don't alter the fact that the King is our prisoner. And be civil when you meet him. He may be your King and mine in more than name if all goes well today!"

Ireton looked at his father-in-law, the commander in battle whom he idolized, the profoundly religious man whose fervour made him almost a saint in the eyes of his family, and could not restrain his astonishment at this complete revaluation.

"I see the necessity for treating with him," he said slowly, "but I don't like it and I don't expect to hear you speak as if you do! You've talked of a Republic for as long as I've known you—you've said over and over that Kings and Bishops and these trappings are no part of a Godly community! Wasn't it you who said if we'd fought this war to restore the King, we'd have fought it for nothing? For God's sake, father-in-law, tell me how far you mean to go with this thing before I come face to face with him!"

Cromwell had been lying outstretched on a large fourposter bed; they were in the Prince of Wales's Cabinet, and the motif of the three plumes was embroidered on the canopy above his head. He had been squinting up at them while he talked to Ireton. Now he sat up and swung his legs over the side, pushing aside the table on which there was the remains of the meal they had eaten.

"What I said at the time was what seemed right at the time," he answered. "I said we must depose the King and live in Christian freedom with each other. I never said we must depose him in order to live under the tyranny of Parliament and have a Presbyterian Church established on the Scottish model! That's not the Lord's intention! Better the King, chastened and powerless, ready to be converted to the truth, with the power of the army to govern, than no King, and those rogues at Westminster dissipating all the benefits we've won. Listen to me. Have you forgotten how they've treated us? Have you forgotten the men denied their pay and ordered to lay down their arms and go back to their homes with nothing to show for their service but promises? And when they wouldn't, what became of the promises but they turned into threats!"

He stood up and began fastening the collar of his hide jacket, stooping to a polished steel mirror to see himself. His face was red with anger and the small green eyes were so narrow that they seemed as if they were shut.

"By God, they shan't cheat the Army! I'd rather put up a thousand dummy Kings than lie down meekly under that pack of aldermen and turncoat aristocrats who see their chance to be rid of us and go their own way now that the fighting's done for them! Button yourself, Ireton, and come. We're going to the King!"

Charles had been given the Royal suite of rooms on the inner courtyard; in spite of the fact that he had given his word not to escape, his captors decided that it was not safe to lodge him near the river, and he had no view except the fountain Courtyard, where a beautiful display of three tall jets rose in the stifling air and cooled the paved yard below his window. He had been the army's prisoner since January, and even before he knew of the friction between the soldiers and the Parliament, he had noticed with surprise how generous his captors had become. He was treated with every courtesy due to him; he was served and waited upon by Cromwell's stiff-faced soldiers as if he were in his own court at Whitehall,

251

allowed his Church of England chaplains to comfort him, and given access to his correspondence. And now the army had sent his three children, so long the hostages of Parliament, on a day's visit to him. It was a gesture that totally disarmed him —even when he heard from Skippon, who had become quite talkative since Newcastle, that there was mutiny among the troops and fierce quarrels between Cromwell, Fairfax, and the civilian leaders of Parliament, Charles felt inclined to accept their kindness without suspecting that it had a motive. And now Skippon had taken his children away and told him that Cromwell himself was at Hampton Court and on his way to see him. The young Princes, James and Henry, had distressed him by crying and kicking out at the soldiers who led them away, but his daughter Elizabeth had curtsied to him with a tragically unchildlike dignity and whispered that she would be brave and pray for him.

He turned to Skippon as the door closed behind them, and said quietly, " Shall I need the child's prayers, Colonel? What does your General want with me? "

" The General comes in friendship, Sire," Skippon answered. He was a fond father and husband himself and he was acutely embarrassed by the scene. He had been constantly embarrassed by the King since his arrival at Newcastle; he was unprepared for the gentleness and resignation with which the King surrendered himself to his custody. He did not for a moment confuse that gentleness with personal fear. Whatever the King's crimes, and his Puritan upbringing had taught him that they were black indeed, he was a brave man himself and he knew another brave man when he met one. If he wasn't soon relieved of this particular post, he was afraid he might begin to like his enemy.

" You'll find a more generous foe in the General than any of those dogs at Westminster," he said. His feelings overcame him again, and he added a piece of personal advice. " For your own sake, Sire, try to find some agreement with him." Then he turned away quickly and left the King alone.

A few moments later Charles and the man who had driven him from his throne came face to face. He had seen many Roundhead prisoners and at first there was little to distinguish the big ugly man from any of them. He was plainly dressed in a buff jacket and breastplate, with a heavy cavalry sword buckled at his side and his helmet under his left arm; a second officer wearing the same uniform and also uncovered, followed a few steps behind him.

"Your Majesty."

To Charles's surprise, the General came up to him and went down on one knee. He took the King's hand, but did not kiss it. He stood up and said, "May I present my son-in-law, Colonel Ireton?"

The younger man moved towards Charles, and Cromwell snapped at him without looking round. "Kneel to the King, sir!"

Ireton knelt and Charles spared them both embarrassment by not giving the officer his hand.

"I have heard a great deal about you, General Cromwell, and about your Colonel, but I never thought that we should meet. As your King, I welcome you, and as your prisoner I thank you for the courtesy which has been shown me since I came into your hands. Rise, if you please."

Ireton had moved into the background, leaving the King and Cromwell facing each other. He had no idea that the King was such a slight man, or would look so young. He was impeccably dressed in dark blue velvet, with the Star of the Garter blazing on his left shoulder. Ireton turned away from him and stared out of the window; he felt confused and disgusted at the manner in which Cromwell had abased them both before their enemy.

"I am gratified that you have no cause of complaint against the army, Sire," Cromwell said.

"If I have," the King answered, "it is only that thanks to them I am your prisoner, instead of you being mine. I must commend Colonel Skippon—he has been a very gentlemanly gaoler."

"Skippon is devoted to me," Cromwell said. "I chose him because I knew I could rely upon him to carry out my orders. You must forgive Colonel Ireton and myself for this intrusion and for any ignorance we may show of protocol; we are plain men, Sire, and not used to speaking to the King. Is it permitted to sit?"

"No," Charles said quietly, "it is not permitted, General. Whatever you have to say to me must be said standing."

"As you wish," Cromwell's eyes flickered. Charles could not

253

be sure whether the expression in them was angry or merely surprised.

"Now, General, what do you want of me?"

"Peace," Cromwell said. "Peace and agreement with the army. I am fully empowered to discuss terms with you and reach a settlement as quickly as possible. That is the desire of Lord Fairfax and all the officers of the army."

"When you speak of the army," Charles remarked, "I presume you mean Parliament as well?"

"No," Cromwell answered, "I do not. Parliament has no part in this discussion. You are the army's prisoner, Sire, and the army alone has the right to make a treaty with you. I advise you not to look to Parliament."

"I am unlikely to do that," Charles spoke with some asperity. "I have little reason to love or trust that particular assembly. I am hardly surprised that you too have found them out. What have they done to you, General? Shown their customary gratitude for services rendered by casting you off?"

"They tried," Cromwell said slowly. "They tried to cast off those who fought and won for them but they have found it's not so easily done. . . They have no use for us, Sire. And speaking plainly, they've little use for you, either. Whereas we may have, if we can settle the differences between us."

"You do indeed speak plainly, General." A slight flush rose in Charles' face but his voice was calm. "And on what terms might I be useful to you?"

"If you will agree to exercise your Royal authority under the protection of the army, we can force Parliament to grant our demands and establish the kind of government for which we fought. You are the King, Sire. As the law stands, you must assent to changes in the Constitution. If you agree to this, the army can see that they are put into effect. Without you, Parliament will continue bickering and trying to cheat us until another Civil War breaks out."

"What changes?" Charles said coldly. "What are you asking of me besides agreeing to a military dictatorship, General?"

"These, Sire." Cromwell called to Ireton who opened a despatch case, and handed him a sealed paper. He spread it on a table and stood back as the King examined it. It was a long document, setting forth the grievances of the army, its demands for pay, its demand for yearly Parliaments and adult suffrage, and its violent refusal of a Presbyterian Church system. It was signed by Fairfax as Commander-in-Chief with Cromwell's signature and those of other high-placed officers. It was so revolutionary that for a moment Charles could find nothing to say; he sensed the impatience of the two men, and after a moment Ireton interrupted him.

"These are the things for which we fought you," he said. "Freedom of conscience and the right of the people to govern their country as they think fit! If Parliament won't give us what we ask, then we'll take it!"

"One moment," Cromwell said quickly. "These are the terms of the first draft. Look at them carefully, Sire. Think what they mean. . . An end to the rule of Parliament—is that so hard for you to accept? The rejection of a system which you yourself started a war to abolish. Do you want the Church of Scotland to take root in England? Are they to burn and hang my men because they read the Bible and interpret it themselves? And what of the King's power? Isn't it better to uphold it with the sword than leave it at the mercy of the men at Westminster who don't know how to do anything with it but destroy it? For God's sake, Sire, keep a clear mind and think what this could mean to you."

"I am thinking," Charles said slowly. He folded the paper and handed it back to Ireton without looking at him. Of the two, he far preferred dealing with Cromwell.

"But all I see in this is anarchy. Religious anarchy and civil anarchy. It is impossible."

"Wait," Cromwell said patiently, "wait before you give an answer." He gave the paper to Ireton and said quietly, "Colonel, leave me alone with the King. That is an order, sir."

When they were alone he suddenly relaxed; he took a deep breath and dropped his helmet on to a chair, and looking straight at Charles he said in a friendly way, "That's better. I should never have brought him in the first place. He's a fine soldier and my own kin but he's a hothead. I nearly boxed his ear for the way he spoke to you. Now, Sire, let us come to this business. These are the rough terms as I said. I can use my own discretion how far they are to go or not, as you like. And if I cannot sit, may I suggest that you do?"

"General," the King said slowly, "you surprise me. You are not the man I imagined you to be at all."

Cromwell laughed. "'Nor are you, Sire. What did you expect? Horns on my head? I'm only a plain Englishman and a soldier. And I do best when I can speak freely."

"I expected someone like your son-in-law, but worse," the King said dryly. "I won't embarrass you by asking what you thought to find in me. What is the true meaning of this document?"

"The true meaning," Cromwell said seriously, "is this. The war was fought between those who wanted their rights and those who wanted yours. As it is now, neither have gained what they wanted. I built the army; I fashioned the best fighting force in the world out of poor working men, and I did it to achieve what I believe is God's Will for this country. I did not believe that the Divine Right of a King was part of God's Will. I don't believe it now. You see how honest I am being with you? Are you offended?"

"No," Charles answered him, "no General, honesty has never offended me. Continue."

"I believe, and my men believe with me, that we should have freedom to worship God in our own way, without the fear of your Bishops or Parliament's clergy bringing anyone before a court of heresy. Listen to me, Sire. The army will permit you to worship as you wish. I tried to show you that by sending your chaplains down here. The army won't ask to govern your conscience as long as you don't try to govern theirs. Parliament is trying to cheat us of our rights, and so we turn to you. Forgive and forget old grievances, I beg of you, and join with us!"

He was watching Charles intently while he spoke: he had got rid of Ireton and mellowed his approach because he had sensed very quickly that bombast would gain him nothing.

He was an expert judge of character, he could tell at first sight if a man had the makings of a commander in battle or was only fit for the ranks, and he immediately recognized courage and conviction in the King. Charles had heard the offer of the army's protection, and the added bribe of Parliament's overthrow without showing any sign of being tempted. And he had nothing to gain by refusing them, and what vestige of hope or freedom he possessed would certainly be lost. Cromwell remembered suddenly the story of the Scots' long siege against the King's religious beliefs, and he looked at him with something very close to respect. As if Charles understood what was passing in his mind, he said at last: "General, before we go further, there is something I must make you understand. Parliament will never grant what you ask, you know that and so do I. But with all the good will in the world I cannot grant it either. You do not believe in the Divine Right of the King. But I do. I believe it as firmly as you disbelieve. I would not keep any man standing in the presence of Charles Stuart. I would never permit him to sit in the presence of an anointed King. I am what God and my Coronation have made me. And I believe that the government of England does not rest with Parliament or with the army or with the common people of this land. I believe it rests with me alone, or with my son if I am dead. I believe that the true worship of God is to be found in the Established Church of which I am the head. What you call freedom I call anarchy, just as I call Presbyterianism heresy. I know very well what you are going to say. I have lost the war, I am a King without a throne, a King who is only useful as a means of bargaining. But I am not going to bargain, General. If the army is disillusioned with its masters at Westminster, they can always come to me. But they must come as subjects, obeying my authority as God intended it to be obeyed. I will not compromise, I cannot. If you are a man of principles yourself, you will have respect for mine and not press me any further."

They faced each other for a moment and neither of them spoke. "I do not believe that is your last word," Cromwell said at last. "I *am* a man of principles but I know that there are times when God requires them to be changed. I swore to overthrow you: I ruined men in my own party who spoke of restoring you after the war with limited powers. Now I come and offer you precisely that. Am I a traitor to my conscience then?" The question was almost a cry, the cry of a man whose faith was increasingly seduced and warped by power. "Am I a hypocrite while you are right? Is God so immutable that He cannot change his command to suit the changes in the battle? How can it be that I see compromise and you do not?"

"I do not know," the King said quietly. "I don't claim to know the mind of God, or hear His voice. I only know what He expects of me, and that I try to do."

"We both try," Cromwell said, and his voice was low. "If

you refuse me, I cannot protect you much longer. I don't expect that to alter your decision. It is a warning, not a threat. I'll leave you, Sire, and hope perhaps some change of heart may come to you. Officially I have no answer from you. I genuinely beg you to reconsider."

"I have a feeling," Charles said quietly, "that you mean that for my sake as well as your own. Believe me, General, I would be no good to you. I stand for a world which has no place in yours. The war may be over but I have no illusions about peace."

"Nor I," Cromwell answered. He looked at the King for a moment. He thought suddenly that Charles seemed very tired and low, not in the least exalted by the triumph of his faith. It was not so with Cromwell or his friends. They drew a fierce and often lyric strength from their beliefs. There was no parallel in his experience with this lonely, drawn man and his sad, reasoned faith.

He felt an extraordinary urge to cry, an urge he had almost forgotten since the war released his energies and liberated his restless soul from its depressed self examinations. It was such a long time since Cromwell had felt what he was feeling then, that he could hardly identify it. His face became dark with visible gloom, his bright eyes were dull under the overhanging brow. He took up his helmet and fastened it under his chin, and every gesture portrayed despair. But it was not only pity, that lost emotion, lost in a hundred battles and countless bloody acts, but despair for himself. The King had refused him, and he had refused more than the army's demands when he did so. He had refused Cromwell's last hope of staying his own ambitions. Now he had no defence against them, and though his disturbance was too complicated for him to understand its nature, his soul was sinking and from now on it would be lost.

"Farewell," he said, and he left the room without kneeling to the King or looking back. When a message reached him that the King had asked for one of his Chaplains to visit him that evening, he refused permission, and told Skippon to dismiss the Anglican clergy from the Palace.

The months of that long year 1647 had passed slowly for the Queen in her exile: long months of frustration, bickering and despair, interspersed by short periods of wild hope followed each other, and these fleeting illusions were the only thing that kept Henrietta from complete retirement from the world. By 1648 the shadows which had darkened England were creeping across France, threatening even that place of refuge and bringing angry mobs of people into the streets of Paris, shouting against the arbitrary rule of the Cardinal Mazarin and demanding their rights. As French internal troubles grew, Mazarin revenged himself upon the little court of unwelcome exiles by suspending the Queen of England's pension. Poverty threatened Henrietta, but the threat came at a time when she was buoyed up once again with hope that Charles might escape his captors and regain his throne. Early in the year she heard the fantastic news that Civil War had broken out again. Wales and Kent were in arms for the King, and Berwick and Carlisle captured by the Royalists. And then a message came from Scotland asking the Prince of Wales to lead an army over the Border and restore King Charles to the English throne. They too had had enough of Parliament's ineptitude.

Part of his mother's frustration was the apathy of the Prince of Wales. Even now, with Scotland in revolt against the power of the English army, with the scattered Royalists in England itself taking up arms again, the Prince only stood with his hands behind his back and hardly said a word. She turned to Rupert, who was with him, hoping that his aggressive spirit would be kindled.

"What chance of success is there? For pity's sake, Rupert, show a little optimism and perhaps my son will stop looking as if he has been defeated even before he sets out!"

"What do you want me to say, Madam?" Rupert asked her. Their old affectionate relationship had vanished, the stigma of his surrender of Bristol had never left him. He was guiltless in his own eyes and in the eyes of everyone who had been with him at the siege but guilty of criminal irresolution in Henrietta's view. On more than one occasion she had said so.

"I want you to tell me whether this counter-revolt can bring the King back to his throne," she said irritably.

"I could tell you that better if the King were at liberty and if the Scottish army had met Cromwell. Personally I don't hold

259

a high opinion of the Scots. I only hope the Prince isn't making a mistake when he goes out to join with Hamilton."

"Oh God!" she said, "oh God, what's happened to you, Rupert? Where is that great heart of yours? Not long ago you'd have leapt at the chance to go back and do battle for your uncle. Now you just stand there talking about those cursed Roundheads as if they were invincible. I wanted you to encourage the Prince, not frighten him!"

"The Prince is not frightened," Rupert retorted. "Nor am I, Madam, whatever people here say to the contrary!"

"If you mean Bristol . . ." Henrietta began and her voice was growing louder as she became more and more angry.

"I mean the whole of my service," Rupert shouted suddenly. "I mean everything I did to try and save my uncle, every battle I fought, every wound I received, every friend I lost! I gave up fighting for my brother to fight for the King and for you, and I'm living here in exile with you without a penny in my pockets or a future, and not one genuine friend among you all!"

"I am your friend," the Prince of Wales said suddenly. "I know what you did for my father and I shall love you and be grateful all my life. Don't trouble about me, mother. I'm not afraid to go to Scotland. I'm not afraid of anything except living out my life in this place. . ."

"Have you no thought for your father?" his mother said. "What about him, lying in prison without comfort or hope. Don't you think of him?"

"I think of little else," her son said slowly. The prison his mother mentioned was not Hampton Court; Charles had escaped from there in November 1647, after all hope of a settlement with the army was gone. According to reports reaching them in Paris, Cromwell himself had advised the King that he might be assassinated because the feeling of disappointment and resentment was so high among the soldiers. They had not heard of his escape until they heard that he was in another prison. Charles had fled to the coast and been forced to take refuge in Carisbrooke Castle on the Isle of Wight. The commander, Colonel Hammond, was a cousin of one of the Royal Chaplains, and without a ship to take him to safety or a place in which to hide, the King had followed the advice of his old friend Ashburnham, and taken refuge in the Castle. But Hammond had another relative besides the clergyman, and that relative was General Cromwell. He had proved himself more sectarian than secular by confining the King he had promised to protect and sending word of his capture to London.

"If only he had come to France," Henrietta said, as she had said a dozen times a day for the past six months. "If only someone had been there to advise him. . ."

"There wasn't time," Rupert said roughly. He was ashamed of his outburst to his aunt. Unfortunately they all lived so close and were so isolated from the general life of the Court, that they rubbed old sores open and flew at each other like starving dogs. This was exile indeed, poisonous, empty, soul-destroying exile. If Henrietta had not been able to think about Charles, write to him, write to others on his behalf and beg and borrow money for one abortive scheme after another, she would probably have died or entered a convent as a Carmelite. He was so sorry for the way he had spoken to her that he came up and put one powerful arm round her shoulders and kissed her contritely on the cheek.

"The King did the only thing he could. He escaped from Hampton Court and no proper arrangements had been made to get him away from England. He went to Carisbrooke because he couldn't wander the countryside until they hunted him down like a dog. At least he's safe and well—his letters are full of good spirits."

"That's only to try and cheer me," Henrietta said wretchedly. "Oh, Rupert, if only I were able to assure him that his son was coming to his rescue with an army. . . If only I dared write and tell him."

"You dare *not*," Rupert said quickly. "You know some of your letters have been intercepted because he's written asking why you haven't sent him any word. If his gaolers got the news of this uprising from you, they might well murder him and try and stop it. Aunt, you must promise me that you will never say a word until the thing is known generally!"

"I promise, I promise," Henrietta said. "Who would have thought those Judas Scots would tire of their English Puritan friends within twelve months—just think how galled they must feel when they remember that they sold my husband for a quarter of a million, and now they've such a need of him to keep their independence that they're mustering an army to set him free. That's irony, if you think of it! Oh, if there's a God in Heaven, He must punish them for what they did at Newcastle!"

She had entirely forgotten that their eldest son was sailing out at the end of the week to join forces with the men she had so bitterly described as Judas Scots. In her utter disregard for anything or anyone but the safety of Charles, she was callous even to her children. And there were three of them with her now. The thirteen-year-old Duke of York had escaped from the enemy's custody and made his way to France through Holland, and the last child of their long love, the poor abandoned baby born at Exeter was reunited with her mother, thank to the Countess of Dalkeith's daring escape with her. And as if the pretty, intelligent little girl were her last link with the man she loved so desperately, Henrietta spoilt and kissed and fussed over her, calling upon her bored attendants to agree that the little Princess was the image of her father. She had very little feeling for her sons at all.

"Just think," she said, and her anxious, care-worn face flushed with the excitement of her dream. "Just think if we were all sailing for England by the end of the year, and I were landing at Dover with the King waiting there to meet me! Twenty-five years ago I landed there as a bride. And I was so disagreeable with him!"

She turned to her son as if she had never told him the story before.

"He wore a very dusty coat I remember, and poor old Madame de St. George was furious. She thought I hadn't been properly received. I forgot the little speech I'd learnt by heart, and burst into tears; your father was so kind and gallant, he gave me his own handkerchief. . . I can see him now. He was so handsome I couldn't believe my good fortune."

Time and the agony of their four-year separation had affected Henrietta's memory of those early years until hardly any painful or disagreeable aspect of them remained. She had once acutely embarrassed the Prince of Wales by describing the day when Charles dismissed her attendants and had struggled furious with her by an open window, as if it were the most charming and romantic incident imaginable.

"When I think back on it"—Henrietta continued, releasing herself from Rupert's arm, "If I had only known what was in the future!"

"Don't distress yourself," Rupert begged her. "Remember one thing—you made the King the happiest man in the world. Few men have ever had such devotion as you gave him, and go on giving him."

"I'd give him my life," she said and her voice shook. "He is the only person in the world who really matters to me." She turned away from them and began to cry. "Please leave me," she said. "Please."

"Come," Rupert opened the door for his cousin.

"My father should have made terms with Cromwell," the Prince said. "He'd have been holding Court at Whitehall now, with all of us beside him. For once I agreed with my mother when she wrote and upbraided him for refusing. He wasn't asked to forswear his own Faith by taking the Covenant. They offered him freedom in return for toleration for themselves. Surely to God it would have been better to save something at the cost of a little honour than to keep his honour and lose all else!"

"To you, yes, because you would have kept your bargain, and to me too because I'd have broken it as soon as I felt strong enough. But not to your father. Your father would not have surrendered at Bristol! He will never surrender."

"If he doesn't," the Prince of Wales said slowly, "they'll kill him. That's why, whatever the odds against us, I must go back and try to save him. . . I wish you were coming with me, Rupert; I should feel that at least we had a chance. . ."

"You've a better chance without me," Rupert shrugged. "The English people are not over-fond of me; you know their name for me? The Devil's Prince. Go on to Scotland and take heart, Cousin. You are their future King; that's all the fame you need to win them. Who knows," he added, "if all goes well with you I may return."

"What will you do if I fail?" the Prince asked.

"I shall stay here and comfort your mother as best I can and train your brother up to take your place. I have no plans, no plans at all."

The meeting of the army commanders and their men at

Windsor on the 6th May, 1648, was like a scene from the Old Testament. Thousands of veterans were gathered for the purpose of prayer and self-examination and a renewal of that faith which had made them the most effective army in Europe. These men, with their dour, fervent faces, were not only representatives of the New Model Army but of the New Model Englishman, so far removed from the rough, unlettered, indulgent commoner of the past, with his liking for women and strong drink and a bawdy joke, that it was impossible to believe that Cromwell's soldiers were the sons and grandsons of the subjects of the great Elizabeth Tudor. There was no swearing, no licence, no camp-followers, no over-indulgence of any kind, and yet the atmosphere was as electric as if a storm were about to burst. The preachers went among them, exhorting them to penance and sacrifice, and every common soldier had the right to stand up and address his brethren. They sang their fierce hymns and exulted in the savage, vengeful God of the Old Testament, a God whom many of them believed had predestined some of his creatures to eternal punishment. Cromwell came among them, and Ireton with him, as penitents whose crime was negotiation with the King. Cromwell's army was not only Puritan but a large section of it were republicans, with a revolutionary view of how their country should be governed. And most of all, the men gathered at that meeting were fanatics of such a dangerous discontent, that had their great General not recanted, mutiny and anarchy would have resulted. Cromwell stood among them and solemnly accused himself.

"In seeking to do what was best for all, I have fallen into grave errors. The considerations of this world blinded mine eyes, and in defiance of my sacred duty, I talked with the unrighteous and kept company with the unclean . . ."

There was an angry roar at this overt reference to the King. Cromwell's powerful voice rose strongly and there was almost a break in it as he abased himself. "I came among you to confess my fault," he said at the top of his voice. "Nay, I glory in that confession, for by confessing it with humble sorrow, I am made whole again and party to the Lord's Council. But the victory His watchfulness procured for us is wasted, washed down the endless gutters of talk and lies and broken promises. And now, my brothers, the enemy rise up to smite us and replace Nebuchadnezzar on the throne from which our faith has toppled him!"

He waited and his audience shouted their approval. The sound was full of hate and fury. "We are at war again," Cromwell roared at them, "the enemy arises in Wales and breaks out in Kent and from over the Border the armies of Scotland are on the march to put the King back in power over us. They fear us, as the weapon of the Lord. They seek refuge with the King, as a cloak for their wickedness and their intent to persecute and regiment the faithful into their abominable form of worship. But I say to you that they and he shall not win victory over us! I say we will gird ourselves and like the Israelites of old, go out and with the Lord's help, smite these Amalekites and when they are smitten—" He took a deep breath—"then we shall call that Man of Blood to a most terrible accounting!"

The rest of his speech was lost—the troops were on their feet cheering and singing, and Ireton came up to him and whispered.

"When you have finished, Lord Fairfax wants to speak to you."

"I have done now," Cromwell answered. He was sweating with the effort of that extempore performance, and he searched in vain for the handkerchief a gentleman was expected to carry.

"It was well done," Ireton congratulated him. "I thank God on my knees to see this change of heart in you again."

"The Lord enlightened me," Cromwell muttered. "May He forgive me for the months I wasted trying to reconcile Him with Mammon."

He felt very tired, and yet there was this wonderful feeling of relief which was almost a feeling of well-being. Parliament was dithering with fright, faced by the upsurge of Royalism among the ordinary people who were not of the Puritan belief, and threatened now by Scotland that unless they reached agreement with the King and restored him, the Scots would establish him by force of arms, Parliament had buried its quarrelling and jealousy and called on the army to protect them. And the King himself was trapped at Carisbrooke.

But apart from Cromwell's own fanatics, most of the ordinary, uncommitted English people were Royalists who hated

the muddle and uncertainties of life without the King. They
wanted him back and they had challenged Cromwell and his
army; it was a challenge that filled the General with such
exultation that he could hardly restrain himself. Peace had not
really agreed with him. Peace and negotiation were not the
means which suited him best, though he could sit round a
table with the wiliest men at Westminster, and manage to trick
them all. But what he really preferred to do was fight them.
It was cleaner in his eyes than the exercise of his considerable
cunning, and the results were final. Dead men did not go back
upon their word. And now there was a Second Civil War, with
the old allies fighting each other, and at last he was free to
take his armies out and smash his enemies in the name of God,
and to dispose of them afterwards as he thought fit.

"Will you go to Lord Fairfax now?" Ireton asked him.
Cromwell looked quickly to the back of the assembly and saw
his old friend and Commander-in-Chief sitting with his head
back and his eyes closed as if he were meditating. Cromwell
did not misunderstand that look. It meant that Fairfax was
displeased.

"How can he talk to me here?" Cromwell said impatiently.
"Go back to him, my son, and say that I'll pay my respects
this evening at five o'clock."

When they met it was in Fairfax's quarters in the centre of
the town. It was often said by the less well-born officers that
the Commander-in-Chief was lacking in the humble disregard
for personal comfort which distinguished that great Christian,
General Cromwell.

The two men had been close friends since long before the
Civil war; from that friendship their famous military partnership grew until the New Model was evolved. Sir Thomas
Fairfax was much altered since the day he walked in Pym's
garden and discovered the potentialities of Hampden's humble
cousin, Oliver. He was known as Black Tom by his troops—of
all the Parliament Commanders he had preserved some semb-
lance of civility to his enemies, most of whom were men and
women he knew very well. His courage and flair in battle were
unfortunately matched by his lack of both in a civilian capacity. In the negotiations with the King and the wrangling
with Parliament, he had gladly appointed Cromwell his spokes-
men and left the conduct of political affairs largely in his

hands. When Cromwell came in he stood up and they embraced, but he was obviously still very irritated. At such moments he was apt to revert to type, forgetting that great Puritan maxim of equality, and when he spoke he did so as an irate peer addressing a subordinate.

"I listened to your speech today," he said. "I damn near fell off my seat when I heard you say that we'd call the King to a terrible accounting. Now, General, be good enough to tell me what you meant by that remark!"

He saw Cromwell's face turn slowly red; the colour began at the edge of his collar and it crept slowly up the powerful neck and into his cheeks. He did not answer at once, he looked into Fairfax's irritable face, so unconsciously proud, and decided that this was not the moment to prove to his Lordship that he might have the higher rank but his General had the power. Not now, he decided, and immediately his hard bright eyes grew mild. He said gently, "How, Thomas, have I offended you by what I said? I meant to depose him in favour of the Prince of Wales, what else?"

His use of the Christian name put Fairfax at a disadvantage, as Cromwell knew it would. He frowned and walked irritably round the room. He had not offered his General anything to eat or drink.

"They're strong words for deposition," he retorted. "A terrible accounting . . . For a moment there I thought you were pandering to these hotheads who keep talking as if they could put the King on trial."

"I told you," Cromwell said, "I meant that he would be deposed. No more, no less. You have my word for it."

"Ah!" Fairfax stopped pacing up and down and breathed a long tired sigh which was full of relief. His thin dark face softened and he sat down on the oak settle by the side of the empty fireplace.

"I should have known, Oliver. The phrasing startled me, that was all. Besides, that son-in-law of yours was ranting on about the King only yesterday, saying he should pay for his crimes like any other criminal, and there were a dozen officers, half of them well known to me all standing there agreeing with him."

"Ireton is young," Cromwell took Fairfax's offer of a stool and balanced his broad body on it, his elbows on his knees.

"He was present when we negotiated with the King at Hampton Court. He was upset by such obduracy in the way of evil. Nothing any of us could say could move him, and I let the negotiations go on for months in the hope that he might come to grace. Ireton cannot forgive him for it, nor for being the cause of a fresh war which we are forced to fight."

Fairfax shook his head.

"There's no use blaming the King for that," he said. "It's the muddling of Parliament and the interference of those pestilential Scots that has caused these outbreaks of rebellion."

"They're more than outbreaks," Cromwell said. "Carlisle and Berwick are in Royalist hands, the fleet's mutinied in the King's favour and about to be joined by the Prince of Wales, and worst of all a Covenant Army is about to march on us! That's not an outbreak, that's a war!"

"You say it almost with relish," Fairfax looked at him. "Are you not tired of fighting, Oliver? Have you no wish to put up your sword and return home? By God, I long for peace! I dream of my home and my lands. I'd put off this uniform tomorrow and return with Her Ladyship and never leave Yorkshire for the rest of my life."

"I have no great estate to care for," Cromwell answered. "I have no yearning for anything but the completion of our work. Think of it, Thomas! Think of the infamy of human nature—only six years ago the whole of England was crying out under the King's tyranny, and now a good three-quarters of it wants him back!"

"We're a peaceful people," Fairfax explained. "'Now the war's over, let's send the army about it's business.' That was the beginning of the trouble."

"Send it about it's business and cheat it of its pay and of the things it fought for." Cromwell snapped back, unable to contain his anger. Once again his old jealousy of the aristocratic classes pricked him. How could a man as enormously rich as Fairfax understand the common soldiers' pressing need for a few pounds pay? And not only the common soldier but the officers who were tradesmen and labourers in civil life; their businesses or their few miserable plots of land were run into ruin through their absence at the war. And then there was himself.

How easy to lay down your arms if you were Fairfax; how

difficult to cast off General Cromwell and go back to parish duties and boundary disputes at Ely in a house no bigger than the inn Fairfax was staying in at that moment! Suddenly he felt a profound dislike for the man who had obtained his first promotion and generously furthered his military career in the early days.

He stood up—he had wasted enough time reassuring this lukewarm patriot that he was not going to kill his King, or let anyone else kill him. When that question was asked again he would, with God's grace, be strong enough to tell the truth. So strong, he thought in his excitement, that the question would never be asked. There would be no one left in England who would dare. He had gone to ask Charles to rule under the Army's guidance because he was still hoping that he might avoid ultimate temptation and seize all for himself. It was a temptation no longer. As he stood in the little inn room on that May day, his temptation was now his only goal.

"I have a favour to ask you, Thomas."

"Ask it," Fairfax said eagerly. He was ashamed of his suspicion of his friend. Cromwell was no regicide, even if he were a little vulgar in his dealing with the commonality, that was his birth, and it was most unfair to blame him. "Ask what you like and you know I'll do my best."

"When the Scots invade, let me go North to meet them!"

For a moment Fairfax hesitated. Normally he would have taken the post as Commander-in-Chief.

"Are you so eager for glory, Oliver?"

"Yes," Cromwell answered vehemently. "But not glory for myself. I want glory for our army and our faith. Give me this command, Thomas. I want it so much that I will go down on my knees and beg you for it if I must! Let me march against Hamilton and the Scots, and if I win then I'll give my sword into your own hands and seek retirement with you!"

Fairfax stood up and held out his hand to Cromwell.

"Take it then," he said, "with my blessing. I will go into Kent and then to Essex and put down the rebels there, while you take the main body of troops northwards to meet Hamilton."

They shook hands solemnly, and Cromwell squeezed Fairfax's so tightly that he winced.

"God will reward you for your generosity," he said.

Carisbrooke Castle rose like a grey cliff on the shore of the Isle of Wight. Its walls were so thick and steep that, as its commander Colonel Hammond wrote to an anxious Parliament, unless the King were a bird, he could not hope to escape from it. Hammond had been his custodian for over a year, and now at the end of November 1648, he was about to take his leave of Charles.

It was not a happy occasion for the Colonel; he was a just man with a profound sense of duty. That sense of duty had made him take the King into protection and then change that protection into strict imprisonment; but so long as he was in command of the Castle, the prisoner's life was safe. But now the Royalist forces were crushed and the Scots annihilated. When he received orders from the victorious General Cromwell to relinquish his post and go to London, Hammond was strongly tempted to let the King escape. It was a temptation which had come to him more than once, when the King's servants were removed and replaced by soldiers picked from the most fanatical regiments in the army. Whatever Hammond thought of his prisoner, he recoiled from the rumours that he would be assassinated in the Castle, or worse still, taken to London and tried for his life.

The Colonel was waiting in the small stone room leading into the King's bedroom. Even now the formalities were preserved, the King was served on bended knee, his privacy was guarded as jealously as his person, and thanks to Hammond's insistence, Parry and Firebrace, his two oldest servants, were allowed to remain and attend to him. The door to the inner room opened, and Parry bowed to him and stood aside.

"His Majesty will receive you now, sir."

Charles was standing by the window when Hammond came into the room; his face was averted, but when he turned and the light fell on it, the Colonel was acutely embarrassed to see that the King had been crying.

"Come in, Colonel Hammond. I'm sorry I had to keep you waiting, but I had some letters to read."

Hammond had been forbidden to give Charles any letters or to allow him to receive anyone not granted permission by Parliament, and by Parliament, he and the whole of subjugated England understood that it was the army and General Cromwell who ordered the terms of the King's custody. Only that afternoon Parry had been brought before him by one of the unyielding troopers and accused of smuggling messages to the King from a boatman who had called at the Castle with provisions. Parry had broken down and begged on his knees to be allowed to give his master the letter he showed Hammond. It bore the royal seal and came from France. It was the first letter he had received from the Queen for nearly two months, and the valet implored him not to deprive his prisoner of his only comfort.

He could see that letter on the small oak table by the narrow window. Charles saw him glance towards it and he said quietly—"My thanks to you, Colonel. Parry brought me this with your permission. I have heard nothing from Her Majesty the Queen for so long . . . I am truly grateful for your kindness."

"I disobeyed my orders," Hammond said. "But since I am going to leave you, it seemed unnecessarily harsh to forbid a wife's letter to her husband. I trust the Queen is in good health."

Charles looked at him with eyes reddened by tears. His face was thin and hollowed by anxiety and his pallor was that unhealthy grey that comes from long imprisonment and little air and exercise.

"My wife is ill, sir. That letter tells me that her allowance has been stopped; she is in such poverty in France that she and my children are forced to stay in bed because they have no money for fuel and scarcely enough to buy bread."

He sat down in the one chair in the room and covered his face with his hands.

"I wish that I were dead before I brought her to this pass."

Parry came up to him. He carried a glass of wine and his hand was trembling so much that he spilt some of it on the carpet. That carpet had come from Hammond's own quarters when he was told that there was no covering on the King's floor.

"Shall I leave, Sire?" Hammond asked. In all the trials and disappointments of which Charles had been a victim this was the first time he had ever seen him lose his self-possession. He was so embarrassed and so shocked by it that he turned round to go.

"No," the King called out to him, "no, don't go, Hammond. I have nothing to hide from you. This is your last night at Carisbrooke and I want to say farewell to you. Forgive me." He drank the wine and took a handkerchief from Parry, wiping his face and lips.

"Forgive the distress of a husband and father. I cannot bear to read it, and yet I have read it twenty times or more since Parry gave it to me. 'I am an embarrassment to them.' That's what she writes. 'They shun me, they neglect even to send what pittance they promised, and while my sister Queen Anne consoles herself with the Cardinal and her amusements, we stay in rooms at the Louvre which are bare of furniture and keep to our beds because there is no wood for a fire to warm us with the snow thick on the ground.'"

"That letter must be old," Hammond suggested. Even to him it was unthinkable that the Queen and her children should be living in actual want. The agony of the unhappy man before him, weeping for the woman he loved as he had never once wept for himself, unnerved the Colonel until he felt quite close to tears. "Look at the date, Sire. It may have been so then but I'm sure the Queen has found friends to care for her by now."

"What friends can she have?" Charles demanded. "She is an exile, married to a prisoner whose last hope of freedom has gone for ever. There is no future for my wife because there's none for me."

"If I had known what was in that letter, Sire, I would have kept it from you," Hammond said. "Whatever our differences, you have enough to bear."

"I shall have more," Charles said. "You leave tomorrow and the lieutenants of Cromwell come to escort me to London. I know what is in store, you see. I knew when he beat the Scottish army at Preston."

"He has beaten them all," Hammond said. "There is not a Royalist left in arms in the whole of England. Scotland itself is utterly subdued."

"He is a great General," Charles said wearily. "A great leader of men in battle. He has but one opponent left and I am he. You should be glad to leave here, Colonel. I know you would not be a party to my death. Will you take some wine with me? Parry, bring a glass and set a stool for the Colonel. Then you may go."

It was a long time since he had refused a seat to Cromwell. He was more tractable in the bleak fortress, where even the company of Hammond was a luxury. And he had long since forgiven Hammond for not letting him escape. Contact with his enemies had taught him to respect those men among them who were truly men of principle. And compared with the new officers who garrisoned the Castle and their men who turned aside and spat when he went out to exercise, Hammond was the soul of Christian gentleness.

"Would you tell me," Charles said, "what can I expect in London? I am shut off from all but rumours now."

It was the one question Hammond did not wish to answer. Cromwell's crushing victory at Preston, where his force of a little over eight thousand men had routed and cut to pieces twenty thousand Scots, made him the military ruler of the country, reducing the protests of Parliament to a frightened murmur. What could Charles expect? With an effort he tried to explain.

"You must expect to answer to the army for what they consider to be crimes against the realm."

Charles raised his head.

"I am the realm. What crimes can I commit against my-self?"

There was no answer to it, and Hammond did not try to make one. On that reply alone he would be doomed. How could he describe the hatred of the Puritans in his own garrison, who spoke of the King as the Anti-Christ, responsible for both Civil Wars and all their bloodshed, and warn him what to expect from them when he still spoke of himself as the personification of the kingdom? It was hopeless; if the King's position had been less pathetic, it would have been unbearably proud. "You do not answer, Hammond," Charles said. "But I repeat my question. How can I sin against myself? How can the King be guilty of treason when the only treason is that committed against the King? I've even heard that they are going to put me to some kind of trial. How far can absurdity go? Who can try me, except my peers, and there are no Kings at Westminster that I know of Hammond, you are a just man and I know that I owe you my life. The news that you were relieved of your command and I was being sent to London made me sure that I was going to lose it. But how will it be done? By murder on the journey? By poison in some prison? Forewarn me if you can. I have no hope of escape now. All is lost for me on this earth and I am reconciled. But I don't want to come on death unawares. Forewarn me if you can; at least then I can meet my end prepared."

"You will not be murdered," Hammond said. "You have my word on that. I know the General's mind. He's not a man to take the easy way and kill you underhandedly. But you asked me what will befall you now that he has won and made himself master. . ."

"Answer me on your honour," Charles said, and he spoke the words as a command, given by the sovereign to a subject.

"The General will bring you to trial," Hammond said. "As for the verdict, God alone can say what it will be."

Charles leant back and put his glass on the table. His expression was calm but there was a glint in his tired eyes which Hammond recognized. He had seen it when one commission from Westminster after another had come to the Royal prisoner with their unacceptable and crippling terms, and one and all had been dismissed.

"No man can try me," Charles said. "God is my only judge and I submit to Him and no one else. Cromwell may accuse me, but his verdict on me can be nothing else but murder. And murder it will have to be. I met the man and I measured him as a true Englishman," his tone was mildly sarcastic—"a man of sound sense and Christian purpose. He knows full well that so long as I live, whether here or in the blackest dungeon, he will not have peace to enjoy his power. He will have to kill me; it is an old rule in history, Colonel, that you cannot have two Kings."

He stood up and Hammond rose quickly. Old habits die hard indeed, Charles thought, as he held out his hand and the Colonel knelt and kissed it.

"Farewell, and my thanks to you for the good care you took of me."

"Farewell, Sire, and may God help you!"

"He has never failed me," Charles said gently. "And now that my time is coming, I shall try not to fail Him. Be good

274

enough to send in Parry as you leave. I want to write a letter to the Queen. I know that you will break another rule and let him send it by the way hers came to me."

By the light of two wax candles, begged or stolen from one of the townspeople at Newport by the tireless Parry, Charles sat down to compose what he felt would be his last letter to Henrietta.

He had always written to her with fluent ease; they both wrote as they spoke. He began as always.

"My Dear Heart, your letter came to me today by the good offices of our messenger and the kindness of the Puritan officer in command here, who is leaving tomorrow, alas! Mine own beloved, the knowledge of your suffering has smitten me to the heart . . ." He faltered, overcome by emotion, imagining the icy room and the horrible indignity of that tumbled bed in which his wife and daughter huddled to keep warm.

What had become of the gay and lovely wife whom he had delighted to wrap in the most costly furs, cherishing her against a breath of wind? Was her hair grey now, like his; had the light and laughter gone out of her smile, if indeed she ever smiled? He had almost forgotten how to smile himself. His laughter had been still for years. His tears fell upon the paper as he took up his pen again. He had written her so many letters and this was undoubtedly his last. He poured out his compassion and heartbreaking regret, blaming himself for her predicament, and then in the next line thanking God that at least she was safe and that their son Charles had returned from the fiasco of the Second Civil War and was able to comfort her. And then he began the hardest part of all and told her that she must no longer try to help him but resign herself that he was lost. Her duty was to work for the restoration of their son; he assured her that he was calm and unafraid.

"So many times," he wrote, "you have reproached me with irresolution, and that reproach was justified, for I never possessed your hardy spirit, seeking always the way of peace rather than the sword. Now by the sword I shall come to mine end, and I do vow to you, the dearest of all human creatures and the sole comfort of my life, that I will bear myself as a King should and you shall have no report of me that is dishonourable. Farewell my love, care for my children and fight for the rights of my son as you have fought so faithfully for

275

mine. Keep nothing of grief in your heart, but only the memory of him who loves you and will never cease to love you, even beyond the grave. Ever thine own devoted husband, Charles R."

He sprinkled sand over the letter and folded it, sealing it with his ring. "Parry!" he called out. The valet came in from the outer chamber and Charles gave him the letter.

"Give this to our friend at the quayside, and tell him to come no more. We will be leaving here and letters must not fall into the new Commander's hands. When you have done, come and help me undress. It's been a weary day."

Chapter 14

T H E Master of England was alone; he had taken up quarters in the Royal Palace at Whitehall as soon as he arrived in London early in January 1649. He had come to the capital bringing his victorious veterans with him, and the city was now under military occupation. One of the army's first actions had been to surround the House of Commons and disband or arrest all those who were of the moderate party, leaving a nucleus of forty-seven picked fanatics to fill the Chamber whose full complement was over two hundred members.

There was no longer any power in the kingdom except the military, and the military was controlled by Cromwell. He had returned after Preston and without a moment's hesitation consolidated his gains by taking the King from Carisbrooke and lodging him under a strong guard at Windsor. He had dealt with the protests of Colonel Hammond by placing him under arrest as soon as he arrived in London.

Cromwell had crippled Parliament just in time, for they were about to make a hurried peace with the King in preference to submitting to the Army.

He thought of Parliament with contempt. Parliament had been easy to dispose of, the people despised them, the army hated them with a hatred only one degree less furious than that they reserved for the King. And now he had the King secure, hemmed in by men who would kill him if he so much as tried to pass a message. He had the King and he had spent the last three weeks in a desperate attempt to make his trial and execution legal.

But nobody would help him. All those who had cried out so loudly against the King's iniquities, became suddenly nervous and hesitant about calling him to an account for them. Cromwell had announced the trial, braving the anger of Fairfax who accused him of breaking his word, and shrugging the insult aside because Fairfax had nothing left with which to fight him but words. But the judges he ordered to sit at the trial had refused, and no amount of threats could make them yield. The English Bar had condemned the idea of arraigning an anointed sovereign as preposterous and illegal and withdrawn from it. Of a hundred and thirty-five Commissioners summoned by Cromwell to act as judge and jury, less than half would take their seats, and some of these were hardly to be trusted.

He began to pace up and down, pulling at his collar. It always seemed to choke him when he was agitated, as if the big muscles in his thick neck swelled. Nothing had changed in his appearance. His linen and hose were coarse and dingy, his plain uniform coat was creased where he had thrown it on the floor the night before; only his breastplate was polished and clean and it shone in the soft winter sunlight which crept into the windows of the room, bringing the reflected shimmer of the Thames outside. He was still the General; humble and untidy and very much a plain Englishman, but there was a look in his face now and a look in the faces of those who were with him which was a token of great change. His brow was deeply lined, and the lines were lines of ill-temper and constant, unremitting concentration. His voice had a loud, harsh edge to it, full of command. The wheedling overtones he once used to Fairfax and his fellow officers had gone. Nobody argued with him now, nobody except a pack of miserable lawyers whose only concern was the letter of the law, and a few fainthearts who were afraid to twist it to suit their own purpose. Cromwell was not afraid, he was not afraid of the law, or of those who accused him under their breath of dangerous ambitions, of Fairfax, or of anyone who tried to thwart him. He had no fear of any living creature but the King of England and that was why he knew, without hesitating, that he would have to kill him. He had no feelings of vengeance or a genuine thirst for what he described so eloquently to the doubters as the guiltiest blood in Christendom. He had nothing but an unwilling admiration for the man who had fallen so pitifully low and yet whose personal stature was greater than ever before.

Cromwell did not hate the King, as Ireton and some of the Commissioners hated him. It was all very well for Ireton to speak as if bringing Charles before a picked tribunal and cutting off his head were an act of Divine justice; Cromwell did not regard the Commissioners as inheriting the mantle of

Judith nor did he think the King was Holofernes. But he knew quite definitely that the victory he had won and the form of government he meant to impose upon his country would be constantly endangered so long as the King lived. If he were buried in the deepest dungeon, those who opposed Cromwell would still take up arms in his name. And though the prisons were full all over England, the spirit epitomized by Charles was not yet dead or even truly conquered; it mocked and defied him even at the edge of the grave.

When the Royalist commander Lisle was executed under the wall of Colchester a few months earlier he had called out to the firing party to come closer, lest they miss him as they had missed him so often in battle. That was the spirit which must stand on trial at Westminster, that was the pride which must be humbled under the common headsman's axe.

It was now the 20th January, and he had given orders the previous evening that the King should be brought to London for his trial. Westminster Hall was ready, the benches were set up and the railings which would divide the Court and the spectators had been hammered into place a week before. Everything was ready but the legal formula without which even he could not deliver Charles to be tried for his life.

There was a knock on his door but Cromwell was too preoccupied to hear it. Some were suggesting that he murder the King or have him poisoned, but Cromwell was too wise for that. The army wanted him to die a public death, and a public death left no doubt in anybody's mind what happened to the enemies of the army and the army's general. When the door opened, he swung round, his face reddening irritably. His son-in-law, Ireton stood in front of him. He looked at Cromwell uncomfortably. "General, excuse me . . . I knocked but you didn't hear me. The Commission are sitting in the Painted Chamber and they have asked for you to be present."

"What do they want with me?" Cromwell demanded. "Don't they know their business?—Can't they get on with it and have done? They've been deliberating about law and forms for three weeks and nothing has been decided! God give me patience—must I write out the procedures for them and act as judge and jury too? Come on, then," he said angrily, "come on and get this business over. Nothing is carried out without my standing watchdog over them. . ."

They sat in the old Banqueting Hall, and Rubens's gorgeous painting glowed above their heads as it had done once above the glittering Courts of Charles; his chair of State was taken down and Cromwell seated himself at the head of the long table in the place where the King had spent so many happy hours watching Henrietta dancing.

One of the members was talking. Cromwell knew the voice —it belonged to Henry Marten, one of the staunchest of the Independents.

"The King began the Civil War in order to win for himself an unlimited and tyrannical power. He corrupted our allies and was the deliberate instigator of that second conflict which has just been resolved by force of arms. He is guilty on both these charges and the whole is simply this, sirs, that the King has committed treason against the Realm. What more do we require than that?"

"The authority to try him. We must establish that authority or else we make the King a victim and ourselves plain murderers."

That was the lawyer, John Bradshaw. Cromwell turned his back on them and went to stand by the window. He was still standing there when the barge drew up at the waterfront steps at the edge of the garden leading to Cotton House. He stiffened and pulled back the curtains to the edge to get a better view. He knew that figure in the middle of a guard of soldiers because it was smaller and slighter than the rest, and dressed in sober black, with a wide-brimmed, feathered hat hiding the face. He saw one of the officers give the prisoner his hand to help him disembark, and then the little company began to walk up the path between the bare trees until it disappeared into Cotton House where he had ordered them to lodge the King.

When Cromwell turned round his face was as grey as the Thames water; his voice sounded very loud and harsh with a strange tremor in it, and the Commissioners became suddenly silent.

"He is come, my friends, he is come! Now we must do that great work which the nation is full of. Therefore we must resolve here and now what answer we will give the King when he comes before us. Do you not know that his first question will be, 'By what authority do you try me?'"

It was not only an order, it was a cry of appeal. His nerves were so shaken by the sight of that figure walking unhurriedly through the freezing garden as if he were about to enter his own Palace at Whitehall, that Cromwell's whole massive body trembled. At first no one answered him. They stared at him, discomforted by the wild, expression and the clenching hands, and then they looked at one another.

"Answer!" Cromwell strode up to them and shouted. "Answer or be ready to let him go free!" and he pointed towards Cotton House. At last someone moved, someone pushed their chair back and stood up. It was Henry Marten.

"We try him in the name of the Commons assembled in Parliament and all the good people of England."

"Enough!" To their astonishment Cromwell laughed and the ghastly pallor began to fade, his cheeks and forehead were as red as fire and there was an unholy, roistering joy in the face which had been grey and contorted a moment before. God had given the sign. Not in the legal quibbling of a lot of doubting old women who lived by their law-books, but out of the mouth of plain Henry Marten.

"By Parliament and the people!" he repeated. "That is our ordinance, and by God's Grace we'll see to it that right is done! Enough now, friends, put up your pens and papers. The trial begins this afternoon."

The Commissioners rose to their feet and left the Hall, some of them bowing to the General, and as the last of them went out Cromwell went up to Ireton and stopped him, putting his hand upon his shoulder.

"By the Parliament and the good people of England, my son! I will meet you at Westminster Hall at one o'clock."

Charles had not been inside Westminster Hall since the time he had sat there listening to the trial of Strafford. He came from Cotton House in a sedan chair, so closely surrounded by Ironside soldiers that his view of the streets was completely obscured. But as he stepped from the sharp January sunlight into that cold dark entrance of the ancient Hall, he shivered and looked around him for a moment without recognizing it. He hesitated on the threshold, and Colonel Hacket, the rough and ill-bred officer who had been his chief escort on the journey to London, attempted to take his arm and urge him forward.

Charles felt that touch, and for a moment his self-control snapped. He wrenched his arm away from Hacket and, stopping, he turned on him so quickly and with such an expression of fury that the man recoiled.

"How dare you put your hand on me! Remember who I am and what you are!"

His eyes were accustomed to the altered light and he saw that the interior of the Hall had been completely transformed. A platform covered the far end of the Hall and there were ranks of benches on it under the great window. These were filled by his judges, and in front of them he saw the mace on a covered table. The body of the chamber was divided by a long gangway lined with wooden rails and guarded by pikemen and musketeers. Behind these rails he saw the people, massed in hundreds pushing and craning to see him come forward to his public humiliation.

Charles had annoyed his guards by taking so long a time about his dressing that he was told he would be late. But at no time in his reign of twenty-four years had appearances mattered more to him than on that occasion. His suit was of deep black velvet, his cloak was also black but lined with bright blue satin and the colour matched the brilliant ribbon of the Garter which hung round his neck, the magnificent jewelled St. George and Dragon ornament suspended from it.

The Garter Star was richly embroidered on the shoulder of his cloak, and his broad black velvet hat was covered in sable plumes. He carried a tall ebony stick with a gold mount and after he had inspected the inside of the Hall, he tapped it sharply on the ground and gave the order to march forward. The soldiers moved even before Hacket could intervene. He found himself pushing forward out of step and Charles turned round and said curtly, "Hurry, if you please, but take care not to come too close lest you brush up against me. I dislike it."

He felt the people watching him, and he was almost overcome by the heat and the smell of them as he advanced down the centre of the Hall. He did not look to either side of him, he walked slowly as he was accustomed to do when passing among his subjects, with his eyes fixed high ahead. For a moment he glanced quickly at the end of the Hall where the Court had sat for Strafford's trial and looked for the little box with its concealing grille which had been built for him and

Henrietta. Its place was taken by a gallery full of favoured spectators who were thus able to look down upon the platform itself. At the end of the platform, facing the ranks of judges, a railed enclosure had been placed for him, with a red velvet chair and a table. As he observed, his back would be to the people in the Hall, and a view of his shoulders and the back of his head was unlikely to invite much of their sympathy.

The soldiers divided, and he walked between them to his chair and sat down. He did not once look at the judges or even behave as if he knew that they were there. Bradshaw was the elected President of the Court and he rose, followed by a rustling and coughing as the other seventy followed, and in a loud voice, louder still because he was nervous, Bradshaw began to read the charges. Charles heard the indictment begin and after the first few sentences concerning the titles of the Parliament and the Court he laid his cane against the side of the chair and getting up he half turned and looked round at the galleries on his left and right. They were full of people, many of whom he recognized from the days when they had attended his Courts at Whitehall. The Countess of Carlisle was not among them however, and Charles remembered that she was in the Tower on the orders of General Cromwell. It was rumoured that the General disliked her and suspected her of intriguing with the Presbyterians. It was also rumoured that he had threatened her with the rack unless she revealed her activities in detail.

Charles put the thought of Lucy Carlisle out of his mind. For if he thought of the past or Henrietta or entertained for a moment more the tragic memories of this place and its associations with the unjust condemnation of his greatest friend and Minister, his contempt for his accusers might change into anger, and he was determined to show them nothing but contempt. Contempt was in his face and in the casual way in which he reseated himself, examined the pen on the table before him to see if the nib was suitable, and then after a moment or two yawned, and got up and looked down the end of the Hall where the ordinary spectators were gathered. He had sat down again, having heard every word of the indictment in which he was accused of starting the Civil War and instigating the second outbreak, when Bradshaw said that he was a tyrant and a traitor, and to his astonishment, the King put his head back and facing them all for the first time, laughed out loud. Bradshaw was so put off by this that he stammered over the rest of the charges, and sat down with his puffy face scarlet. He collected himself and leaning forward he addressed the King.

"What answer do you make to these charges brought against you?"

At the back of the last row of benches, Cromwell leaned forward. He had felt sure from the moment Charles entered the Hall that the King would refuse to plead. He was even human enough to be angry at the contempt and indifference Charles had shown for his elaborate and intimidating set-piece. The elegant, dignified figure in his splendid black, with one ancient Royal Order blazing on his breast and shoulder, made the ranks of soldiers and gentlemen and the President Bradshaw look ridiculous merely by sitting with his legs crossed and gazing at the ceiling while they spoke.

But now he had to answer. The man who on public occasions had such an impediment in his speech that he had addressed his Commons as seldom as possible and deputed others to read long speeches for him, must now stand before an audience of many hundreds and answer for his own life. Cromwell sat forward to see and hear. He confidently expected that nervous strain would render the King incomprehensible.

The King folded his hands over the top of his cane and his voice carried very clearly and distinctly to the furthest corners of the Hall. He spoke slowly but without a trace of hesitation.

"If you will tell me by what authority you ask that question, and by what authority I sit here, I shall be willing to answer you. But first, remember that I am your King." There was a second's pause and he stood up. Cromwell thanked God that he had had the foresight to place him as he did, so that he was practically hidden from the majority of the people present.

"Remember," Charles' voice rang out, "that I am your lawful King, and the sins you bring upon your heads and the judgment of God upon this land. Think well on it before you go further from one sin to a greater, and tell me by what lawful authority I am seated here. Then I will answer you. But in the meantime I will not betray my trust." Cromwell saw that the King's pale face had coloured slightly, and for the first time the stern tones wavered and he showed some sign of emotion. " I have a trust committed to me, by God and by old and lawful descent. I will not betray it to answer something new and unlawful."

" I knew it." Henry Marten was seated on the other side of Cromwell; they were divided by a backcloth emblazoned with the arms of the new Commonwealth of England. He leaned across to whisper. " I knew he would refuse to answer. What will Bradshaw do now? "

" Proceed without it," Cromwell snapped back. " It doesn't matter what he says. The Court will find him guilty! "

" Amen," Marten murmured and sat back.

Bradshaw spoke up as soon as the King had re-seated himself. He was sufficiently irritated by the nature of the King's answer to make an elementary mistake, which Cromwell detected immediately the words had left his mouth.

" The authority is that of the people of England by whom you were elected King! "

" No, Sir! " There was a note of mockery in the King's voice. " I deny that. This is not an elective but an hereditary Kingdom for these last thousand years. That answer will not do at all. I stand more for the liberty of my people than any here who pretend to be my judges! "

Lisle, who was one of the few lawyers present, left his seat by the President's chair and came up to Cromwell.

" He knows the law too well," he whispered. " If this continues and he's to be condemned without pleading, it would be better to do it in his absence."

" That old fool," Cromwell said under his breath. " Elected by the people . . ! God have mercy on us! Doesn't he know how to try a case? Tell him from me, Lisle, that if he gives the King such another opening to make him and us look ridiculous, I'll arrest him and put another in charge of the trial. Say that the proceedings can be cut short today. Go back and tell him now! "

Without seeming to watch them, Charles saw that hurried conference and for the first time he distinguished his principal enemy among that crowd of faces in front of him. Unlike the aristocratic spectators above him, there were very few of his judges that he recognized. He could see Ireton's pale, thin face watching him with hatred; Waller, the Parliament General, and the notorious troublemaker and pamphleteer,

285

Robert Lillburn, were among them. The rest were officers, country gentlemen of middle-class degree, and a few labourers. He leant back in his chair and looked straight up to where Cromwell was sitting.

"The Court adjourns," the President called out, and the judges struggled to their feet again. "You are hereby summoned to meet at this place tomorrow at the same hour for the continuance of the trial. I would advise you, Sir," he added, pointing his finger at the King, "to change your mind and plead when you appear again."

The King stood up and ignoring the President, he directed his reply to that figure by the backcloth in the last row.

"You may bring me here, but a King cannot be tried by any superior power on earth. Produce that power, and I will answer you."

Charles turned and as he did so, the gold top of his stick came off and rolled a few feet away from him. In all his life he had never stooped and picked anything off the floor. Until that very afternoon one of his sullen guards had served him on one knee, and called for Parry to bend down and tie the ribbon of his shoes. He hesitated, waiting for someone to move, and then Hacket stepped up to him.

"My cane," Charles said. "There is the top. Give it to me, if you please."

Hacket's face flushed, and then for the first time since he had taken the King into his personal custody he looked at him and smiled. "No, Sir," he said slowly, "I will not. And there is no man here who will. Henceforth, you will stoop for yourself!"

Lord Fairfax had not gone near Westminster Hall. He remained in his London house, avoided by most of his army compatriots who felt that he had incurred Cromwell's enmity by his attitude and that it was no longer safe to be on intimate terms with him. He showed considerable courage in receiving a messenger from France on the second day of the trial. To his surprise and embarrassment the man gave him two letters, one of which was from Henrietta. The Queen's letter did in fact, upset him, and in spite of his intense dislike of her in the past, he could not read without a trace of sympathy that anguished, hysterical appeal in which she threw herself upon her knees, begging his intervention for the King, but it was the second letter which roused him from his retirement and made him summon Cromwell and Ireton and two of the other generals to a meeting at his house that night.

Though he had not gone to the trial, his wife had taken her seat in the privileged gallery for the past two days, and as he waited for Cromwell, Lady Fairfax came back to report on the second day of the proceedings. Fairfax loved his wife, he admired her courage and he even admired her for defying him and going to hear the King defend himself. He was also ashamed because she could not understand why he did nothing to stop something which they both regarded as an abominable crime. Unlike him, Lady Fairfax had the courage to say so to Oliver Cromwell's face. He heard her step on the stairs and going to the door he opened it and took her in his arms. She was a handsome woman with sparkling blue eyes and a commanding character, and she pushed her husband unceremoniously aside while she unfastened her cloak.

"Sweetheart," he said anxiously, "I've been waiting for an hour or more. The business was over at four o'clock. Why aren't you home until past five? I began to think something had befallen you."

She laughed angrily.

"Something nearly did! I sat there listening to those murderers shouting the King down and refusing to let him speak in his own defence."

"Has he answered the charges then?" Fairfax interrupted.

"No, of course he hasn't! All he asks is that they listen to his reasons for not answering. But they dare not, the scoundrels, because they know he could prove that they had no right to try him, or anyone in England for that matter. I've never seen such a parody of a trial. I listened and I watched His Majesty sitting there full of dignity and patience and when they called out the roll of judges, they had the impudence to call your name!"

She paused for breath, and Fairfax saw that she was trembling. She was far more agitated than she would admit. He took her hands and said gently: "What nearly befell you, my dearest? Be calm and tell me."

"When they called out your name, trying to implicate you in their vile doings, I couldn't bear it and I got up from my seat and shouted out, 'He has more sense than to be here! Oliver Cromwell is a rogue and a traitor!' The next thing I saw was a group of soldiers down below taking aim at me."

He caught her in his arms, and her hardy spirit faltered and she began to cry.

"They would have fired on me, Thomas, only someone ran up to tell the officer who I was. He shouted up that the next time I interrupted them I should be shot!"

"Good God!" Fairfax kept repeating. He was so incredulous that such a thing could happen to a woman, and that woman his own wife, that he was tempted to think she exaggerated. "Don't trouble yourself, I'll have this man arrested, I'll find out who he is!"

"I saw the poor King look up at me," she continued, drying her eyes and growing calmer as he comforted her, "and I'll swear he smiled. Thomas, what are we going to do? What will become of us all if we allow the King to be murdered and the right of free speech taken away from us? Is this what we fought the King to gain? Is this why you killed some of your own friends on the field and why my own cousins fought for the King at Marston Moor and will not ever speak to me again? Thomas, I beg of you, do something to stop this creature Cromwell before he involves us all in his guilt."

"I may be able to now," Fairfax said slowly. "I know how you feel about this, and I don't blame you. But you wouldn't believe me when I said that I was powerless. Now you've seen the temper of the men that Cromwell represents. That man who would have murdered you for speaking out is typical of them all. If I came out for the King, there's not one who would follow me. But now I have something with which to bargain for him."

"What?" she asked quickly. "What do you mean, bargain for him?"

"I have a letter from the Queen and another from the Prince of Wales. I've sent for Cromwell and Waller and Ireton and Whalley to show the letters to them. Then we shall see what can be done to save the King."

She put her arms round him and for the first time since the King had come to Cotton House to stand his trial, Lady Fairfax forgot her disappointment in the husband she loved, and kissed him warmly on the lips. She had risked her own life to try and shame him into action; now he was about to prove that he was still the brave and honourable man who was even admired by his enemies in war.

"Please God you will succeed," she said. "I know you won't falter. When are they coming? I want to go to my room before. I wouldn't trust myself to see them."

"They should be here at any moment," Fairfax said. He spoke quietly so as to hide his anger and anxiety from her. The thought of those muskets levelled at her box made him feel physically sick.

"Go upstairs, sweetheart, and rest. Trust me to do whatever I can for the King."

Less than a quarter of an hour later Cromwell and the three other officers were announced. They greeted Fairfax politely, and Cromwell emphasized that their old friendly relationship no longer existed by formally bowing to him.

"Good evening, gentlemen. I regret the need for bringing you here at such an hour and disturbing your conduct of business, but I received something which is very pertinent to that business—I mean the trial of His Majesty the King." He looked round them and his angry eyes lingered on Cromwell. It was Ireton who answered first.

"You mean the trial of Charles Stuart, my Lord. We no longer have a King!"

"Call him what you will," Fairfax snapped, "and I will call him what *I* will. General Cromwell, I suggest that we all sit down. I have something to show you all."

He went to his writing cabinet, unlocked it and brought out the letters sent by Charles's wife and eldest son. He held out the first to Cromwell.

"A messenger from the French Embassy brought these to-day," he said. "This is from the Queen, begging for her husband's life. Whatever our opinions of the writer it is a moving letter, and as such it is worth reading."

"If it contains nothing of importance, my reading it would be a waste of time," Cromwell said curtly. "Surely, Lord Fairfax, you did not bring myself and these officers here to tell us that this pernicious woman is trying to interfere in English affairs yet again!"

His eyes were as cold as steel as he looked at his old friend. There was nothing in them but dislike and contempt. As he had once said to Ireton, it was a great pity that Fairfax had survived the war.

"No," Fairfax answered, and his face was turning red. "I know you better than to think that a woman's tears would move you. The second letter is my reason. It is from the Prince of Wales." He held it out and after a moment, Waller, the tough and brilliant campaigner of the First Civil War, squinted at it and then exclaimed: "Letter! What letter? there's nothing but a signature on a blank page!"

"Precisely!" Fairfax dropped it on the table in front of them. "On that page we can write what terms we like above the signature. That's what the Prince offers in return for his father's life."

There was a moment's silence.

"It is an advantage well worth having, gentlemen. If you want to make permanent peace, that letter is your charter. Put down what settlement you will and the Prince will honour it. You can depose the King in his favour, you can extract a total abdication from the Prince and his heirs, if that is what you want. Think what this means in relation to the life of one man."

"It's a trick," Ireton said. "I would not trust a word of it."

"Now, now!" Cromwell turned round and admonished him. "You are too prejudiced, Ireton. This is no trick! It comes from a distressed and noble boy, ready to forswear himself and all his rights to succour his father. Nobody doubts that. . . But my Lord Fairfax made the point. What does this mean in relation to the life of the King? Now that, gentleman, is a different matter."

He sat back in his chair and folded his arms and looked mocking at Fairfax.

"I say it means nothing at all. There is no settlement to be made with any of the Stuarts. England has done with Kings. Far from accepting the Prince's offer, we are bound to reject his right to make one at all, and to answer that if he should ever show his face in the country after his father's execution, we will hunt him down and kill him as a traitor. Nothing can alter his father's guilt or snatch the people's lawful victim from their vengeance. The trial must continue and Charles Stuart will be convicted and sentenced before the end of the week. This letter is superfluous. I suggest that you destroy it or return it with a suitable answer whence it came. And now, Lord Fairfax, I must ask you to excuse us. We have much work to do."

"It is not work which will bring you or any of us any profit," Fairfax said slowly. "You are determined on the King's death. So be it. I will return the Prince's letter."

Cromwell bowed and began to walk towards the door. Fairfax stepped in front of him suddenly.

"There is one other matter, General. My wife was in Westminster Hall today. There was an incident when she spoke out and some of your troops nearly fired upon her! I would like an explanation from you if you please!"

Cromwell faced him calmly. He restrained an impulse to push the infuriated man aside without bothering to answer him.

"I heard about it," he said. "My regrets to you and her Ladyship. It seems she made remarks which would have put a humbler person into the Marshalsea for contempt. The officer in charge was not aware that a woman of quality would cause such a public disturbance and he was only trying to keep order."

"What was his name?" Fairfax demanded. "I'll have him disciplined!" He was trembling with helpless rage. Thanks to his own faith in the man standing before him, and to his own blindness of that man's true character and motives, he was as impotent to protect his wife as he was to save the King.

"Axtell," Cromwell answered. "Punish him by all means, my Lord. But for her own safety, I suggest you keep Lady Fairfax at home until the trial is over. I cannot guarantee protection for her if she makes another demonstration. Your servant, my Lord. Come, gentlemen."

He did not go up to his wife after they had gone. He stayed on in the room and lit the candles by his writing cabinet and tried to begin a letter to the Queen and the Prince of Wales explaining that there was nothing he could do for Charles. But he had written nothing when his wife came to him. He did not speak at first, he did not know how to tell her that he had failed. He did not need to; she looked down over his shoulder and said quietly: "You must find that letter very difficult, Thomas. I knew he had refused to listen to you when you stayed down here."

"He mocked," Fairfax said bitterly. "He sat there grinning and then dismissed the whole appeal with a few words. 'England has done with Kings.' That's what he said."

"And he's to have his way," Lady Fairfax straightened and moved away from him. "What has become of you, that you let such a creature get so far? Will you stand idle while he kills the King and think you will be safe if only you keep quiet? What manner of man are you?"

"Man enough to have that wretch who threatened you to-day brought up for punishment!" It was a feeble answer and a feebler attempt to pacify her. He saw her expression and he caught her hand and held it tightly.

"Believe me, sweet, there's nothing in the world that I can do to save the King. The army has him and the army is determined to put him to death. Even without Cromwell, there would be Ireton and Waller and the rest. For the love of God don't reproach me as if I were a coward!"

"You are not a coward," she said coldly. "Only a fool and a laggard. I shall go down to Westminster tomorrow. If that vulgar brute thinks that a few muskets can frighten me away he is mistaken!"

"You are not to go," he said quickly. "Cromwell told me he cannot protect you if you make another scene. I forbid it!"

Lady Fairfax smiled sadly at him. Whatever happened to them in the future, their relationship would never be the same again.

"Thomas, I fear you are in no position to forbid anything. I shall go every day until the trial is over. If I am shot or arrested, it will be well worth while if it persuades you to do something at last!"

Three more days had passed since that first day, and the assembly sitting at Westminster Hall knew that it would not meet again. Charles had not listened to all the proceedings because he had been removed on one occasion after coolly and persistently interrupting in order to make himself heard. He was no longer distressed by anything but the ordeal of walking through the lines of hostile, jeering Puritan soldiers on his way to the Hall and back. The first time they began to shout insults at him, he flushed and half turned, and then quickly collected himself and walked on as if he had not noticed. That afternoon on January 27th the Hall seemed to him to be oppressively quiet; he glanced round and was sure there were more soldiers present than before, and as he took his place, several of those sitting on the judicial bench avoided looking at him. Charles settled himself in his chair and composed himself. Evidence of his supposed crimes had been offered on preceding days, and witnesses had testified that his Standard had been raised for war in Nottingham, and he himself had been present at Edgehill and Newbury. There was nothing more to be said against him, and he had spent most of the previous night on his knees praying because he knew that this was the day on which his sentence would be passed.

As he looked at them all, the soldiers, the ill-assorted group of judges sitting a little above him, the faces, some of them unhappy, many curious and a few vindictive, which watched him from the galleries on either side, Charles felt little sensation beyond that of great weariness and a deep, painful disgust. It would be necessary for him to fight the verdict, even to make a last attempt to forestall it, and he was ready to do this. But he did it in the name of the Sovereign power he represented; personally, he had little inclination to live, when the future could hold nothing but a lifetime of close imprisonment and lasting separation from those he loved. He had spent a lot of the time thinking of Henrietta, and he was so sure of the outcome of the trial that thoughts of her no longer pained him. They were a sweet relief, a refuge in which he escaped the hatred, insult and humiliations which increased with every hour. His memories of her were so vivid that they and not the grey cold Hall and the droning voices of his enemies, were the reality in which he lived.

Now the evidence was given, the speeches were over, and Bradshaw gathered his papers together and settled himself. Charles knew that he was about to pronounce the sentence and before he could do so, he stood up.

"One word, before you speak, Sir. A hasty sentence may be repented but it can never be recalled. Before you do this thing, I ask that the Commons and Lords may be assembled and I will speak before them both. I adjure you to allow this if as you pretend you value the liberty and peace of this kingdom."

There was a sudden movement among the judges; he saw one man try to rise from his seat and those on either side of him try to press him back again. It was Colonel Downs, a veteran of the Civil War and `a man of staunch principles. Those principles had been outraged every day in which he sat at Westminster and by every word exchanged between the King and the President of the Court. Cawley and Wanton were sitting with him; they were old friends of his and when he started to get up they almost struggled with him in their fear of what he meant to do.

"Leave me alone! Are you men, to sit here and agree to this?" Charles heard him distinctly, and equally distinct was the reply of Cawley, "Sit down, for God's sake! You will destroy yourself and us with you."

"If I die for it, I must do it!" Downs was on his feet and the whole Court was silent and expectant, staring at him. He was extremely pale but he turned to Bradshaw who had twisted round in his seat to see what the disturbance was and said at the top of his voice: "My Lord, I am not satisfied with this sentence . . . I cannot give my consent to it!"

"What is the matter with you, Sir?" Downs looked below him and saw Cromwell rise out of his seat. His back was to the King. "Colonel, what are you doing? I must ask you to be quiet!"

"I cannot be quiet!" Downs looked beyond him and for the first time he met the King's eye direct. "I want an adjournment."

"Very well then," Cromwell snapped at Bradshaw. "Adjourn for half an hour while we hear this gentleman."

Charles was removed to an ante-room to wait; it was nothing but a railed-off space in the outside passage, where a chair was put for him and Parry waited with his cloak.

"A glass of wine, Sire," he said anxiously. He came forward with the cup and ewer, and went down on his knee before Charles.

Charles took it and thanked him. "Get up, my good Parry. Do not kneel to me here or you will offend these people. They will only deal roughly with you when I am gone."

"Sire, I will kneel to you so long as God gives me the strength to bend my knee," Parry answered. "May I ask you a question?"

"You may, gladly," Charles replied gently.

" What is happening in that place? Why have you come out here to wait, Sire? "

" The Court, or whatever it calls itself, has been adjourned. Some poor fellow's conscience troubled him and he spoke out in my favour. God knows, it was a brave thing to do. I was very much moved by it. But it will not come to anything. He will either be arrested or he will do what he is told like the rest."

Within the half hour, Colonel Hacket reported that Colonel Downs' doubts had been satisfied and that the Court had reassembled. The King's presence was required.

Charles stood up and gave his empty glass to Parry.

" Have no fear for me," he said quietly, " for I have none for myself."

In the name of the Commons and the people of England, Bradshaw pronounced Charles a traitor, a tyrant and a murderer responsible for all those who had died in the war and sentenced him to be beheaded.

There was a piercing cry of protest from the gallery, where the intrepid Lady Fairfax, with the tears streaming down her face, cried out in defence of the King who stood before his judges, and was at that moment trying to speak out. He was not allowed a last defence. As his voice rose in an impassioned denial, wrung from him by the crude and vicious terminology employed against him and which impugned his Royal honour, Bradshaw stood up and shouted to the guards to take him out. And outside in the passages a cry of hate and triumph greeted him. The soldiers, relieved of discipline for the moment, crowded round him, shouting and jeering.

" Execution, execution! "

The smell of them sickened him. He drew back from the faces pressing close round him, blowing tobacco smoke into his eyes, and hedged in by his guards he pushed forward as quickly as he could.

" Execution! Execution for the tyrant! "

That was an officer, the fanatical Colonel John Hewson, who elbowed his way between the men guarding the King and came close up to him. His eyes were blazing with hatred; he had watched his detested enemy deriding the Court which to him was an instrument of Divine justice. He saw him even then preserving his damnable dignity, and it was too much for him. He came within a foot of the King and spat into his face.

The King's expression did not alter. He showed no sign except that a slight flush appeared as he wiped the spittle away from his cheeks and forehead.

"Now, tyrant, pay for your crimes!" Hewson hissed at him. Charles looked at the maddened, livid face of his tormentor and said gently: "God has justice in store for you as well as for me."

He moved on, and Hacket ordered his men to close their ranks so tightly round the King as they emerged into the winter daylight that he was almost hidden from the crowds outside. As he stepped into the sedan chair which brought him from Cotton House, Charles saw that most of the silent crowd massed in the streets and gateway of Westminster fell upon their knees; many of them were weeping openly.

In the chair he leant back well out of view and closed his eyes. Without looking at it, he threw the handkerchief soiled by Hewson's outrage on the floor, and tears of pain and weariness ran down his face. It was the first and only time in the last week that he had wept, but when Hacket opened the sedan door and curtly ordered him to get out, he showed no trace of anything but dignified indifference.

"Thank God!" Charles remarked, as if he were making conversation. "I shan't have to go to that wretched place again."

Chapter 15

THE sound of hammering at Whitehall Palace began at dawn on the morning of Monday, January 29th. The scaffold was to be built as high as possible so that the crowds should see as little as possible, and their view would be obscured still further by a rail hung with black cloth. The wooden struts rose up against the walls of the Banqueting Hall and the centre of the platform came under a window which was broken down to make it long enough for a man to step straight through it. The General had made his usual thorough preparation for the execution which was to take place on Tuesday the 30th, and having satisfied himself that he could put the King to death efficiently—the preparations included staples and ropes with which to tie the King to the block if he resisted—Cromwell showed his lack of personal enmity by sending him to sleep at St. James's Palace for his last two nights on earth, wishing to spare him the sound of that incessant hammering. He also ordered the disappointed Hacket to keep his troops out of the King's rooms and he allowed the former Bishop of London, Edward Juxon, to bring Charles the consolations of the Anglican religion.

For Charles, it was a blessed interval of peace, free of the attentions of his tormentors. He gave himself up completely to spiritual preparation, and he found the closest union with a churchman in the gentle, steadfast Juxon that he had known since the death of his beloved Laud. Together they prayed, and Juxon exhorted him to forgive as he truly hoped to be forgiven and to put aside all fear and hope and earthly considerations. There was little need for this advice. Charles was weary, and yet his spirits soared with a strange cheerfulness; he was resigned, but there was no sign of despair or even of recrimination. And out of the past the one crime of his life was claiming its just retribution; he confessed to Juxon that he deserved his own death for having condemned the guiltless Strafford. His peace was made with God and his conscience; he was happy and ready to exchange the crown torn from him by men for the crown of eternal life.

And on Monday, the night before he was to die, he was allowed to see his children.

Their last meeting had been at Hampton Court, and that too was by courtesy of Cromwell, who was such a good father himself. Then, three children had come to him, now there were only two, for his second son James had escaped long before and was safe with his mother in France. Charles had been waiting impatiently by the window, but it was too dark to see their arrival. When he heard the sound of steps outside his room, some of them light and quick, he turned quickly to Juxon who was standing at the side of the room.

" Pray that I don't break down before them! Whatever their last memory of me, it must be one of courage! "

" It will be, Sire," the Bishop answered. " Prepare yourself, they're in the ante-chamber."

They came into the room alone, the little Princess Elizabeth, aged thirteen, holding her nine-year-old brother Prince Henry by the hand, and they hesitated, staring at their father as if he were a stranger. It was nearly two years since they had seen him last. Charles walked towards them slowly, and bending down he took his daughter in his arms. He felt the child stiffen as if she were going to pull back, and then suddenly she threw her arms around his neck.

" Papa! Oh, Papa! "

The little Prince came clamouring to be kissed and embraced with his sister, and for some moments Charles knelt and held them to him, and the Bishop moved to the door and slipped out, leaving them alone.

" Elizabeth, come, let me look at you—and Henry too. How big you have both grown! Why, my son, you're quite the man," he said gently, stroking the little boy's head. " Come and sit down with me, here."

They went with him to the fireplace, where a heap of logs were burning brightly, and Charles lifted the boy upon his knee and held his daughter close to him, his arm round her waist, hers round his neck.

" My children," he said at last, " my dear children, now I am truly happy."

Elizabeth's eyes were big and blue and very like his own;

there was a shade of red in her brown hair. "You are a true Stuart," he told her proudly. "And you, my little son. You are of the Blood Royal, and that is why I must speak to you, not just as your Papa who loves you, but as the King to a Prince and Princess of England. Come closer still, Elizabeth, and listen to what I tell your brother. When I am gone you must remind him of it at all times."

The firelight blazed and flickered on the small face turned up to him, its forehead shadowed by long curling locks of hair. It was the face of a puzzled little boy who had to be made to understand death and the rights of Succesion to a Crown. Charles bent down and kissed him on the forehead and then began to speak very quietly.

"Sweetheart, they are going to cut off your father's head." The boy's eyes opened but he did not speak. "They are going to cut off my head," Charles repeated slowly. "Mark, my child, what I am saying; they will cut off my head and afterwards they'll try to make you King. But remember this; you must not be a King so long as your brothers Charles and James live. Do you understand, sweet one? You must never let them make you King. Give me your promise."

The little Prince's frightened eyes began to fill and then to overflow with tears. He put his knuckles to his mouth and bit them, gazing at the gentle, serious face above him.

"You must not be King, my son," Charles prompted him, and the child choked through his tears and promised.

"I will be torn to pieces first, Papa."

"You are my son and a brave and good boy," Charles whispered to him. "Hold fast to me now, and do not cry. Elizabeth, my daughter, now I must speak to you."

"Tell me what you want me to do," the little girl begged him. She leant her head against his shoulder. "I will do anything you say, Papa."

"First, I want you to promise not to grieve for me," Charles said. "I shall die a glorious death, my child, remember that. I shall die for the liberty of my people and their ancient laws and for the truth of our Protestant religion. You must never forget these things or be tormented by what happens to me. I repeat it again, sweetheart, it will be a glorious death and I am ready for it. Your father is not afraid, nor must you be."

"No, Papa, I'm not afraid, I promise you."

"And you must forgive my enemies as I have forgiven them," he said. "That is God's commandment and we must obey it. Never forswear your faith my child; guard it jealously and live by it always."

"I will, Papa, and I will see that Henry does so too."

"Take care of Henry," Charles told her, and taking her hand he placed it in her brother's. "Hold fast to each other after I am gone, and never forget what I have told you. And give this message to your mother, Elizabeth, whenever God pleases to reunite you and you can tell her in your own words. Tell her," he said slowly—and for a few seconds he was far away from them, back in Whitehall in the happy, vanished past—"tell her that my thoughts have never left her for a moment, and that my love for her will be the same to the last day of my life."

Then there was silence; he sat with his son gathered into his arm, the child's face hidden against his coat. The little Prince was too tired and overwhelmed to cry any more. He held on to his father as if he would never let him go. The Princess Elizabeth moved and climbed on to his knee and they sat all three together without speaking for some moments.

At last, very gently, Charles set them down.

"On that table there's a box," he said. "Come with me and we will open it. I have a few gifts for you."

To the Bishop he had shown some signs of distress the previous evening because he had nothing to distribute to those who had served him. Money and jewels had all been taken from him. He possesed nothing but his suits of clothes and the few jewels he wore. The box contained some broken Garter Stars and two ornaments of St. George set with diamonds which were also broken. His rings, and the magnificent Garter ornament, were all he could bequeath to Henrietta.

"Juxon!"

As he opened the box and kissing each child divided the few ornaments between them, he signalled the Bishop to come in.

"We have said our farewells," he said quietly, "and I have given to them all I have left to give in this world, except my blessing. Kneel down, my little ones."

He stood with his hand upon their heads, the dark and the fair, and asked God to protect and succour them in their orphancy, and as their father, he blessed them and asked that they would pray for him.

The Princess Elizabeth who was to die in his old prison at Carisbrooke Castle within a year, and the Prince who would not survive into his manhood, answered him together.

" Amen, Papa."

" And now good-bye, my little ones. By tomorrow it will all be over. Do not forget me." He turned away from them and called out in a shaking voice to Juxon, "Bishop, take my children away now, I beg of you. . ."

Juxon caught both their hands and led them out. They had a last sight of their father who turned round, putting his handkerchief back in his pocket, and waved to them. He was smiling.

Chapter 16

N o message from England had reached Henrietta in Paris for three weeks. Her letter begging for Charles' life and asking permission to come back to England and see him, had not been answered; nor had the offer made by the Prince of Wales received the courtesy of a reply. Alone with her few attendants in the Louvre, Henrietta passed the time in a miserable condition of suspense, until her natural optimism reasserted itself, and she insisted to her household that since they heard nothing, some miracle must have intervened to save the King from the trial which she had heard mentioned at the very beginning of January. Who could say, she demanded of her embarrassed ladies and gentlemen, that her next word from England might not be a summons from the liberated King to join him. Harry Jermyn, for so many years her faithful and devoted friend, and all those who had followed her into exile, suspected that no news was only the silence of calamity. But they did not contradict her. January passed, and by the first week in February it was cold and overcast, a month of driving snowstorms. Paris itself was troubled by civil disorders and the French Court had left it and taken up residence at St. Germain. Only the Queen of England waited in her quarters in the deserted Palace, waited day by day and week by week for the news from England which never came.

On February 8th Harry Jermyn suggested that she send a messenger to Queen Anne at St. Germain in the hope that the French Court might have received some word from their ambassador in London. She had agreed to send a special courier to her sister-in-law that morning without any premonition that he might return to her with the worst possible news in the world. Silence had come between Henrietta and the thing for which she lived; all her life, through the crisis and upheavals of the past, she and not Charles had been the realist, but now her mind would not admit disaster. Now she took shelter in her dream that somehow he was safe, and the

hints her friends had tried to give her were ignored.

While she waited for the courier's return, she occupied herself writing a long letter to her daughter, Princess Mary of Orange. The little woman sitting at her table by the fire in her large, echoing reception room was only thirty-eight, but her dark hair was nearly white and her brilliant eyes were faded and red with years of weeping. The letter almost wrote itself. Her thoughts came flowing out through her pen, full of hope and pathetic obstinacy. Mary must pray for her father, she urged, and discount any rumours that evil had befallen him. They were merely the lies circulated by his enemies who hoped to dishearten his friends. She herself was not alarmed, though she had heard nothing from him for many weary weeks. This silence was only to be expected, she wrote proudly, as he was closely guarded for fear that his loyal subjects would break in and rescue him.

Henrietta no longer filled her letters with details of some new expedition, some new negotiation which would bring Charles his freedom; now her sole insistence was that in spite of everything, he was alive and well. And though, she said again, there had been no news for a long time, she was confidently waiting at that moment for the return of a messenger she had sent to the Queen of France. She was certain that he would bring her some good intelligence of her beloved.

Outside the door of Henrietta's room, a little group of stricken men and women talked in whispers; the Queen's favourite ladies Mademoiselle Orpe, and the Countess of Dalkeith were weeping. Her confessor, Father Cyprien de Gamache, put his hand upon Harry Jermyn's arm.

"I will go to the Queen and tell her, if you prefer it, my son. But we cannot delay any longer."

"No, Father." Jermyn's round face was grey and sunken. "I know my duty. I am Her Majesty's Chamberlain; I am the one who must tell her. The King would have wished it."

"God help her," Lady Dalkeith whispered. "Only this morning she was talking of sending yet another letter to De Grignan in London in the hope that he could smuggle it through to the King. When she hears this I think she will die. . ."

"That is her bell now," the priest said. "The moment has come. Go to her, and we will retire to the Chapel and pray."

Jermyn nodded and turned away from them. His hands were

trembling as he opened the Queen's door. Henrietta looked up from her writing table, but he was still in shadow and she could not see his face.

" Ah, Harry—I've written a letter to my daughter Princess Mary. I wanted to reassure her about the King. Will you see that it is sent off by the morning? And what time is it—it must be very late! What has become of that courier of mine; St. Germain is only an hour or two's ride. He should have returned long ago! "

Jermyn closed the door very quietly and came into the room. Henrietta was not looking at him; she was collecting her papers, setting the letter addressed to Holland on one side. She passed one thin hand over her forehead, and the gold wedding ring shone for a moment in the candlelight.

"I am so tired," she said. "I should begin a letter to the King, but now it is so late. What is the time, you didn't tell me? "

He looked down at her lined and drawn face, ravaged by pitiless anxiety, and suddenly remembered the first time he had ever seen her, dressed in a gown of scarlet satin, her neck alight with diamonds, sweeping down the spacious corridors at Whitehall on the arm of a young, adoring King. For a moment his throat constricted and he could not speak.

"It is past eight o'clock, Madam."

She pushed back her chair quickly and came round the table towards him.

" Eight o'clock! Then where is the messenger? He must have come back hours ago." She looked closer at him and said suddenly, " What's the matter with you—are you ill? "

Jermyn went down upon one knee before her, and took her hand in his. He kissed it reverently.

" Your Majesty," he said gently, and it was the first time that Henrietta had ever seen him cry. She stared at him, unable to speak, unaware that her whole body had begun to tremble.

" Your messenger returned over an hour ago. God forgive me, but I must be the one who brings his news to you. But first, I beg of you—sit down. . ."